PRAISE FOR

Incognito

"A finely wrought narrative about stepping into the realm of faith. [Raynor] shows us how following a hunch can lead to a life of beauty, purpose, and yes, adventure. This is an inspiring read."
—Barbara Hall, creator and executive producer of *Joan of Arcadia*

"Andrea Raynor's engrossing memoir switchbacks the reader through the realities, passions, pettiness, lessons, disappointments, and triumphs on the way to ordination. . . . Whatever your perceptions are of the men and women who wear the collar, they will be challenged in this honest and soul-searching romp."
—Lee Woodruff, author, blogger, and television personality

"When Andrea Raynor learns to look within for guidance, she truly arrives at the spiritual life which is home. I want a sequel!"
—Joan Steinau Lester, author of the novels *Black, White, Other* and *Mama's Child*

"In her wonderful memoir, *Incognito,* there is nothing disguised about the heartfelt way Andrea Raynor shares her life, faith, doubts, and unlikely path to ministry. Get ready to be inspired, entertained, disturbed, and maybe just a little changed by this refreshingly honest take on a world few get to glimpse with such clarity."
—Edward L. Beck, faith and religion contributor for CNN and author of *God Underneath: Spiritual Memoirs of a Catholic Priest*

"*Incognito* is a refreshingly candid glimpse into the sometimes mysterious and always miraculous making of a minister. . . . Sprinkled with humor and insight, it is a divinely warm and inspiring story that opens a window onto life behind the collar and will leave you wishing for more."
—Roberta Gately, author of *Lipstick in Afghanistan*

incognito

lost and found

at harvard

divinity school

Andrea Raynor

HOWARD BOOKS
A DIVISION OF SIMON & SCHUSTER, INC.

new york   nashville   london   toronto   sydney   new delhi

Howard Books
A Division of Simon & Schuster, Inc.
1230 Avenue of the Americas
New York, NY 10020

First Howard Books hardcover edition March 2014

HOWARD and colophon are trademarks of Simon & Schuster, Inc.

For information about special discounts for bulk purchases, please contact Simon & Schuster Special Sales at 1-866-506-1949 or business@simonandschuster.com.

The Simon & Schuster Speakers Bureau can bring authors to your live event. For more information or to book an event, contact the Simon & Schuster Speakers Bureau at 1-866-248-3049 or visit our website at www.simonspeakers.com.

Interior design by Jaime Putorti
Jacket design by Connie Gabbert Design
Jacket photograph by Shutterstock

Manufactured in the United States of America

10 9 8 7 6 5 4 3 2 1

Library of Congress Cataloging-in-Publication Data
Raynor, Andrea.
Incognito : lost and found at Harvard Divinity School / Andrea Raynor.
pages   cm
1. Raynor, Andrea. 2. United Methodist Church (U.S.)—Clergy—Biography. 3. Harvard Divinity School—Biography. 4. Women clergy—United States—Biography. I. Title.
BX8495.R33A3 2014
287'.6092—dc23   2013027870
[B]

ISBN 978-1-4767-2345-7
ISBN 978-1-4767-2364-8 (ebook)

For Katherine,
who lived it,
and Andrew,
who survived it

contents

incognito

preface

Saugus, Massachusetts, 1985. I am standing at a bus stop waiting for the bus that will take me back to Cambridge. It's cold and the light is beginning to fade. I pull my jacket a little tighter around my body and tuck my chin as the November wind tosses my hair and sneaks down my back. After a few minutes, an old white Chevy rolls to a stop in front of me. The windows come down, and I see three young men smiling and gesturing at me.

"Hey, baby, whatcha doin'? Wanna ride?"

"No, thanks," I say casually.

"Aww . . . you sure? It's awful cold outside . . ."

Their manner is flirtatious, but good-natured. I guess them to be a few years younger than I—but even at twenty-four years old, I'm often mistaken for nineteen. I lean forward slightly to take a closer look at them. Their friendly faces and thick Boston accents somehow make them appear sweet and comical rather than threatening, and so I smile and say, "No, I'm good. But thanks anyway."

Suddenly the guy in the front seat does a double take. His eyes fly open. "Whoa!" he exclaims. Apparently, when I leaned over to look inside, something was exposed. Was it a glimpse of my bra that caused the stir? The curve of my breasts? No. It was my clergy collar. "Hey! Are you a priest?" he asks, incredulous. Then I feel it—the instantaneous *pop!* It's as if all the air has been let out of my party balloon, as if all the lightness has been let out of me. I stand up straight again (my knee-jerk reaction), sigh, and brace myself. No longer do I feel like a girl at a bus stop; I feel like a freak. "Yeah. Yeah, I am," I reply, rather flatly. There is a pause. *Here it comes*, I think. What *it* is, I'm not sure, but I figure they're going to have some fun at my expense. I look away, preparing myself for ridicule, but the fresh-faced boy in the back remains undaunted. "That's okay!" he calls with a big grin. "I'm in Christ—hop in!" This takes me by surprise and makes me laugh out loud—we all laugh. A flood of relief washes over me. *I am still me*, I think. *Even in this collar.* Just then, the bus pulls up. As I wave good-bye and board, I am still laughing.

1

metamorphosis

About halfway through Pennsylvania, my father glanced over at me looking agitated, his eyes darting between my face and the road. "And stay away from the Unitarians!" he snapped.

We were on our way from Cincinnati, where sanity rules, with its Methodists and Lutherans, its Episcopalians and Baptists, its Catholics and its Jews—people who have a clear idea of what they believe in—bound for Cambridge and Harvard Divinity School. Right off the bat, my parents smelled trouble.

To begin with, anything east of Pittsburgh was suspect. Cambridge, while not conjuring a particularly negative association itself, meant Boston. And Boston? Well, everyone knew it smacked of liberals and heretics, atheists and academics (which, let's face it, were one and the same thing in my house). It reeked of old money, the Kennedys, and the benign anarchy of thousands of college students living in alarmingly close proximity. To make matters worse, Boston was a stone's throw from New York City, where, if you believed my father, danger lurked on every corner and it cost an arm and a leg just to get a peanut butter sandwich.

Cincinnati, on the other hand, was nestled comfortably between Kentucky and Indiana in the bosom of the Midwest. It was the Queen City, gracious and dignified, warm and modest, a place where no one honked a car horn unless in trouble, and rush-hour traffic moved with such precision it appeared to be following the cues of an invisible conductor. The Midwest stood for patriotism and family and God . . . but the East? It was the unknown region, a place from which some never returned. This perception, of course, made it all the more mysterious and alluring, like the Forbidden Zone in *Planet of the Apes*.

With each passing mile, the excitement over my being accepted to Harvard was beginning to be replaced with anxiety—not my anxiety, mind you, but that of my parents. They had the foresight to know that these years would change me and the wisdom to let me go anyway. In retrospect, I don't blame them for worrying—I could not then fathom the fears and the heartache of parenthood. All I knew was that we were hurtling toward the future in a blue Ford van, propelled by time and karma and hope, and that somehow I was on the cusp of adventure.

I dangled my arm out the window as we drove and let the warm air fling it around like a rag doll's. I shut my eyes and turned my face to the sun as my hair danced wildly on my head, unfettered and free, Medusa's giddy sister. Meanwhile, outside our speeding blue capsule, the terrain was changing subtly, hypnotically. Even at seventy miles an hour, it felt as if we were crawling in the wake of Earth's galloping spin. Flat farmland slowly morphed into rolling hills, signs pointed the way toward unfamiliar cities, trees waved from the sidelines cheering us on. Although their leaves were still green, they could barely contain the explosion of color that was planned for October—and I was feeling the shift, too, feeling my own metamorphosis waiting for its time.

For three hundred miles, we drove east across Pennsylvania; meanwhile, the gods flipped the sun over our heads like a glowing gold coin in a game of cosmic tiddlywinks. I wanted to reach up and snatch it in my hand, feel the weight of it, and send it skipping across the horizon. I felt elastic and fluid, a secret playmate of the universe disguised as a twenty-two-year-old girl from Ohio. As the sun made its graceful exit through the western door, the sky changed from blue to blood orange to inky black as if undressing and dressing again for the evening.

In response to my father's warning about Unitarians, I had just nodded my head. To be honest, I wasn't even sure what a Unitarian was. I had never met one and wasn't sure if they were a secret society, a New Age religion, or a cult. Judging from my father's tone, the Unitarian Church was, for all practical purposes, an oxymoron.

"Is that like a Moonie?" I asked, genuinely curious, but aware that I sounded like a simpleton. I felt about five years old again—which wasn't necessarily a bad thing. (In retrospect, I realize that I was confusing the Unitarian church with Sun Myung Moon's Unification Church.) Dad seemed relieved to slip back into his role as teacher, protector, and authority on most things. I leaned forward to listen from the back, my arms draped around the seats that held my parents, head bobbing between the co-creators of my DNA. And, for a few minutes, the world was right again. Common sense prevailed. Although

I don't recall my dad's answer, I do know that, instead of fortifying my resolve to stay away from Unitarians, it secretly intrigued me. Unitarians now belonged to that same Forbidden Zone—of which Harvard Divinity School was the epicenter.

Against the dark velvet curtain of the evening sky, I projected my dreams of the future. Harvard became the shiny crimson apple hanging from the tree in the Garden. Despite the warnings, my mouth started to water for it. I wanted knowledge; I wanted exposure to new ideas; I wanted to know what frightened my parents. Oddly enough, I had already discovered that I was naked; in fact, so had they. Maybe this is part of what scared them.

It had been a tough few months since my graduation from Denison University, starting with a disastrous Parents' Weekend in the spring. It was always an awkward and somewhat stressful time on campus. The frat houses did their best to clean up for the weekend, even though little could be done to eradicate the smell of stale beer and old socks. Bongs were put away, party girls hid their cigarettes and sashayed around in sweaters and pearls, and everyone, including the professors, tried to act natural. Parents smiled politely as they were led around the campus like circus ponies, and even those who were alumni looked awkward and out of place. On the surface, they were received kindly, but secretly, the campus was on high alert until the last Lincoln Town Car or BMW or airport limo disappeared down the hill. Then it was *Exhale. Prime the keg.*

I had no bottles or drugs to hide, but I had my own reasons for feeling stressed at the prospect of their arrival. Not only was the deadline for my senior honors thesis fast approaching, but also I knew my parents weren't crazy about the coed dorm in which I lived or meeting the guy I was dating.

My older sisters had had the good sense to go to more conservative schools, where the dormitories were not only single sex but also had strict rules for visitors of the opposite sex. These included keeping the door open and one foot on the floor (I kid you not). In light of this, Denison must have seemed to them like a high-end Sodom and Gomorrah.

Regarding the new man in my life, my parents were wary, to say the least. They still hadn't forgiven me for breaking up with my high school boyfriend a few months earlier. Now, *there* was a guy who could be trusted. Scott was a local boy whom my parents knew and adored, and whose grandfather had worked with mine long before we were ever born. He'd been a high school football star who went to church and came to Sunday dinners; who helped my dad with the grass and blushed when my mother teased him. Whoever this new guy was, he wasn't Scott. To make matters worse, he was from Connecticut.

That being said, the day managed to go off without a hitch. I introduced my new boyfriend, Andy, who looked (in my mind) exceedingly handsome, with his dark, curly hair and his giant blue eyes. Naturally shy, and understandably nervous, he seemed dangerously close to jumping out of his navy-blue blazer and making a run for it. My parents were cordial but cool—as cool as their midwestern manners would allow. After an awkward but painless visit, Andy left to join his own parents. I introduced my friends, most of whom they had met before; we walked around campus; we chatted with some professors. The day passed.

Before saying goodnight, we made plans to go to church together the next morning. They were to pick me up at 10:00 a.m. for the service. Later that night, Andy came over to study, and I worked like a madwoman on my thesis—a ninety-page paper on Latin American liberation theology. I had a mere seventy pages to go. For the first time all year, both of my roommates happened to be away for the night. One was sleeping with her English professor and the other had recently decided to drop out and hitchhike to Tennessee for unknown reasons. *For once, I won't have to go to the library,* I thought, *or sit out in the hall typing so as not to wake them.* It was going to be a long, quiet evening of work.

About two in the morning, Andy asked if he could stretch out and rest on my bed while I worked. "Sure," I answered, hardly looking up.

"Just wake me up when you stop for the night, and I'll head home," he said as he pulled off his shirt and climbed into the loft.

"Okay. You rest."

Another two hours passed. It was four in the morning and my brain was starting to shut down. *Must sleep. Must sleep.* I looked up at Andy sleeping soundly and couldn't bring myself to send him stumbling into the darkness of that early morning. *I'll set the alarm for eight thirty,* I thought. *That should be plenty of time to get him out of here before my parents come.* With that, I collapsed next to him in a dead sleep à la Romeo and Juliet.

That fateful decision changed and altered the course of my life in ways I am still trying to come to terms with. Was it destiny or just the way things went—karma or merely the random turn of events that make up a life?

At 8:15 a.m., just before my alarm was to go off, there was a tap on my door; then it quietly opened. We didn't lock our doors back then; no one did. In fact, I don't ever remember having a key, although I must have. The outside door to the dorm was also unlocked, as usual. My mother still had her hand on the doorknob when she looked up and saw the bare boy chest of the young man, whom she had just met the day before, lying in my loft. If she wasn't impressed with him in a Brooks Brothers jacket, then one can imagine how she felt about him half-naked. I popped up and said, idiotically, "Uh, hi, Mom . . . come on in." But she didn't come in. Instead, she just said, "Oh . . ." quietly, like someone who's been shot in the heart but has yet to feel the sting of the bullet. Then she backed out just as quietly as she came and shut the door— which happened to be covered with a life-sized black-and-white poster of Clark Gable, dressed as Rhett Butler, from *Gone With the Wind*. For a moment, I was frozen in place, staring wild-eyed at Clark, the obvious irony of his "I don't give a damn" attitude completely lost on me.

The next few minutes in my room could only be described as sheer pandemonium. I jumped out of the loft and flew out the door into the dark hallway. Andy, whose huge eyes went even wider with panic, frantically pulled on his shirt. Then, clutching his socks and shoes, he climbed out my window, where the fire escape happened to end. My roommates and I used it as a sort of balcony, decorating it with plants and wind chimes. Now, for the first time all year, it was truly being used as an emergency exit. Because I went to find my mom, who was sitting on the steps with her head in her hands, I missed the visual of Andy slipping and sliding down the fire escape. It had been raining during the night, and the metal steps were quite slick. Little did he know that my father was sitting in his van at the bottom of the stairs observing the whole scene! With socks in hand and shirt half-buttoned, Andy fumbled with the lock on his Toyota before zooming off. He had seen the van parked at the bottom of the stairs, but the windows were tinted and he couldn't be sure that my father was sitting inside. Powerless to keep his head from swiveling wildly between the van and his car, I'm sure he was quite a sight.

Turns out my parents had decided to come early to take me to breakfast. Because cell phones were still a thing of the future, and because our dorm had only one pay phone on the first floor, there was no way for them to call me ahead of time. Now each of my parents was wondering whether the other one had seen Andy's awkward exit out the window. I quickly dressed; my mom and I walked out of the dorm and got into the van. Not only was my heart in my throat—it was squeezed between every other organ in my body. I was about to regurgitate my entire circulatory and digestive system. Needless to say, it was a very icy breakfast, a silent ride to church, and an uncomfortable good-bye. No mention was ever made of the morning drama, nor did they send their warm regards to Andy.

Telling my parents that I'd been accepted to Harvard was the thing that finally broke the ice between us—being named Phi Beta Kappa also helped. Those two calls prompted the first conversations we'd had since that ill-fated Parents' Weekend. It was impossible for them not to be proud of me, and I was immensely relieved to have something exciting to report. When my mom asked how they would ever be able to pay for Harvard, my dad simply said, "We'll sell the house!" Luckily, they didn't have to—I was able to get enough in the way of scholarships and loans to cover my three years there.

The ride to divinity school will always be preserved in my mind, like a leaf pressed into a book. Even then, I knew that I would look back on it and try to recall the words my father said to me, try to reconstruct the contours of my mother's face as she looked out her own window, contemplating her own dreams, while I watched the chrysalis of my childhood recede in the rearview mirror. Actually, I was probably more hermit crab than butterfly. Instead of unfurling my newly formed wings in a flash of brilliant color, I would undergo my transformation more gradually, shifting and shedding shells as I inched my way along.

I was not a child then, but I was still my parents' daughter, raised on the promises of God, grounded in the rich Ohio earth, taught to be kind and to show compassion, to set a good example for others, to work hard and to achieve whatever I put my mind to. Steeped in the mystical yet carved by religious tradition, I was ready to be born, to break out of the parameters that had both constrained and protected me, formed yet inhibited me. It was time to grow up. It was time for a larger shell.

Eventually, the van grew quiet, while the wheels turned and the motor hummed its monotone lullaby. But it wasn't icy, as it had been on that Sunday, just a couple months before. It was cozy and full of thoughts colliding, like a silent orchestra warming up for a concert. Strapped in our seats, staring into the darkness, we were in our own private theater waiting for the curtain to come up. *What is my mother thinking?* I wondered. *What worries make my father furrow his brow as he drives?* I didn't ask because I probably didn't want to know. All I knew was that I was ready. Ready for transformation, ready to step out of the van and into my life, forever colored by crimson.

2

hds 101

I don't remember watching the van pull away from the Divinity School, but I'm sure that I must have stood there for a moment to wave as my parents disappeared in the blue tin, contained in their private world with their private thoughts, in a life that was increasingly separate from mine. This was okay. I was ready to embark upon my own journey. It hadn't taken us long to move my things into the small single room to which I was assigned in Rockefeller Hall, one of the Divinity School dorms. I hadn't brought much with me—some clothes, sheets and towels, and a few personal items. The tight quarters didn't bother me; they were simple and austere. Besides, I was quite happy to have my own space for nearly the first time in my life.

As the fifth of six children, I had always shared a room with my sister Jennie, who is thirteen months older than I. Only when she went to college and I was a senior in high school did I have the room to myself—at least until the summer. I never minded this. Jennie and I were inseparable.

We played on the same sports teams, we were cheerleaders together, we shared our clothes (until I outgrew her), we double-dated; she was part sister, part mother, part friend. The sound of her steady breathing in the darkness of our room had been my lullaby since before I could remember.

Jennie also had a habit of talking in her sleep, famously reciting the periodic table the night before a high school chemistry exam to the tune of "My Favorite Things." Sometimes, on evenings when she was particularly vocal, I would try to coax her into revealing her secrets, but I was never too successful. Her (unconscious) revenge came in the form of screaming bloody murder on a fairly regular basis in the middle of the night. That was something I never got used to. When this happened, our parents would run into the room, turn on the light, and try to wake her, after which she would quickly settle back into a blissful sleep. That worked out well enough for her, but I would be left with my heart pounding and the covers pulled over my head. Maybe it was because I had lived in such close quarters all of my life that I made a good roommate in college. I could sleep through just about anything—talking, typing, laughing, loud music. After spending the last year at Denison in a triple, however, I was ready for some personal space—ironically, I found it in the smallest room I'd ever lived in.

Each room in Rockefeller was furnished with a single bed and a desk. My desk faced a large window overlooking the trees that lined a quiet street behind the dorm. There was a closet with sliding doors and a small built-in chest of drawers. I'd brought a tiny refrigerator, which I put in the corner (and behind which a mouse came to live for a time). Beyond that, there was barely enough space for a couple of people to sit on the floor. My room was one of a suite of four single rooms that shared a bathroom and shower. There were three such suites on each floor, all of which shared a common kitchen. The twelve of us, eight women and four men, were each given a cabinet in the kitchen in which to store our food; mine, as it turned out, was chronically empty. I was the Mother Hubbard of the second floor.

I walked back into my room and began to hang some posters on the walls and place a few things on the desk. I propped my door open so that I could hear the friendly chatter of people milling about. Some were introducing themselves, others were clearly reconnecting after being away for the summer. I caught a few snippets of conversation between two men already engaged in a theological discussion in the kitchen.

"Don't you find it interesting that Heidegger's concern for authenticity inhibits his description of the relationship between self and other, while Sartre purposely avoids the concept of authenticity altogether?"

"Yes, but that's part of why Heidegger's employment of hermeneutical phenomenology is so important when it comes to examining the meaning of being."

The words that they were using and the sophistication of their thought made my stomach lurch. The phrase *I don't belong here* flashed in my mind like a neon sign. *This may be a very short stay* was another one. The possibility of being sent home in shame, a failure after one semester, seemed very real. The fact that I was even there at all was the most staggering thing that had ever happened to me.

I had always been a good student, but I started out at Denison as a bio/premed major, with the hope of becoming a doctor. It seemed the natural choice for someone who was smart and wanted to help people. During January of my freshman year, I spent what was known as January Term at Cincinnati Children's Hospital Medical Center. For four weeks, I watched surgery while standing shoulder to shoulder with the surgeon, focusing on what I knew of anatomy to keep me from feeling faint. To recharge, I would often spend my lunch hour feeding and holding the babies in the neonatal and burn units. I loved being at the hospital; the scrubs seemed to fit and I felt at home in the medical setting. Halfway through my sophomore year, however, it was becoming increasingly clear that the sciences were not my strength. I snoozed through zoology, excelled in math and physics, but did a face-plant in chemistry. For the first and only time in my life, I dropped a class—chemistry—and with it the biology major. Because I was not someone who took these things lightly, or for whom college was mostly a social experience, this was devastating. Driven to achieve, I felt as if I'd just driven off a cliff.

One of the hardest parts about the decision to step off the premed track was telling my parents. They had always been genuinely supportive and encouraging of this goal; having a doctor in the family was going to make them very proud. *What would they tell people?* I wondered. Would they think me a failure or secretly believe that I hadn't tried hard enough? Did I think this about myself?

I remember slowly making my way to the pay phone down the hall from my room. As was often the case on a Sunday afternoon, it was in use—but at least there was no one else in line. Through the glass door of the phone booth, I could see a girl sitting there. She was wrapped in a yellow bathrobe, her hair still wet from the shower, her face fresh and animated, and she appeared to be in no hurry to end her call. For once, I wasn't impatient as I waited my turn. The girl in the little booth could talk her head off for all I cared. I slid down the wall and slumped onto the floor, dreading the conversation that was to come. To disappoint myself was one thing; the thought of disappointing my parents made me miserable.

When Shower Girl finished her call, I slipped into the small booth and sat on the wooden bench facing the phone. It was still warm, and the faint scent of the girl's shampoo lingered in the tight enclosure. After dialing the number, there was a momentary pause while the operator put through my collect call. The cheerful sound of my father's voice as he said hello brought an instant lump to my throat. Yes, he would accept the charges, I heard him say. My mom, as she always did, got on another line, ready to settle into our regular Sunday conversation.

"What's up, Andrea?" Dad asked playfully. Although I had always gone by Andie, once in a while my dad would call me by my full name. He was the only one who ever did, and from him it sounded almost like a pet name. My voice was shaking a little as I began to explain to them that I was going to drop the bio major. They listened thoughtfully, unsure of whether to encourage me to keep trying or to support my decision. Before long, I began crumbling under the pressure I had imposed on myself (and the disappointment they had tried to conceal). Then the floodgates opened. With the phone pressed to my ear and my eyes shut, I began to cry. I didn't know whether I wanted to hang up or to hold on. The wires connecting us stretched across Ohio cornfields, Native American burial grounds, and the expanse of my childhood. I was on the brink of something I did not yet understand. My words came out bent and thick with emotion. "I just . . . I . . . The sciences are just not what I am good at."

Lost in my misery, I was startled by the sound of someone tapping on the glass pane of the phone booth door. "Hey, any chance you want to wrap it up in there?" A scruffy boy with hair like an unmade bed and a benign face was peering into the booth. I jumped involuntarily, then nodded, lifting my finger to indicate that I'd only be one more minute. "Look, Mom, Dad—I have to go. Someone's waiting for the phone— but I'll call you next week." We said "I love you"; then I hung up, restoring the receiver to its rightful place, a plastic priest ready for the next confession.

"Sorry to rush you, man," said the boy as I stepped out of the booth. "I just gotta catch my 'rents before they toddle off for the afternoon. Got a bit of a cash flow problem."

"It's okay," I said, feeling slightly self-conscious about my blotchy face and runny nose. "I didn't mean to be on so long."

As we switched places, I noticed that he smelled slightly of stale beer and yesterday's pizza, which made me glad to have beat him to the phone.

Even though part of me felt as if I had failed, I finished most of my general requirements with flying colors by the end of that year. When I returned to school the next fall, I finally started to relax, allowing myself to enjoy college, enjoy the journey, and see the unknown road as one of adventure and promise. I spent the spring semester of my junior year in Vienna, although I still had little idea of what I wanted to major in, much less do with my life. When I returned to Denison for my senior year, I became a religion major by default— it was the only thing I could cobble together in order to graduate on time.

I had consistently taken courses from the religion department each year because I found them compelling, but I had no interest in majoring in the subject. *What could I do with that?* I wondered. I briefly considered going to law school, even spending a January term at the Cincinnati courthouse, but I found the chaos and the procedures overwhelming. I wanted to do something big with my life, something important and challenging, something successful that would be the payoff for all my hard work. Being a religion major seemed both predictable and disappointing, highlighting my failure in the sciences—but I simply didn't know what else to do.

My parents were supportive as I began to explore where this path might lead. Mostly what they wanted was for their children to be happy. Jennie had become a nurse; my oldest sister, Laurie, a lawyer; and my younger brother, Joey, was a junior in high school. My two older brothers were tradesmen. The fact that I was now a religion major opened new possibilities. I had animated talks with my dad about the classes I was taking, his lifelong interest in all things spiritual enthusing our phone calls with energy. My mom reminded me that two of my aunts had gone to seminary and had served as missionaries. She also told me that my grandmother remembered a female lay preacher making the circuit in Kentucky as far back as the early 1900s.

It made sense for my parents to ask if I was considering the ministry. Methodists were more progressive than many Protestant denominations when it came to the ordination of women, for which permission was granted in 1956. Although there had never been a female pastor at my church, it didn't seem out of the realm of possibility. The ordination of women to the Episcopal priesthood, on the other hand, was still in its early years.

The ripple effect of Carter Heyward and the magnificent eleven (who were ordained in 1974) was inspiring other women to bang on the door of the Catholic church. They are still banging. As a United Methodist, I took it for granted that ordination was open to me—whether I was interested in it or not—and my parents were very encouraging. Having a minister in the family would be *almost* as good as having a doctor; but I had absolutely no interest in becoming the humble parson.

I loved the ministers that I had known throughout my life, but I never aspired to be one. *Surely God has bigger plans for me*, I thought. The church was like a giant fishbowl, one that members could dip in and out of each week, but where the minister remained behind glass, forced to sink or swim in full view. Ministers had kind but weary faces. They lived in parsonages supplied by the church, with families who could be uprooted at the discretion of the bishop. They might answer to God, but they were often run ragged by their congregants. It was an oddly public profession, given the nature of its deeply private connection to, and conversations with, the Divine. What's more, I saw how the more intellectual ministers were often criticized. Sometimes it seemed as if the minister was judged more for dramatic or comic flair than for biblical scholarship; but the thought of being a stand-up comedian in the pulpit or some sort of dramatic orator made me want to escape through the stained-glass windows.

Pushing that image out of my head, I dove into my studies. Because of the haphazard way in which I had chosen my major, almost every class I took my senior year was a religion class. The only exception was acting, which I needed to fulfill a requirement. Perhaps I was unconsciously linking ministry and theatrics, which strikes me as funny when I think about it now.

I took acting my final semester—and that is where I happened to meet Andy. Although Denison was a small school, I had never had a class with him before. I'd seen him around campus, I'd known his best friend, Bobo, since our freshman year, I knew his former girlfriend; but our paths had never crossed. When I walked into acting class on that first day, I saw Bobo and went over to say hello. Sitting next to him was this lanky guy with an interesting look and a sweet, alluring energy. He smiled as I greeted Bobo, and watched as we exchanged a few pleasantries. "Hey, man, I'm sorry," said Bobo after a minute or two. "Don't you two know each other? Andie, meet Andy." As we shook hands, I looked into his eyes, and I remember thinking, *Couldn't his name be something like Bob?*

As my days at Denison began to dwindle, my interest in the study of theology and world religions only increased. My advisor, Dr. Walter Eisenbeis, was a brilliant German scholar and theology professor, who had been just as supportive my freshman year, when I was a biology major, as he was when I switched to religion. "We need ethical and moral doctors, too, you know," he'd said with a smile upon our very first meeting of the school year. He was a soft-spoken, bespectacled man who challenged me to think about what I believed and why, and who opened me to a more scholarly and intellectual approach to faith by introducing me to thinkers such as Tillich, Otto, Bultmann, and Eliade. After I switched my major, I told him that I wasn't sure what I wanted to do with my life. The only thing of which I was certain was that I wanted to find work that would be healing or socially relevant. I also felt as if

I was just beginning to study the field of religion. He advised me to take the Graduate Record Examinations and apply to divinity school.

"But I have no interest in becoming a minister," I practically moaned, a strange sense of desperation starting to trickle down my chest like ice water.

"That's okay," he reassured me. "There are many things you could pursue from there."

"From where?" The image of the Methodist seminary in Kentucky where my aunts had gone, and from where some of our more conservative ministers had graduated, flashed in my mind. My sister Laurie had been an undergraduate at the college there, and I remembered her stories of having to wear dresses to class and abide by strict rules regarding visitors and curfew. As a free spirit herself, she retained her sanity by finding creative ways to break those rules. After two years, even that got old, so she transferred.

"I don't know, Dr. Eisenbeis," I said. "Maybe I should have stuck with premed."

"Harvard Divinity School would be perfect for you," he responded matter-of-factly. Said in his familiar German accent, it almost seemed possible. "Harvard is a school where you can explore new ideas and be challenged. It is not narrow-minded theologically, spiritually, or academically, and not everyone goes there to become a minister. I am certain that you will feel right at home."

"That would be incredible—but do you think I'd get in?"

"You will never know unless you apply."

I filled out the application with the same sense of expectation one has when buying a lottery ticket: *Hey, it's a long shot, but you never know.* My application fee was waived due to the amount of financial aid I was receiving, so I had no excuse not to apply. I halfheartedly began to fill out applications for other schools, but I never managed to finish these. It was less a calculated risk than a prayer. Harvard had been a place that existed only in movies, in books, and in the imaginations of people like me, people who came from modest homes and hardworking families hundreds of miles away. It hardly seemed real—or possible—until now. In some ways, I was so distracted by the thought of going to *Harvard* that I ignored the fact that I would be headed to divinity school if I got in. That reality would only sink in as the shock and euphoria of being accepted gradually diminished to manageable proportions.

The acceptance letter was delivered to my college mailbox in the spring. I had worked in the campus mail room, and I could picture the hands sorting the letters and placing them into the open slots on the other side of the metal façade, where combinations were needed to unlock their treasures. I took the thick white envelope from my box and sat on one of the couches in Slayter Hall, the student union. I was too anxious to wait until I got back to my room. When I opened it, I realized that I had hit the jackpot.

As the time approached to actually go to Harvard, I often wondered what divinity school and my fellow students would be like. I confess that I had stereotypical images floating around in my head, most of which bore a striking resemblance to something out of Cecil B. DeMille's *The Ten Commandments*. This was strange, considering I grew up in a religious family that didn't exactly fit the mold; in fact, we were unconventional in many ways. Although we went to church every Sunday and my parents lived their faith, my best high school friends attended the same Methodist youth group, and our ministers were approachable people, we also explored the mystical realm through meditation and spiritual inquiry. As a family, we often sat around the dining room table in the light of a candle and held hands while my father received messages from the Great Beyond. Even at four or five years old, I thought it quite normal to communicate with the dead or to experience unexplainable occurrences in the house. My parents were (and still are) intellectually curious spiritual seekers, who are also faithful Christians. Hence, I shouldn't have been surprised to find that the Divinity students were not caricatures of religious practitioners, but rather normal people who happened to be very bright and very interested in exploring and discussing all things theological, spiritual, social, and political.

Dr. Eisenbeis had described the Divinity School as a place where I would find deep tolerance and respect for different viewpoints, lifestyles, and avenues of personal expression. He said that people of every faith and no faith sat side by side in class. Tibetan monks in saffron robes would raise their hands next to Orthodox Jews and Catholic priests. Conservative Christians might engage in genuine dialogue with Muslims, while academics and atheists gave ear to mystics explaining the unexplainable. I'd also read that there was a lively gay and lesbian caucus, African American and liberation theologians, feminist scholars, and activists working for peace. Thinking about it gave me a "hold on to your hat" type of feeling—it was exciting and a little scary, but I also felt the strength of my roots, the depth of my faith, and the giddy possibility of spreading my spiritual wings. My parents might have been concerned about some aspects of Harvard's liberal reputation, but they were excited for me, proud of me—they just didn't want me to leave God on the intellectual autopsy table.

As I was unpacking my things, I began to meet my suite-mates, all of whom were about my age. This was not a given, because many people came to study at the Divinity School after having had careers as lawyers or teachers, businesspeople or parents. There was a man of about forty who'd just moved into the men's suite on our floor. I remember thinking that he looked really good . . . *for his age*. Makes me cringe when I think about that now. He was gentle and quiet, the sage down the hall. What was nice about sharing the suite with women my age was that we all seemed to be at similar points on our journey.

Katherine had already moved into the room on my right. She was from Vermont, six feet tall, blond and athletic look-ing, with smooth, tanned skin and aquiline features. The first time I met her, she was wearing hiking shorts and a bandana, and she seemed to be in a hurry to get somewhere. *So this is what someone from Vermont looks like*, I remember thinking (id-iotically) to myself. I had only met one other person from Ver-mont, a place that seemed right out of a made-for-TV Christmas special. Katherine was already surrounded by what appeared to be a coterie of friends. Her intelligent green eyes were not unlike my own, but she had a unique way of looking at you, as if she was intently listening to what you were saying while absorbing a myriad of other data using her formidable intuition. In the coming months, I would frequently hear her typing on her typewriter (yes, typewriter) into the wee hours of the night—not papers, necessarily. Often she was writing poems, lovely and interesting, brilliant and beautiful. The smell of smoke would sometimes escape from under her door—there were no rules against smoking in the dorms at that time—making her seem all the more artsy and intellectual to me. I eventually learned that she was the oldest daughter of the distinguished writer and theologian Frederick Buechner, who had briefly taught at the Divinity School some years before; she didn't make too much of this.

The room to the left of mine belonged to Silvia, a petite Jewish lesbian, with dark, lustrous eyes and short black hair. She was planning on becoming a rabbi. Serious and studious, Silvia didn't really seem to care for me very much—at least in the beginning. Maybe I was too girly, too wrapped up in some drama or another involving men, too midwestern. She would look at me without a word, then shake her head or roll her eyes. That's why her occasional acts of kindness would surprise me. She probably knew that I was one of the more impoverished students in our dorm. I couldn't afford to join the food co-op, and I rarely cooked. Sometimes it seemed I rarely ate. Knowing this, she would occasionally leave food outside my door, like one feeding a stray cat. Chocolate banana boat was one of the more famous selections. For some reason, she got it in her head that I really liked this, though I'm not sure why. It was a miracle that I never managed to step on the squishy foil offering left at my door, turning her mitzvah into a regular "ring and run."

On the other side of Silvia's room was Carla's. Carla was a world unto herself. At first I thought it would be Carla, a fellow midwesterner, with whom I would become closest. Born and raised in Michigan, she was short and plush, with a sensuous air and no sharp angles to her body. She had creamy skin and straight black hair that hung below her waist; her mother was Japanese, her father American. Carla intimated that her mother had been some sort of geisha—something that she seemed to channel as well. She was soft-spoken and quick to smile, pretty in a natural and earthy way. When I saw a young man leave her room the morning after our first night there, I breathed a sigh of relief; when I saw a different one leave the next morning, I liked her even more! *Okay. This is not a monastery*, I thought to myself. *We've got some elbow room here.* Carla and I decided to share a phone to keep down expenses. We split the monthly charges for the line and paid for our own long-distance calls when the bill came. The phone, a red retro-style model with a long cord, could reach to either of our rooms. When I was using it, the line had to cross in front of Silvia's door—this could not have helped my standing with her.

Carla and I were fond of each other—but at times she had a strange façade that made me slightly uneasy, as if she was keeping her true self hidden behind a mask of innocence. This prevented us from being genuinely close. She was quietly am-bitious, driven, and intent on getting what she wanted. I wouldn't have judged this, but, once in a while, an underlying competitiveness would pop up unexpectedly and hit me like a sucker punch.

But this was all ahead of me as I placed my cowboy boots in the closet with the sliding doors and hung up my corduroy coat. As I turned to survey my new living quarters, I noticed a jar of Nutella sitting on the desk with a spoon and a note. *Wel-come to Boston!* it read. *Can't wait to see you. —Love, Andrea.* Andrea (pronounced with the accent on the second syllable: An-*dre*-a) had been my roommate in Vienna our junior year in college, and we had eaten our fair share of Nutella there. Orig-inally from Long Island, she had just graduated from Ithaca College and was planning on applying to a master's program at Brandeis. I could not believe my good fortune to have landed so close to her again. It was typical of Andrea to make such a thoughtful gesture, and I smiled thinking of her getting to my room before I did. She was always better at finding places than I was.

Before long, there was a knock at the door. Two friends from Denison were standing there smiling—Tom and Burki. All three of us had been accepted into the Divinity School at the same time, which was quite unusual. Tom was a musician who had been in a band at Denison with Andy; Burki was a history major and a potter. Tom had brought his guitar with him and began strumming and humming while Burki and I chatted.

"So, what are you taking this semester?" I asked Burki as we sat cross-legged on the floor.

"I'm not sure, really," she answered. "I'm mostly interested in Buddhism and the study of Eastern religions—but who knows where that will lead?"

"How about you, Tom?" I asked. I couldn't help but smile thinking of the first time I met him. It was my freshman year at Denison in a class taught by Dr. Eisenbeis. We were discussing whether key biblical passages, such as those recounting the resurrection and the virgin birth, were historical fact or symbol of faith. Tom was a year older than I was, articulate and razor sharp, and he was pressing me about the intellectual validity of my beliefs. I had never been challenged in that way before, and I took his words as a personal attack, rather than an academic volley. And yet, here we were four years later, friends, starting a new chapter at Harvard.

Strumming his guitar, Tom shook his head and laughed. "I don't know, man. It's a goof. We'll see what happens."

We continued to chat as Tom played, and my room felt cozy and blissful.

Katherine later remarked that her first impression of me was that I, too, had an established circle of very cool friends—and I guess, in some ways, she was right. Having Andrea in Boston was like having a sister close by (one who felt free to kick me in the pants when I needed it), and Tom and Burki were eminently hip. Perhaps it was understandable that, in the beginning, Katherine and I would sort of skitter sideways past each other—neither wanted to intrude on the other's space.

That first day, however, was full of good omens, all signs pointing toward what would be the most incredible period of my life. By the time the sun had set, my parents were more than halfway home, my walls were echoing with laughter, Katherine was typing next door. I'd looked up the definitions of *exegesis* and *hermeneutics*, and I hadn't met anyone who really knew what they were doing at Harvard. This was a good thing. We were all on an adventure. Who knew where the Spirit might lead?

3

mapping the course

The next day, I made an appointment with my advisor, Dr. Rusty Martin, to discuss what classes I would be taking. Rusty, as his name implied, was a redhead with an easy air and a warm pastoral presence. He had visited Denison when I was a senior to speak with any students who might be interested in the Divinity School. A representative from the University of Chicago was also there the same day. I met with the man from Chicago first. He was erudite but rather smug. When he asked what I planned on doing with a divinity degree, I told him (honestly) that I wasn't sure. A momentary but unmistakable frost hung in the air between us, during which a few icicles formed in his eyes. Then, crossing his arms, he leaned back in his chair and said, "Well, my dear, if you do not intend on teaching theology or continuing on to a PhD, then I strongly suggest that the University of Chicago is not for you." Not only was I rattled—and slightly annoyed about the way he called me "dear"—I was completely turned off. If this was the attitude at Chicago, I shuddered to think what the guy from Harvard was going to be like.

Bracing myself, I took a seat in front of the redhead from Harvard, who looked disarmingly friendly, and I repeated the same thing about not knowing what my future plans were. Instead of a chill, however, a distinct warmth emanated from him—turquoise blue, Caribbean warm, unexpected as a good pun. It was as if the sun had popped out from behind the clouds, melting the frost left by Chicago. In response to my admitted lack of direction, Rusty smiled knowingly, as if I had given the perfect answer. "Don't worry," he reassured me, with a wave of his hand, "most people don't know what they want to do when they get to Harvard. Just come, and we'll figure it out." I was hooked.

I decided to enroll in the two-year master of theological studies (MTS) program. Many students who are planning on working toward a doctorate, as well as those who are not pursuing ordination, choose this path. Most of the mainline Protestant denominations, including mine, require pastors to earn the three-year master of divinity (MDiv) degree. Unlike the MTS, this requires proficiency in a relevant theological language, submitting a thesis, and completing two years of field education. Field studies were not graded like academic courses, although supervisors at the chosen sites did evaluate the students at the end of the year. One could choose a setting such as a church, a nonprofit organization, a school, or a social service agency. The idea was to gain practical experience in an area of interest, which would then enhance one's intellectual and academic pursuits. Because I was enrolled in the MTS program, this was not required of me.

On the trip from Ohio to Cambridge, I had read some of the course offerings from the Divinity School catalog aloud to my parents—but that had been like reading a menu of food you'd never heard of or tasted. Now that I had arrived, things felt different. The banquet table was right in front of me; I just needed help deciding where to dig in. Rusty suggested I begin with a scripture course and perhaps something in practical (applied) theology. I was immediately drawn to an offering on The First Epistle to the Corinthians, as well as one entitled Jesus and the Moral Life. The latter was taught by Harvey Cox, a well-known writer, professor, and American Baptist minister. I was familiar with his book *The Secular City*, and the thought of actually studying with the man who wrote it was exciting. In addition, a course entitled The Writer as Theologian: Aesthetic and Religious Visions of Reality caught my eye, as did another called Peace: Research, Education, and Action. I was intensely interested in the relationship between faith and politics, scripture and everyday life. It was going to be an exciting first semester.

When we had settled on my courses, Rusty brought up the subject of field study. "As you know, field education is not required of MTS students," he began, "but I see that you are eligible for the Federal Work-Study program. I'm wondering if, instead of getting a job, say, in the bookstore, you would like to do a field placement. Not only would you be paid, but you would also be gaining some valuable experience."

"That would be great," I told him. "I definitely need to work—and I'm familiar with Work-Study from college."

"The other benefit," he continued, "would be if you decided to switch to the MDiv program. That way you would already have one year of field education under your belt."

"Does that happen often?" I asked. "Do people switch from one degree program to another?"

"Oh, sure. It's quite common. Sometimes your path only becomes clear once you are here."

His words gave me goose bumps; I knew that this would be true for me. In that moment, I let go of any lingering uncertainty over whether I could cut it at HDS, as well as my anxiety about not knowing what I wanted to do with my degree. Instead I began to surrender, in a deeper way, to the path that was unfolding—and I was learning something new about faith. I had always had faith in God, but now I was being challenged to have faith in the future, faith in myself, and faith that the way would be illuminated. The only thing required of me was to show up with my best self and an openness to inspiration.

I jumped at Rusty's suggestion to apply my Work-Study benefit toward a field education. The prospect of doing something relevant in the world, even if it meant working for minimum wage, was hugely exciting. At Denison, I had worked in the mail room, had organized packages, and had made phone calls to alumni for the Annual Campaign. That was Work-Study to me. Now Rusty had opened the door to another possibility—both for work and potentially for the future. We discussed the types of placements I might be interested in, such as working for a hunger organization, working on behalf of the poor, working in a clinic. I was motivated by a sense of calling and by an eagerness to put my personal theology and understanding of scripture into action.

"How would you feel about working with the homeless?" he asked.

An immediate *Yes!* bubbled up from the deepest part of me. "I think I would really like that," I responded. "I volunteered at a juvenile detention facility for boys when I was in college and was a counselor at a camp for inner-city children when I was in high school, but that's about the extent of my experience with marginalized or disregarded populations."

"Then I'm going to suggest you contact Dik Behm, director of the Pine Street Inn. Pine Street is the largest shelter for the homeless in Boston. It's not in the best area of town, but you'll be okay; we've sent many students there over the years. There is a small women's side but it's primarily a men's shelter. Would you feel comfortable working on the men's side? That's where they need the most help."

"Yes, I think so."

"Good. Then give Dik a call. He's a Div School grad, too, and a wonderful guy. I know you'll like him."

I left Rusty's office feeling that the future was opening to me, that it was entirely plausible that I would succeed at HDS, and that two years of study here might not be enough.

As instructed, I called Dik Behm at the Pine Street Inn to set up an interview. He suggested that I come around 11:00 a.m., since that would be a quiet time at the Inn. I wasn't sure what he meant by this, but I followed his instructions as to which T to take and what to do once I arrived. It was a beautiful September day, warm and sunny and green, the kind of day that makes even the shabbiest of neighborhoods appear somehow friendly and humble, rather than scary and dangerous.

The Pine Street Inn was no longer located on Pine Street in Chinatown, Dik had told me, but on Harrison Avenue in Boston's South End. The shelter had moved into the old Boston Fire Department headquarters a few years earlier when the need for beds overwhelmed the original space. The building's tower stood above most of the surrounding rooftops, serving as a beacon of hope to the shivering and the hungry, and a silent witness to compassion.

Though not familiar with the area, I found the building fairly easily. Dik had told me to look for the iconic tower, which had once offered an important aerial view for firefighters in the early 1900s. It was a strangely beautiful building, one that appeared permanently out of place—as if it had been dropped accidentally from the sky—like something once bound for greater things but now stuck there like its nightly visitors. Built in 1892 and modeled after the city hall in Siena, Italy, it was Italian Gothic Revival in a formerly Irish Catholic, and then gay, and then African American, neighborhood. In some ways, it remains an unconscious reminder that we are all transplants and visitors here.

Aside from a man dozing on a park bench in the sun, I saw little evidence of the multitude who would be populating the shelter come nightfall. The entrance, too, was somewhat hidden from view—I had to ask a woman on the street how to get in. She smiled and pointed down an alley between two buildings. Though it was empty, I was relieved to see that it was well lit by the sun shining above it. When I reached the glass door of the shelter, it was locked, so I rang the bell and waited to be let in.

I watched as a man, who looked to be in his early forties, approached. He was wearing jeans and a short-sleeved button-down shirt, his strawberry–white blond hair and beard, coupled with his warm smile, giving him a slightly angelic appearance. We waved through the glass as he opened the door; then I crossed the threshold to the only sanctuary many in Boston would ever know.

"Andie?" he guessed. "Hi, I'm Dik. Glad you found us."

We shook hands; then he led me through a large room to the left of the lobby. I noticed a young man, clearly a staff member, seated on a long bench next to an elderly gentleman. He was straddling the bench so as to face the older man and was making notes on a clipboard. Without looking up, he gave a wave with his penned hand as we passed. "That's Ernie, one of our counselors," Dik said as we continued walking. "He's trying to determine if the man has a veteran's benefit that he isn't accessing or even aware of. Many of our guests have been off the radar for so long that they don't realize there may be some assistance available to them." I nodded, trying to take in the reality of someone my grandfather's age, someone who had served his country in battle, living on the street.

Dik ushered me into a small office, one that allowed for little more than a desk, and motioned for me to take a seat on one of the two folding chairs. The walls were painted a pale industrial vanilla and were bare, save for a couple pieces of paper, one of which looked like a schedule of sorts, tacked on a small bulletin board. Oddly enough, even unadorned, the space felt welcoming and safe, like a shoulder to lean on or an ear to listen. That was what Dik filled it with—not with things, but with his wise, gentle presence.

"I notice you call them 'guests'—the visitors to the shelter, I mean."

"Yes," he replied. "That's very important here. Paul Sullivan, one of the founders of Pine Street—which opened its doors in 1969, by the way—insisted upon that term right from the beginning. By referring to those seeking shelter as 'guests,' we are reminded to treat the men as we would want to be treated; namely, with kindness and respect."

"What kinds of things would I be doing here?" I asked.

"Well, it's not so much what you will be doing that is important, but what you will be learning," he said softly.

". . . learning about yourself, about others, about simply 'being with' those who are suffering."

Looking into his eyes, I knew that I was already learning.

Dik described the day-to-day workings of the shelter and gave me examples of what a typical shift might entail. I, in turn, asked him about safety, about how much time was required of me (approximately fifteen hours a week), and, eventually, how he had come to do this work. Dik confirmed what Rusty had told me, that he was an HDS grad who never aspired to be ordained. Instead, like me, he was motivated by his faith to do secular work that was spiritually grounded and socially relevant. He had found that at Pine Street.

At the end of our interview, which felt more like a discussion between teacher and student, Dik suggested that I pray about whether this was the right setting for me, saying he would do the same. We got up and walked back through the large room where the counselor had been seated with the elderly guest. This time, it was empty, save for three giant beams of sunlight pouring through the large windows of the old firehouse, like celestial specters of Jacob's ladder. *Pine Street had once been home to firemen*, I thought, *brave souls dedicated to saving lives. Even though they have moved on, their legacy continues.* Looking at the sunbeams, it felt as if the men had simply ascended those ladders, as they had so many others, and kept going. Instead of walking into fire, they had walked into Paradise—but had left the ladders just in case.

4

the frenchman

A week into my new life, and before hearing back from Dik, I found myself on the T, en route to Harvard Square. I was coming from a visit with Andrea, who was living in a cool little apartment in the North End, commonly known as Little Italy. It was a great neighborhood, one that felt both European and distinctly Old Boston at the same time. The Freedom Trail led to cobbled streets that were narrow and winding. The smell of espresso and pizza floated from the open doors of shops, old men sat in the windows sipping coffee and shooting the breeze in Italian-drenched English, while young people strolled past with their backpacks and Sony Walkmans. Meanwhile, the Old North Church held court like a dignified patriarch, its ghosts hidden in the gleam of polished wood, empty pews, and daytime tourists. But at night . . . at night it was almost impossible not to hear the echo of footsteps ascending the steeple stairs once again, a brave sexton armed with two lanterns in one act of defiant courage. The North End was alive—alive with families who had been there for generations, alive with ghosts who had been there for centuries.

Andrea let the people in the neighborhood think that she was Italian, which she could easily pull off with her dark hair and her olive skin. It wasn't a total stretch. Her mother *had* been born in Florence, although it was while her Jewish grandparents were on the run from Nazi Germany.

"I don't know how they'd feel about a Jew living next door," she said dryly, with a shrug of her shoulders, her blue-green eyes as unblinking as a cat's. "It's generally a pretty safe neighborhood. Everyone seems to look out for each other . . . *if* you're not black or Hispanic or some other minority." She shook her head and gazed toward the window. "Someone I know had a friend over the other night who was black, and when she went to leave, her tires had been slashed. Nice, huh?" I felt suddenly naïve and vulnerable. This was not Denison. I was no longer living on a secluded and idyllic campus. Who was watching? Who was lurking in the doorways? What racist bully would slash some poor girl's tires? But Andrea just waved it off. "What are you gonna do? If they want to think I'm Italian, it's fine by me—but it won't change who my friends are."

She made tea, and we sat in the quiet of her apartment, drinking in our good fortune to be living so close to each other again. The sun danced through the open window to the music of our spoons scraping the honeyed bottoms of ceramic cups. We were at the beginning of yet another adventure, and this was an important pinpoint on the map. I readily conceded that Andrea's apartment was infinitely more hip and cozy than my sparse room at the Divinity School dorm. Not only was she living alone in her own place, a milestone postponed for me by graduate school, but Andrea had a flair for making things look homey and arty at the same time, her European roots blending with her New York bohemian sensibilities. She was boho chic before the term was coined. Her one-bedroom apartment was filled with spider plants and hanging cooking pots, with tapestries and books, and with interesting objects from her travels. The furniture was worn and comfortable, extending a friendly flop-down-and-talk kind of invitation, the kind that made it hard to leave. It was a place to exhale and recharge; like Andrea, it was familiar and intriguing, cultured and intelligent.

We hugged good-bye and made plans to see each other again in a few days; then I made my way back toward Haymarket and the Green Line. I loved the ease of traveling by the Boston subway, which was a good thing because I didn't have a car. I felt mobile and light and totally alive, as if all the cells in my body were shimmering. When the train came, I boarded, smiling like the village idiot. It didn't bother me that people seemed to have none of the midwestern politeness upon which I was milk-fed; I found it oddly fascinating. Old and young alike shoved past me without even a halfhearted murmur of "Excuse me." When a small elderly woman, who was barely five feet tall, elbowed me impatiently, I wanted to giggle. It was like being in a foreign country again. Who was I to judge its customs?

I found a seat and surveyed the bouquet of passengers. There were college students engaged in loud, playful banter, and others with their heads in books. There were two elderly Asian women, speaking in a language filled with diphthongs, next to a Latino laborer, who was staring straight ahead. Women in power suits with sizable shoulder pads and pencil skirts stood in sneakers, their colorful pumps tucked securely in totes, and someone I couldn't see was playing the Clash on a tinny boom box that must have seen better days. We rattled along to "Rock the Casbah" and "Should I Stay or Should I Go," till I had to change trains at Park Street Station and board the Red Line toward Harvard Square.

When the doors opened at the Charles/Mass General stop, about a dozen more people pushed their way into the car. A clear-eyed but weary-looking pregnant woman awkwardly wedged past several standing passengers. I noticed her belly brushing up against them and imagined her baby but a few layers of skin and muscle away. Another month, and people would be oohing and aahing—but today, she was just another body taking up space. Instinctively, I hopped up to offer her my seat. "Thanks!" she mouthed, with a little smile and a roll of her eyes, sighing gratefully as she took the load off her feet. Just as the doors were about to close, I noticed a man still in the process of trying to board. He had one foot in the car and one on the station platform, and he was struggling with a ridiculous amount of luggage and random boxes. No one seemed to see him or to care. I felt like I was in some weird dream where I was the only person who could move. I quickly helped him shove the last few boxes onto the train just before the doors closed. He nodded his head but never really met my eyes; instead, he was frantically looking over his packages, like a worried mother duck, as if counting to make sure they had all made it on board. Then I heard him give a curt little "Merci."

Hmmm . . . a Frenchman. Interesting. A slight man with a rather large mustache, he looked to be in his late twenties or early thirties. In some ways, I couldn't believe my eyes. He was the embodiment of a comical character out of a Peter Sellers movie. Because he had clearly forgotten about me, I took the liberty of observing him without apology. He was sweating profusely, occasionally dabbing at his forehead with a handkerchief, a gesture that made him look like he had stepped from another century. It was obvious that he was sweating due to a combination of stress and the fact that he was wearing a rather heavy overcoat, most likely out of necessity, because he could not have carried one more thing. His eyes darted anxiously between his belongings and the subway doors, and I wondered how he had managed to lug all those boxes from wherever he had come from—Logan Airport? South Station? *He's probably a graduate student,* I thought, *an intellectual who hadn't really thought this whole move-to-Cambridge thing through.* Maybe he was the type of person who could understand quantum physics or who was working on the cure for cancer, but could not find the glasses that were sitting on his head. There were so many different kinds of people in Cambridge; he was just one more anomaly.

When we arrived at Harvard Square, I was not surprised to find that this was the Frenchman's stop. He began moving boxes off the T with the ferocity of one passing buckets of water at a raging fire. I joined his one-man assembly line; I couldn't stop myself. We grabbed the last of the boxes, and the train continued on. I watched for a moment as its lights disappeared around a bend in the tunnel. Meanwhile, people walked around and past us without missing a beat. *Maybe they think we're together. Maybe he's invisible. An invisible Frenchman. Maybe no one can see him but me!* I obviously knew this wasn't true, but I found the whole experience curious, absurd even. *Wait till I tell Andrea about this one!*

Feeling rather good about myself, I took a couple steps toward the stairs that led out of the subway and up into the sunshine of Harvard Square. It'd been a full day already: I'd seen my friend, I'd given up my seat for a pregnant woman; I'd helped a foreigner. Life was good. I took another step. *Don't look back!* I told myself. But I couldn't resist the temptation; I was powerless. It was like trying to look away from an accident. I had to see how the Frenchman was managing, regardless of the consequences. *Surely someone is going to meet him here on the platform.* Standing about ten yards away, I watched as he mopped his brow and rubbed his chin, clearly surveying the problem of how to move all his belongings up all those steps. He began stacking things in impossible piles, then rearranging them again. It was like watching a stage act, an improvisation that was relying heavily on stereotypes. I was cast as "the nice girl from Ohio," while he was "the hapless French intellectual." *Okay*, I sighed, *I'm in. I'll play my part.* Besides, I was still blissfully happy, still giddy about the life that was unfolding for me at Harvard.

He didn't look up as I approached him on the platform. "Where are you going?" I asked, in my most friendly tone. No answer. "Do you need some help?" Hesitating for a moment, he pulled a wrinkled piece of paper from the pocket of his trousers and held it up for me to read (but clearly not to touch). It contained a scribbled address. I vaguely recognized the name of the street, but wasn't sure how to get there. I was still trying to learn my way around. "Okay. I'm not sure where that is. Do you know?" Nod. "Would you like some help?" Nod. "Okay," I offered cheerily, hoisting the largest, heaviest, most awkward box imaginable. It was covered with duct tape and a French airport sticker. As I shifted my grip, the man piled two smaller boxes on top, as if I were a pack animal; then he loaded one onto his suitcase, which he was forced to carry because it had no wheels. He tucked a final box under his arm, and we staggered forth toward the light of the Square, like the Holy Family, determined to keep moving but unsure of the final destination.

Every few steps, one of the boxes would fall, and we would have to stop while he attempted to balance it again. I was aware of the passing glances of strangers, who seemed mildly entertained by our procession. We looked ridiculous, part of a circus troupe that had gotten squeezed out of the clown car. All we needed was a funny honking horn and a couple giant red noses. I was following him as best I could, but it was hard to see over the boxes, and the Square was filled with people.

We made a turn off the main street and went down a cob-bled road; then we retraced our steps. I was beginning to regret my offer of help. My arms were aching, and I, too, was starting to sweat. I asked to see the address again, a request that was promptly ignored. Somehow, improbably, we arrived in front of a garden apartment. The Frenchman pressed on without saying a word. An outer door led to a narrow, poorly lit hall-way. I let the boxes slide to the floor while the man fiddled with the lock. I couldn't feel my arms. I was aware that my face was the color of a plum, and sweat trickled down my spine.

I had woken that morning to a beautiful September day— one of those days lodged magically between summer and fall. The air was warm, but devoid of the blistering heat of August. It carried the faint hint of cooler nights, of gloved hands and the rustle of fallen leaves. I had chosen a long denim skirt, one that snapped all the way from the waist to the hem. It was straight cut with a high waist, falling to my ankles. I wore it unsnapped to about my knees, accompanied by a short-sleeved black turtleneck sweater. The sweater was made of a synthetic material, which didn't breathe very well, and which made me feel suddenly trapped by the heat. I hadn't intended on wearing it for heavy lifting, just as I hadn't intended on schlepping some stranger's belongings all over Harvard Square in my five-dollar Chinese slippers.

I leaned against the wall, waiting for him to get the door open and praying that we were in the right place. Voilà! (and thank God), it opened! He straddled the doorway as we resumed a version of our bucket brigade, shoving the boxes and suitcase just inside the apartment. I noticed that he seemed—oddly—in no less of a hurry than he had on the subway platform, even though no train was coming. Once everything had safely crossed the threshold, I stood up straight and exhaled with a relieved and triumphant smile. I expected him to smile, too, in a "Whew, we did it!" kind of way. But almost immediately, without saying a word, without raising his head or looking at me, he quickly squeezed through the door himself, as if he were his own last parcel, and promptly shut it in my face. Then I heard the lock turn on the other side.

I stood there for a moment—incredulous, speechless, shocked. I stared at the painted wooden barrier, as if it were an illusion, as if the little man had simply vanished behind a curtain, like a magician, and would soon reappear to my cheerful applause. But he did not. Instead, 1B hung there like a tarnished signpost, like a strange hieroglyphic that I could not read, but which obviously meant "Keep Out!" I'm not sure what I had expected at the end of this pilgrimage, but it wasn't this. My mouth hung open as I stared at the door, while a rapid series of feelings and thoughts ran through me—indignation, hurt, surprise, anger, confusion . . . then laughter. I turned and walked back down the hall, shaking my head and just laughing. Had he been afraid—afraid that I might actually rob him? Was he a misogynist, a man who felt entitled to the servitude of women, or was he a recluse, one who realized that he had no choice but to accept the help of a stranger?

I stepped back into the sunlight, knowing that I would never understand what had just happened—at least on the part of the Frenchman. Maybe it was none of my business. In fact, I knew it was none of my business. I was only responsible for my own actions. I stretched my arms and shook some of the life back into them; then I tried to waft some cool air into my sweater. I was regretting the acrylic turtleneck. *There is a lesson here for me somewhere*, I thought. *I am a divinity student. Acting with kindness and compassion is its own reward; it is food for my soul.* With that affirmation, I was genuinely grateful for the actions of the Frenchman, grateful that he hadn't thanked me. It was hilarious. It was all about spiritual growth, about self-discovery, about the Zen slap, the Divine one-liner that makes the lightbulb go on. Inside, I was laughing my head off.

I made my way back to the center of Harvard Square and the open-air tables in front of Au Bon Pain, where old men were perpetually engaged in serious chess games against any worthy opponent (some of whom looked homeless), while punk rockers hung out around the entrance to the T. One guy's giant spiked Mohawk seemed to defy gravity. It was as if he were wearing a helmet with a dozen pointy blue spears. He lounged casually against a newsstand in his skinny black jeans and unlaced combat boots, smoking a cigarette and tossing his head back when he exhaled. Next to him were a couple of girls sitting crossed-legged on the ground. They were dressed in black torn tights adorned with safety pins, and sleeveless T-shirts. Wearing fingerless gloves, silver chains, and leather chokers, one had hair the color of a pink neon flamingo, while the other's was jet black and shaved on one side. Near the corner, a guy was channeling Coltrane, playing a jazzy rendition of "My Favorite Things" on the saxophone, his case open to catch the change thrown his way.

Stepping from the Square into Harvard Yard through the Johnston Gate was like passing through an invisible barrier into another world. It was a transition that I always found profoundly striking. The air seemed cooler, shaded as it was by dignified trees and by the stately brick buildings that lined the Yard; and anything outside the gates became almost instantly muted, as if Widener Library itself was whispering "Hush." The faint strains of the saxophone and the chaos of the Square were soon swallowed up, absorbed, and rendered silent, like a drop of water in the ocean.

As I walked through the Old Yard, past the famous John Harvard statue, my body was cooling down from the strain of helping the Frenchman, but my little Chinese slippers were beginning to give me blisters, so I took them off. The sidewalk felt nice beneath my feet. I continued on my way with long, light strides, like someone about to dance, swinging the shoes in front of me and smiling. *Walking, walking, walking*, I intoned, the words inaudible but alive, round and light, floating on the breeze, iridescent, illuminated. For a moment, I was back at Denison, walking through the grass with my mysticism class. A Buddhist monk was teaching us about awareness and meditation as we followed him around (to the amusement of our fellow students). As then, happiness seeped from the center of my earth, pushing its way to the surface like a flower through the cracks. *Be present, free the breath. Bring attention. Sidewalk beneath my feet. Walking, walking, walking.* I glided past the Harvard undergrads, only mildly cognizant of them. They were part of the kaleidoscope, moving bits of color, like leaves floating by on a river. I didn't linger on their faces, and I'm sure they didn't linger on mine. The college students were in their own world, a subset of this experience, one with which I had little contact. Although I wasn't much older than they, I felt worlds apart . . . and I really couldn't care less about how I looked walking barefoot through the Yard, swinging those cheap shoes in my cheap sweater.

About the time I emerged from the Yard near the Science Center, I felt someone's gaze, like the warmth of the sun on my cheek. Instinctually, I wanted to turn my head in the direction of that warmth. It was like being gently awakened from a dream—the dream of moving through Harvard Yard, the distant dream of the Frenchman, the dream of Andrea's apartment. Something silently, steadily caressed my face, summoning my gaze to the other side of the street with a gentle, magnetic pull. It took me a moment to register what I was seeing; the light obscured the details. Sunspots and shadows had to clear. Surfacing from the trance of my walking meditation, what reached me first were not the features of his face but the expression. The closest thing that comes to mind is sheer delight. Someone was clearly delighting in the way that I was walking in my bare feet, swinging those shoes. I smiled back. We were walking parallel to one another, on either side of a road that was beginning to converge. "Everything that rises must converge," wrote Flannery O'Connor. We were rising, made buoyant by the moment and by the sheer joy of being alive, and we would converge.

This is how I met Tomas. Our paths literally crossed when the roads on which we were traveling came to a point at a crosswalk. He was tall and lean, with a forest of wavy, dark hair that bobbed about his face in random wildness when he walked. His eyes were dark and narrow—a warrior's, an artist's—but when they looked at me, they were laughing in a startled kind of way. I could see it from across the street; I could feel it. We were forced by our respective paths to walk toward one another. As we moved closer, I noticed the long, deep dimples that ran down his cheeks like twin rivers when he smiled. He looked over at me and gave a little shrug of his shoulders, as if he couldn't believe it, as if he'd stumbled upon something that he didn't even realize he'd been looking for.

He was wearing jeans and a thin, short-sleeved T-shirt. It was a pale yellow that looked beautiful against his skin, skin that was the color of creamy coffee. He was not barefoot but wore shoes of soft brown suede, tied with leather laces around his ankles. When he took his hands out of his pockets, I could see that they were beautiful. But mostly what I saw was goodness. Without a doubt, this stranger smiling at me from across the street was good.

When we finally converged we shared an awkward little laugh as we waited for the crosswalk to signal that it was safe to go. I liked standing next to him. It was that simple. The light changed and we crossed the street. Then, turning to face me, he broke the silence, saying, "Hi . . . my name is Tomas. I would like to know you." He spoke with the gentle musicality of his native Spanish. "Are you a student here?" I looked up into his face and sighed. A rapid series of thoughts and images ran through my mind, including all the reasons I should not tell this man anything about myself. He was a stranger, he looked older than I; I was meeting him on the street. I had a boyfriend. *Be careful! What if he's a freak?* "Hi. I'm Andie," I heard myself saying. "Nice to meet you." I shifted my shoes to one hand so that we could shake.

"I saw you walking like that, without your shoes, and I had to meet you," he said.

"Oh, yeah . . . that . . . well, my feet were killing me so I just took them off. I mean, why not?" He smiled again, the rivers running. He looked at me sweetly, as if I were utterly fascinating. Meanwhile, I became increasingly self-conscious standing there sweating in my private inferno. The image of a head sticking out of a choking black chimney came to mind. I would have given anything to rip that sweater off and make a run for it. To make matters worse, I could feel that my face was still a lovely shade of Harvard crimson (ugh) and I had an unsightly pimple on my forehead (which I was trying rather unsuccessfully to keep covered with my bangs). Each time I tilted my face to talk to him, the bangs would part and the cyclops would emerge, so I kept looking down, and felt anxious to go on my way.

"You seem different from other people I see here. You are . . . free."

"I don't know what I am," I said, laughing. "I just know that my feet were hot." *Can he see that huge zit on my forehead? Please kill me now.*

"I would like to see you again. Do you have a number where I can reach you? I'm a music student at Longy. It's not far from here. I'm a cellist."

I hesitated. Every sensible reason to refrain from giving him my number ran through my head at lightning speed. *Don't be an idiot. You are so green. You can't give your number to the first guy you meet on the street. Then again, it would be a shame not to see him again, not to stand next to him again . . .*

"Tell you what. Why don't you give me *your* number?" I finally said, squinting and cocking my head to one side in yet another vain attempt at hiding the cyclops. I wanted to come off sounding confident and savvy, but instead the words tumbled out awkwardly, like dice badly thrown.

Awkward or not, I figured that taking his number would give me time to think about it. I wasn't ready to release him to chance, but I also wasn't ready to be foolish. Tomas found a pencil and a scrap of paper in the pouch he was carrying across one shoulder. It was of a natural woven material in an earthy tan and blue. I noticed his hands were shaking a little when he wrote his number for me—something I found secretly endearing. I felt a pinch. The moment stitched him to my heart with a delicate silver thread, nearly imperceptible and yet undeniable. I tucked his number into one of the shoes still dangling from my hand. We shook again and gave a little wave. He went left, I went right, swinging my buried treasure.

5

love and other disasters

When I got back to my little room, there was a note on the door in Carla's handwriting: *Dik from Pine Street called. Scott called. Knock if you need the phone.* We were each other's answering machine. The only way to leave a message was to catch one of us home. Taking the note, I followed the trail of phone cord that disappeared under her door. Even if I hadn't heard the soft ripples of a conversation coming from the other side, I was in no hurry to return those calls. All I wanted to do was to rip my sweater off. I unlocked my door, stepped inside, and did just that. Then I ripped my skirt off, too—*pop, pop, pop, pop, pop*—the snaps offering a satisfying finale to my escape from the inferno. I put my hair up in a ponytail, washed my face, and surveyed the pimple on my forehead in the mirror. I pushed my bangs around, trying to determine just how bad it must have looked in the afternoon sun. Oh well. Nothing to be done about it now. I pulled on my giant Superman T-shirt, which was the largest, most comfortable thing I owned, took off my bra, thought about washing my

feet, then figured I'd do it later. Before throwing my shoes in
the closet, I took out the scrap of paper with Tomas's number
on it. The handwriting was distinctly foreign, with its flagged
ones and its crossed sevens. I liked it. Looking around, I decided to stash it in the journal on my desk.

I plopped down cross-legged on the floor, a pillow behind
my back, and leaned against the bed. It was quiet. The sun
bathed the room in a warm, golden glow as it began its de-
scent. I thought about returning the phone calls. I was both
anxious to hear back from Dik and a little nervous as well. He
epitomized my idea of a Harvard Divinity School graduate,
one who was putting his degree into action with intelligence
and compassion. Since our interview, I had been praying
about working at Pine Street, picturing myself there and imagining what it might be like. I was drawn to the contrast that it
provided to the Divinity School, knowing that it would be a
reminder of those who were suffering and would ground me in
a sense of calling. *If Jesus were walking the planet today*, I
thought, *I'd be more likely to find him hanging out at Pine Street
than sipping tea at the Div School.* Looking at Dik's phone
number, I hoped that he saw potential in me, that he was calling to confirm the placement and to tell me when I would be
starting.

Then there was Scott . . . my longtime Cincinnati guy.
Though we had broken up several times, including my senior
year at Denison, the finality of this really hadn't sunk in; not
completely anyway. In the back of his mind, he had probably
thought that I would return to Cincinnati (where I belonged)
after graduation and go back to being the person he fell in love
with. He could then forgive me for dating Andy—after all, I'd
only been with Andy about three months, as compared to the

six years I'd spent with him—and once I had ended that unfortunate interlude, he would welcome me back like the prodi-
gal girlfriend. This, of course, did not take into account what *I*
wanted. My decision to go to Harvard had been the last straw
for Scott—and the honorable escape route for me. Why
couldn't I go to grad school in Cincinnati? he wondered. Why
not Xavier or UC? Why did I have to be (in his words) such an
"opportunist"? I tried to explain, tried to hide my indignation
but, in reality, there was no discussion. I was going. Even
though I wasn't sure about where things were going with
Andy, to think that I would pass up the chance to study at
Harvard was absurd.

I felt certain that God had a purpose for me, that I had
been given certain gifts and talents, and that I had a responsibility to use them to do some good in the world. "You can do
anything you want to do" had been my father's mantra for as
long as I could remember. "Don't let anyone tell you differently." Not only did he believe in me, but he expected great
things from me—none of which ever had to do with how
much money I'd make. It was always about living up to one's
potential, about the spiritual journey, the adventure of becoming oneself. Even with this support, however, I often felt apologetic and rather embarrassed by my strength. It was my freak
flag—one that I was reluctant to fly (at least not too high), because doing so seemed immodest. I was raised to achieve—but
to do it without fanfare.

I had always been driven, academically and personally, and
yet rather passive in my relationship with Scott. Perhaps it was
because I was sixteen when we started dating, while he was
eighteen and a freshman in college. He was sweet and trustworthy, tall and handsome. I waited for him to come home

from college on the weekends, which took me out of the loop of the high school parties and the usual dating dramas. I didn't mind much. Everyone knew him; our families loved us together. We had all the private jokes of a couple that had been together forever, which (in teen years) we had.

The trouble started when I began wanting to stretch my wings. By my junior year in college, I had become restless. We broke up in the fall and decided to date other people; then I went to Vienna for the winter and spring. When I returned to Cincinnati in the summer, before my senior year, Scott was there waiting for me, even though I had not asked this of him. I can still see him leaning against his silver Mazda RX7, looking every bit the athlete in his six-foot-three frame, long legs crossed casually at the ankles, strong, tanned arms folded loosely across his chest in a gesture that was either paternal or challenging (or both). It was clear that he expected me to come to my senses and stop this nonsense about needing a break. But I'd returned from Vienna with a carpetbag of experiences and a heart like a magician's cabinet, full of secrets and hiding places. Put me in the box and I just might disappear.

It began to dawn on me that I was growing increasingly remote and privately furious. It wasn't his fault, really. I was a natural caregiver, finding genuine pleasure in catering to him, in going with the flow, and in being easy company. This had worked well for the most part, but now the stakes were higher. Now I was on the verge of the rest of my life. My seismic terror over the prospect of hurting his feelings (or anyone's feelings, for that matter) was in a standoff with my innate spiritual compass. It was an epic battle.

Scott was steady and consistent, and he had a clear plan for the future, which included marrying me and having a couple of kids by the time he was thirty. But I didn't want the future in black ink—I wanted it in fluid, living color. I wanted it to surprise me and to unfold in ways I had not thought of. Like the Yellow Brick Road, I wanted it to manifest one illuminated brick at a time. I began to believe, fairly or not, that Scott was in love with the sixteen-year-old me, not the one who was emerging. "You've changed," he said sadly, toward the end of the summer, his sigh like a nail in our coffin, punctuating the fact that this change was not for the better. "I'm growing," I whispered, trying to remind myself it was true. What did he expect me to do? My ire at the thought of staying home rekindled my resolve. Even if I hadn't met Andy, it was time. I needed some space; I needed some freedom. And yet, the irony that I might be in school again with a long-distance boyfriend, this time one in Connecticut, was not lost on me; it was unsettling, something I tried to throw to the back of my mind.

Somehow, these issues didn't seem so pressing when I was sitting in my small room in Rockefeller Hall, where there was so much space for me. I allowed the stillness to silence the noise in my head. *Just breathe*, I told myself. My eyes came to rest on my makeshift bookcase, where Tolstoy quietly beckoned me from his place on the shelf. Gratefully, I shook off my introspective hand-wringing and resumed my reading of "Father Sergius," the story of a prince who became a monk, who cut off his finger to stave off temptation. Sergius was a man who struggled to find true faith and a genuine existence, someone with inner demons, with doubts, even though he appeared saintly to others. The themes resonated with me. Tolstoy was one of the first writers we were studying in my class The Writer as Theologian. I found his work dark and compelling, visceral and spiritually challenging. The other challenge was getting to class on time. Unfortunately, it began at 8:00 a.m., tough for me since I have never been a morning person. The good news was that it was on the first floor of my residence hall, and I could literally roll out of bed, Superman T-shirt and all, and be there with one eye open. Luckily, Professor Guy Martin was not only a brilliant teacher but one of the kindest people you could ever meet. If I was late, he would just nod and give me a patient smile. But, in truth, I never wanted to miss a word that he said.

When the light disappeared from my room, I shut my book, turned the lamp on, and stretched. Images from the story were still quite vivid in my mind—and I felt like it was taking me a while to transition back to the present. Sometimes life was oddly solitary. Poking my head out the door, I was happy to hear friendly voices in the kitchen. A few people from down the hall were beginning to make their dinners. Ours was the closest suite to the kitchen, which I always appreciated. The sounds of cabinets opening and closing, or a teakettle singing, or people talking made life in the graduate dorm feel homey. The only time it wasn't great to live so near the kitchen was late at night when I would flip on the light and catch the mad dash of cockroaches scattering for cover like petty criminals who'd just gotten busted. Or worse, if I took one barefoot step too many in the dark, I might feel something moving underfoot—the sacrificial lamb offered up to make me jump. City cockroaches were new to me, as were the dog-sized rats that brazenly tooled around the Boston sidewalks at night. Give me an Ohio garter snake any day of the week!

Carla had put the phone back in the hall outside her door. I pulled it into my room and called Pine Street to speak with

Dik. He had already gone for the day, so I left a message—but I couldn't quite bring myself to call Scott. For some reason, I felt out of body when we talked, and I found myself concentrating really hard on conjuring an old self. It was like trying to put on a pink polka-dot dress that used to look cute years ago but no longer fit. His voice was clear and steady, while mine was steadily receding into the distance. I was never good at endings, and I had a terrible time expressing my feelings if I knew someone else's feelings would be hurt. *Maybe I'm just a coward hiding behind a pretense of compassion*, I thought. I started to dial his number, then slowly placed the phone in its cradle and set it back in the hall. I could always say that I didn't get the message . . .

I grabbed my towel and shampoo and started for the bathroom, but then I heard Silvia's alto voice coming from the shower. She was singing one of her favorite songs, the newly released "Total Eclipse of the Heart," in her signature monotone: *"Once upon a time I was falling in love . . ."* At that moment, Katherine came striding around the corner. As was often the case, she seemed semi-breathless and in a bit of a rush. She stopped short when she saw me standing in the hallway, then let out a silent, nodding laugh when I put my finger to my lips and pointed in the direction of the shower. We stood there for a moment, listening to Silvia's voice echoing in the bathroom, the words rising through the running water like steam, occasionally interrupted by the dropping of soap: *"Every now and then I fall apar-ar-art . . ."* It was funny and touching and revealing. Silvia's full-throttle commitment and lack of self-consciousness as she sang out in the shower did not seem to jive with her minimalist, deadpan persona. Standing there listening to her, it struck me anew that we

were, all of us, multi-textured creatures, expressing and ex-
perimenting, sharing and withholding, learning and growing. I felt so lucky.

"Hey, how's it going?" I asked Katherine as the water came
to a sputtering stop on the other side of the bathroom door.

"Good. Good. Well, actually I'm a little freaked out. My
ex-husband is coming by to visit me later, and I haven't seen
him in ages."

"Your ex-husband?" Katherine was only twenty-four years
old at the time.

"Yes. Long story, short marriage. Good guy, wrong girl."
Katherine hunched her shoulders, curling herself like a comma
in a cringing smile, and giving me a knowing look.

"Oh!" I said, with a raise of my eyebrows. "You want me
to stick around?"

"No, I'll be fine. But it might be interesting for you to
meet him. Would love your take on him. If you're around, I'll
introduce you."

Just then, Silvia emerged wrapped in a towel and glowing
from the heat of the shower. Her dark, wet hair was slicked
back, and a few drops of water still clung to her eyelashes.
She looked like Snow White's alter ego. Her skin might have
been white as snow and her hair black as night, but she
wouldn't have been caught dead cleaning up after seven little
men—or anyone else, for that matter. She paused, surveying
us with benign detachment. "Katherine. Andie," she said in
her clipped, official-sounding voice before disappearing into
her room. This, of course, made us laugh, albeit silently.
Then I told Katherine to knock on my door if her ex showed
up. She disappeared into her room, I slipped into the shower,
Silvia continued to hum, and Carla emerged to make dinner.

Our doors opened and closed like Japanese fans, revealing and concealing, or like the wings of a butterfly preparing to take flight. For a moment, I imagined our suite was a convent, a sanctuary from the heartache and uncertainty of relationships, a safe haven in which to rest—and, in many ways, it was.

6

---

the alley

My jeans suddenly felt too tight and my legs like hollow branches filled with cold jelly, somehow stiff and rubbery at the same time, as I walked down the alleyway that led toward the Pine Street Inn. Dik and I had finally connected on the phone, confirming that Pine Street and I were a good match. Now it was time to start my field education in earnest. What I hadn't considered was that it had been quiet there the day of my interview, an "off" time at the Inn, when the only people inside besides staff members were the very old or those needing special help. Most of the guests were not allowed into the shelter until after 3:30, when the doors were unlocked. Because there were not enough beds to accommodate all who sought shelter, the lines would start forming hours before the doors opened. The first three hundred men to enter would get a bed ticket; the remaining two to three hundred would have to make do on the floor. Although this wasn't the most comfortable accommodation for many of the guests, it struck me that no one was ever turned away, no one was told, "There is no room at the Inn." The weary "Josephs" of Boston could always find a place to rest, while the "Marys" were welcomed on the (smaller) women's side.

I was scheduled to arrive on the men's side at 2:30, prime time for a full assortment of waiting guests. When I rounded the corner and looked down the alley, I reminded myself, *It will never be as hard as it is today.* Sometimes a sense of calling gives us courage; sometimes, youthful optimism blinds us to danger. I had a little of both going on. I believed that I should be there, that this was where God was calling me, and my conviction helped keep me moving forward, one wobbly step at a time.

There were over a hundred homeless men already lined up against the wall as I began walking what felt like the gauntlet of despair. The men ranged in age from twenty to seventy and were in various mental and physical conditions. Some were having animated conversations with themselves, others were swaying to the groove of music that only they could hear, and still others had the bleary-eyed stare of the stoned or the intoxicated. Plenty of guys just looked bored or hungry. I began my fieldwork with that first step down the alley. Lesson number one: *Don't be scared. Hold your head up. Smile, but be confident.*

When I got to the door, I felt as if a thousand hands had passed over my body; it was strange. This feeling would dissipate over the course of my experience there. I either became less self-conscious or more confident—or both. I didn't exactly become immune to the stares or numb to the reality that I was one of the few women working there, but as time went on, I grew to know and love many of these men. They became individuals to me. They were not "the homeless"; they were Willie and Martin and Frank and Gerard. I knew their names; I knew their stories and tall tales. I cared about them as people—and they cared about me. The less time I spent in my head and the more time I spent in my heart, the better things went.

Once inside the shelter, I sought out Barbara, the counselor in charge. She was fondly nicknamed Barbowie for her love of David Bowie. It amazed me how small the staff was compared to the number of guests. There were only about six harried staff members working each shift, as well as a rotating cycle of volunteers who came from local churches and community groups to serve dinner. Barbowie tossed off a quick introduction to Ernie, whom I recognized as the man who had been sitting with the elderly gentleman on the day of my interview. Before I could mention this, she indicated that I should take a seat at the front desk so that I could see how the shelter functioned from the moment the doors opened. She wasn't overly friendly, but she wasn't unwelcoming, either. The message I got was simply "Keep up. Stay out of the way. Figure it out."

Barbowie sat on a stool behind the tall, battered desk, which stood about chest high, and I found myself a seat. A Boston police officer arrived, exchanged a friendly hello, and took his place at the door. Barbowie explained that an officer was posted there every day to frisk the men for weapons or alcohol when the shelter opened. "Some things still get through, of course," she said matter-of-factly, "but we do the best we can to make it safe for the guys." Shelter violence was a grim reality—but weighed against the chill of winter and an empty belly, most found it worth the risk. "These are the bed tickets," she explained, holding a stack of small papers. "First come, first serve. When they're out, they're out."

Across from the front entrance was a small office with a Dutch door. It was open on top, and I could see a woman busily organizing what looked like a medicine cabinet, with bandages, tape, and pill bottles spread out on the counter. I waited until Barbowie seemed finished with what she was doing, then asked what the office was used for.

"That's our clinic. If someone needs basic first aid or medication, they go to Norma there. If they need socks or gloves, or maybe a pair of pants (if they're lucky), they go in that big room to the right of the door. That's where a lot of the guys hang out. There's a TV and some benches, and the clothing closet where we can give out a few things, depending on donations." Before she could explain anything else, the cop said, "Ready?" as if he were about to lift the curtain on a show, and he opened the door.

Immediately, the shelter came alive. After a quick frisk, guests began shuffling inside. Each man paused at the desk to collect his bed ticket before moving on to the big room where dinner would be served. Barbowie greeted many of them by name. She was tough and loving at the same time, a straight shooter who was passionately committed to the shelter, to the guests, and to the well-being of those who remained on the street. I snuck a sideways look at her, her blond hair, the color of straw, pulled back in a long, loose braid; her clear, naked face beautiful without trying. I made an effort to stay out of the way. I didn't want her to think she had to babysit a divinity student on top of all her other work.

When most of the guests were inside, and the bed tickets were gone, Barbowie told me to go find Ernie and ask him if he needed help. I didn't take her quick dismissal personally, although it was an odd sensation to be cut loose. I'd felt safe somehow behind the desk, separated by protocol, tucked under Barbowie's wing, whether she wanted me there or not. Trying to hide my uneasiness, I slid from my stool and wandered into the large room opposite the TV lounge, where dinner was about to be served cafeteria-style; then I spotted Ernie talking to some of the guests.

All the workers at the shelter seemed to be young, and Ernie was no exception. He looked to be in his late twenties, with a helmet of dark hair and a black mustache. I studied his face for a moment. At first glance, his thick glasses and gap-toothed smile were disarming; they made him appear friendly and approachable. Upon closer study, I noticed he was also quite attractive behind those glasses, with a quirkiness that hinted at a more complex personality. He had a nice chin, and a face full of compassion when he interacted with the men. It was striking to see, actually. In the midst of all that chaos, all that sea of hurt and need and people clamoring for *something*, his posture spoke volumes. It said that someone was actually listening; someone genuinely cared.

The room was quite full now and growing noisier. There was a restless energy as guys looked for places at one of the long tables or waited in line for food. Ernie suggested that I help some of the older men retrieve their dinners. So I carried trays and got coffees and shook hands and eased into my work there. When I ran out of things to do, he told me to just sit, listen, hang out, be an ear. Trying not to feel self-conscious, I sat down next to one rather odd-looking fellow. His skin, his beard, and his clothes all seemed to be the same shade of dirty gray, giving him a strangely monotone appearance—a monument to the streets. He shot me a shy, sideways smile when I sat down on his bench, and I tried not to react to the strong smell of urine and filth that emanated from him. I had just introduced myself when Ernie approached with an amused look on his face.

"Uh, I wouldn't sit so close to Billy, there. He's going upstairs for a scabies treatment in a minute. Sorry, Billy; no offense."

"None taken" was Billy's friendly response.

Ernie motioned for me to come with him; then he leaned in and told me how the staff tried to treat those with known infestations. He also explained how all the men who were sleeping upstairs had to be checked for scabies, lice, etc., before getting into bed. Most guys were used to the routine, he told me. Those with bed tickets were ushered upstairs to the sleeping area. Each man put his clothes in a bin, which was then placed in a large oven overnight to kill off any bugs; this also cut down on the number of concealed weapons that managed to make it past the frisk at the door. Everyone had to shower. No shower, no bed. It was that simple. The men were given something to sleep in and would retrieve their (deloused) clothes in the morning. "I just told one guy upstairs to take off his vest," Ernie said with a little smile. "Then I saw that it was moving! Turns out it wasn't a vest; it was cockroaches. I kid you not. He had a vest of cockroaches." This might have been an extreme case, but more than once during my time at Pine Street, I saw a cockroach scramble out of someone's shirt or disappear down a collar.

He led me over to two old-timers sitting on a bench against the wall and introduced me to Stevie and Leo. "Look out for this girl, will ya, fellas? Show her the ropes." Then he disappeared back into the packed room, like Jonah swallowed by the whale. I could not have known then how grateful I would be for that introduction, because these two men became home base, my touchstones, throughout my time at Pine Street. Whenever I wasn't sure of what to do with myself, they always had a place for me on the bench. They told me of their lives, they entertained me with exaggerated tales of being sailors or soldiers or salesmen. They told me whom to watch out for, and they worried about me when I left each evening.

As we talked, Stevie smoked cigarette after cigarette, his eyes a patriotic red, white, and blue, his hands rough and chapped. He had the slim frame of a chain smoker, and the wet, phlegmy cough to go with it. "One of these days, I'm bound to cough up a lung," he'd say, only half kidding. He usually sat with one skinny leg crossed over the other, an elbow on his knee, gesturing with his cigarette as he talked. Sometimes his stories were so fantastical that my eyes would widen, and I would find myself incredulous. "Really? Really, Stevie?" I'd stammer.

When he could take it no more, Leo would interject, "Aw, cut it out, Stevie!" Then, turning to me, he'd gently say, "He's pulling your leg, honey. You gotta learn not to be so gullible."

"But she's from *Ohio*," Stevie would say, with mock indignation and a croaky laugh. "She can't help it!"

Stevie loved to tell me colorful stories about being in the merchant marines, traveling the world and having adventures, but he became strangely vague when asked about his family. "Yeah, I got a coupla kids. All growed up now. I haven't seen or talked to them for years. Probably for the best." *Drag on cigarette, eyes looking off into space.*

Leo, on the other hand, was tall and rather round faced, an old Irish version of Oliver Hardy. He was sweet and pleasant, with smooth baby skin and a mostly bald head, which he usually kept covered with a beanie. He looked about ten years younger than Stevie, although it was hard to tell ages at the shelter—life on the streets had a way of aging men beyond their years. I guessed Leo and Stevie to be about sixty and seventy respectively but, more than likely, they were in their late fifties and sixties.

I wasn't sure why Leo was at the shelter, whether he had simply fallen on tough times or had a diagnosis that was difficult to read on the surface. Maybe he was illiterate but too embarrassed to admit it; maybe he had a panic disorder or was bipolar. Maybe it didn't matter—from all appearances, he seemed like anyone's friendly uncle. He said that he had a daughter, a real sweetheart, who was always begging him to move in with her, but he didn't want to be a burden. "Besides," he said, "I'm used to being on my own." Sometimes he'd stay with her for the weekend—but he was always back at Pine Street by Monday, back in his spot next to Stevie. Unlike his buddy, however, Leo didn't smoke, and he often remarked about how tough the shelter air was on his lungs. "My daughter took me to the doctor the other day," he explained. "The doc told me I had the lungs of a man who smoked two packs a day. Can you believe that? I've never smoked a day in my life but I've been breathing this air for five years."

He made a scary point. I knew that the air in the shelter was toxic, but Leo's condition confirmed it. The vast majority of the men smoked, and smoked continuously. With hundreds of men in an enclosed space, it took only about fifteen minutes for a haze to fill the two common rooms; it was like moving through low-lying fog. The ceiling and walls were stained yellow-brown, like so many of the men's hands and teeth, from nicotine and tar that had nowhere to go. When I would leave the shelter and board the T for Harvard Square, I was often self-conscious about how I smelled—which was basically like a giant ashtray. I was a life-sized pack of Luckies. So saturated was I with smoke after a night of work that even my bra reeked. As soon as I got home, I would immediately strip down, put my clothes in a plastic bag to be washed, and stand in the shower while the fumes literally rose off my body—my hair, my skin, my eyes, my throat. It took quite a while before the mist in the shower stopped smelling like cigarette smoke. I said a prayer for Leo and the guys each time before getting out.

That first evening passed without incident. Barbowie said I could go home around nine; in the future, my shifts were usually 3:00 to 10:00, twice a week. When the cop at the door offered to escort me to the T, I declined, saying that I'd be fine. Thankfully, I was—but I later shuddered at my naïveté. I really didn't know enough about the area to say that. I waved good-bye to whoever was standing near the door, which seemed to go largely unnoticed, and began walking back up the long alleyway, which was now dark and deserted. Only the ghosts of the men remained. But I was not afraid of ghosts. They accompanied me, they walked with me, and I knew that they were teaching me. There was danger on the street, yes—real danger lurking in the shadows—but I felt safe at Pine Street. Maybe that's why Stevie and Leo continued to come night after night, year after year. Besides the need to get out of the cold, they knew they had a place there. They were known there. And they had developed a friendship that made life a little more bearable. Although I had yet to fully discover my own purpose for being at Pine Street, there was room for me at the Inn. I was there to help, I was there to learn; that much I knew. What I couldn't have imagined was that I was there to meet God.

7

love is patient,
love is kind

A couple weeks had gone by since my chance encounter with Tomas, and I had yet to call him. I was blissfully absorbed in my studies and my work at Pine Street. Katherine's ex had come and gone, leaving hardly a ripple on the surface of our pond. A tall, bearded, flannel-shirted man, he was handsome and appropriately awkward as we shook hands in the tight hallway. The next time I saw Katherine, I forgot to ask about him. The hallway between our rooms was like a stage upon which various characters routinely appeared and disappeared. Some were minor, bit players, never to be seen again; others provided comic relief; still others became regular parts of the ensemble.

Andy would become a familiar guest star. The first time I saw him after moving to Cambridge was both sweet and difficult. It was early October, and I hadn't seen him since June. After our graduation from Denison, I had flown to his family's house in Greenwich, Connecticut, to visit him before he left on a backpacking trip to Europe with his friend Bobo. My parents weren't crazy about my going to Greenwich, but I was stubborn in my resolve.

That trip proved to be a crucial cementing of the delicate mosaic we were building. The first pieces of our puzzle were still locking into place; if bumped by time or neglect, they might become jumbled, losing their significance and beauty. Seeing each other outside the context of college life confirmed that something vibrant and real existed between us. It had not been a "spring fling," as so often happens in the last days of college. My being accepted to Harvard extended the possibility that we could have an ongoing, viable relationship.

I smiled seeing how nervous he was about showing me his house and how apologetic he was about being from Greenwich; he didn't want me to think him a snob. Ironically, I was clueless about Greenwich's reputation for affluence, not that I would have cared, anyway. I was more concerned about seeing his mom again; we had met only briefly at Denison. I hoped that she would like me, despite the fact that I wasn't from the East Coast or a debutante.

When we arrived at the house, which was lovely but not ridiculous, Andy's German shepherd, Abby, came out to greet us, wagging her tail. Although ten years old, Abby was elegant and graceful; we made friends immediately. (Katherine later nicknamed her Queen Elizabeth, when Abby accompanied him once for a visit.) Andy told me that his mother also loved cats, and that they had two of them, which I took as a good sign. When we stepped inside, his mom and stepfather were gracious and welcoming. They were clearly impressed that I was headed to Harvard Divinity in the fall; at least it showed that I had a brain and some ambition. Andy's stepfather had gone to Yale, which provided an instant basis for friendly teasing and made for easy conversation. They were Episcopalians, intellectuals, and open-minded about women in the ministry—not that that was my intention, I assured them. The fact that Andy had no plans yet and no job prospects probably helped my standing with them.

We tried not to dwell on the future too much during the visit. Instead, we talked about his upcoming trip. He gave me his itinerary and I wrote down the names of places to stay and things to see in various cities, which were still fresh in my mind from my semester in Vienna. I promised to send letters to the American Express offices in the countries that he would be visiting, crossing my fingers that they would get there ahead of him, as this would be our only means of communication through the summer.

The next morning, we took the train from Greenwich to New York City, sitting close together while laughing and canoodling, occasionally drawing the eyes of the passengers across from us. I'd never been to New York, but it only took about an hour or two to realize that my much-anticipated mugging and murder were not a given. He thought my fear very funny. Eventually I stopped clutching my purse so tightly to my side and began to relish the vibrant flow of the city. We spent the day walking around Greenwich Village; we picked up his Eurail pass; we enjoyed the sights. When my cotton skirt was blown to my waist, Marilyn Monroe–style, as I walked over a subway grate (causing a passing bicycle delivery-man to point and hoot), we burst out laughing. Everything about the day seemed magical.

Before I knew it, he was dropping me off at the airport to go home. We held each other a long time in the parking lot, not wanting to part. Just before we did, Andy balanced his camera on top of his car, put the timer on, and ran to my side before it clicked, taking a picture of us arm in arm.

"I'm going to take that with me to Europe," he said.

"You'd better wait until you develop the film before you say that," I said, laughing. "What if I look bad? Then you'll never come home!"

"I don't care what it looks like; I just want to remember this moment. Besides, you always look beautiful."

That was almost four months ago. Since then we had only spoken by phone a couple of times. Miraculously, he had gotten all but one of the letters that I had sent to the various cities in Europe, and I had received numerous postcards from him. This gave our relationship a romantic, almost unreal quality. But now he was on his way to the Divinity School to visit for the first time. It was almost as if he were going to be stepping out of one of the pictures I had looked at so often in his absence. Those were moments frozen in time, but I was not frozen. I was already living in another world—and I was uncertain about how that reality would merge with the fantasy.

He called as he was leaving Greenwich so that I'd have an idea of when he would be arriving, the silky quality of his voice awakening my sensory memory of him. It was about a three-hour drive—close enough to make our relationship possible, but far enough to require determination. I tried to do some studying in the interim, but felt distracted and antsy. When I heard Katherine's voice in the hall, I stuck my head out the door.

"Hey, Katherine—happy Friday!"

"Oh, hi!" she said, pausing to lean against her door, keys in one hand, a giant coffee in the other. "What are you up to this weekend?"

"Well, actually, this guy that I'm dating is on his way here, even as we speak."

"Really? Who? Scott?"

"No, Andy, from Denison," I said with a little laugh. Katherine had heard me agonize about Scott and had seen the telephone messages that Carla routinely stuck on my door.

"The musician?"

"Yes. We haven't seen each other for months. He was backpacking in Europe with his best friend all summer; and I came straight from Ohio to here."

"Cool. Are you excited?"

"Yes . . . but a little nervous, too."

Just then, the buzzer rang near the kitchen, indicating someone was at the door downstairs.

"Oh, boy," Katherine said with a conspiratorial smile. "Bet that's him. Good luck!"

"Gulp," I answered, opening the door to the stairwell. "Say a prayer!"

"Always!" I heard her yell as I went flying down the stairs.

Someone must have let him in because he met me on the first-floor landing. I saw him taking the steps two at a time, his long arms hanging loose in his jean jacket as if they were barely attached, his upturned face providing a beautiful backdrop for his blue eyes. He wrapped himself around me and held me to him, our bodies perfectly aligned, and we stood there kissing in the shady in-between.

"I can't believe you're here," I said, barely able to look at him directly. I suddenly felt shy, as if I'd rather take him in from a distance first.

"I know. I made great time. You can really fly on the Mass Pike."

His dark chestnut hair was a mess of long, loose curls, and he had grown a little scruff (I don't think it would have actually qualified as a beard) while in Europe.

"Come on," I said, taking his arm. "Let me show you around."

We continued up the stairs to my floor, where I introduced him to a couple of people who were sitting in the kitchen. I tapped on Katherine's door, but when she opened it, she was engaged in a phone call.

"Hi," she whispered, tipping the phone sideways with her left hand while extending her right to Andy. "Sorry," she mouthed, pointing to the phone with a roll of her eyes. I waved it off, letting her know it was okay.

Next I showed him my room, leaving the door open in case Carla or Silvia were around so I could introduce them, too.

"Wow . . . this is so cool. I like your view," he said. He was standing in the middle of the room with his hands in his pockets. As he was looking around, I was looking at him. He was hip and mercurial, liquid, sanguine—an intriguing combination of nervous energy and Deadhead cool. He was so alive, I could practically feel the blood pulsing through his body when we'd stood arm in arm.

"I told Tom and Burki you were coming, and they said they'd stop by. They seemed anxious to see you," I said.

"Sure, that'd be fun—maybe I'll get my guitar out of the car. I can't believe you're all here together."

After retrieving his guitar, he sat on my bed strumming it as we waited for Tom and Burki. Meanwhile, I studied his face as he played. It always struck me as slightly fairylike or mythical, something out of a Victorian painting or a Shakespearean tale. I don't mean fairylike in a feminine way—he was King Oberon's mortal child, ethereal, translucent. Standing six feet tall, he was thin as a rail but broad shouldered, with large, strong hands and smooth skin Saran-Wrapped across his cheekbones. His nose was straight and sturdy, trustworthy somehow in its prominence, affirming his masculine strength. He needed this because otherwise he was almost pretty with his large, sapphire eyes and dark lashes, and his perfect lips, which frequently curled into an impish grin.

As we relaxed into each other's presence, he told me about his travels with Bobo and showed me some pictures. Sitting close together, we began to reharmonize, to synchronize, and to find one another again. I wanted to touch his face and body like a blind woman, to smell him, and to refamiliarize myself with this lanky boy-man. I was almost surprised that he did not feel like the past to me, and although I couldn't fathom the future, I was grateful that he was there, in the lovely present.

Soon there was a tap on the open door—it was Tom and Burki. After hugging our hellos, they found a spot on the floor and quickly settled in. "Hey, man, guess what?" Tom said after a few minutes. He was scratching his blond beard and trying to contain the broad smile that was pressing at the corners of his mouth. "Burki's pregnant! We're going to have a baby. Pretty crazy, huh?" We all let out an excited whoop. Questions such as "Are you happy?" "Was it planned?" "Will you stay in school?" were fired in rapid succession. They were the first of our friends to embark upon this path. They told us that the baby was a surprise, but not an unwelcome one, and we all marveled over this new wrinkle in the fabric of our world.

"Wow, man, congratulations," Andy said, shaking Tom's hand.

I hugged Burki—then I looked at her, at her lovely face and clear eyes. *This must be what Mary looked like*, I thought, *full of mystery and wonder*. What was my friend pondering in her heart, what secret thoughts? She was only twenty-one, young for our class, when we graduated from college and started divinity school. A natural beauty, with light brown hair and blue eyes, Burki never wore makeup and was usually dressed comfortably in something like jeans and a cotton peasant shirt. I looked at her in awe. There was a life growing inside of her at that very moment. Each second, and the milliseconds in between, a human being was being formed, a story was unspooling, both separate from and part of her. What was it like to suddenly be *two* instead of *one*? That *is the mystery of incarnation*, I thought. That *is holiness*.

As her pregnancy progressed, Burki would sometimes come to my room to rest. She and Tom lived off-campus, and there were times she simply needed to lie down. I could not then imagine the fatigue of an expectant mother, especially in the early months, but I was happy to share my room. After Max was born, I would sometimes watch him so that Tom and Burki could study. This was especially helpful during exam times. While his parents studied, I would push him around Harvard Square in a stroller, pointing out this and that, take him for ice cream, or wander down by the Charles River to watch the rowers glide by. I welcomed the opportunity to step out of my head for a couple of hours, step out of the world of academics and homelessness and romantic uncertainties, and simply feel his little fingers curl around my hand. Years later, Burki asked Max if he remembered me. "I can't picture her face," he said, "but I think I remember the sound of her voice." The image of that connection always touched me: my voice behind him in the stroller, his little ears giving me the opportunity to sing.

After our friends left, Andy and I took a walk into Harvard Square. It was like stepping into a living Jackson Pollock painting, with young people and color splattered everywhere. As soon as we crossed from the Yard to the Square, we became part of the painting. The Friday-night scene was pulsing and fun, with just enough grunginess to give it an edge. Andy put his arm around me and I felt the familiar flash of skittishness, my fear of being tethered, of commitment—but then it passed as I exhaled into the us-ness of us. I'm not sure if he felt my urge to run like a cat through the street, but he held me there firmly. Perhaps he was unconsciously reassuring me that he was *in* it: in the relationship, regardless of the distance. He was always more transparent and honest than I was, but he'd also been in free fall since our graduation. He'd returned from a great summer in Europe to the dim reality of *What's next?*

"I don't know what I can do with this English major," he confided as we walked, our strides in easy synchronicity, our eyes looking ahead. "I'm thinking about applying to journalism school but I'm not sure if that's really what I want."

"Well, you're doing some writing now, aren't you?" I offered, trying to be encouraging.

"Writing obits for the local paper isn't exactly writing! Can you believe I'm doing that? What a trip. And working at the Love and Serve, that natural food restaurant in Greenwich, is cool, but not exactly what I want to do with my life. You're so lucky to be here."

I did feel lucky. I didn't know what I wanted to do either, but I knew that I was on the right path. He was living at home, feeling a little isolated; I was at Harvard, surrounded by interesting people. He was struggling, trying to figure out the next step; I was taking them two at a time. Maybe part of that tight hold, then, was fear . . . fear that I would slip away, fear that his life had no clear direction or that he would get lost.

The next day, Katherine, Carla, and a few other people from my dorm were going to Walden Pond, the lake made famous by Thoreau. "Let's go," I suggested to Andy. "It will be fun—and I'd love for you to get to know some of my friends." He seemed amenable, but I noticed that he wasn't entirely enthusiastic about the idea. I chalked this up to his natural shyness.

It was a perfect fall day. The leaves were just beginning to change colors, reflecting on the water with staggering beauty. We'd brought food to share, books to read, journals to scribble in. The feeling was relaxed and happy. We hiked, we sprawled on the ground; we got to know each other a little better. There was not a lot of God talk, but I could tell Andy was feeling rather out of body and out of place. He became self-conscious when people asked him about what he was doing, and this self-consciousness made him retreat into himself. I knew that he was just shy and probably felt uncomfortable, but he came off as aloof, which irritated and embarrassed me. Fairly or not, I felt that he wasn't really trying. By the time he got in his car to go home, I was ready for some space. I needed a *lot* of space. I was chock-full of mixed signals, both wanting a relationship and holding him at arm's length. Deep down, as I watched him pull away, I was grateful for the three hours that separated us.

When he called a few days later, there was palpable tension between us.

"What was going on with you at Walden Pond?" I asked. "You were acting so weird."

"I'm sorry. I just got so freaked out," he replied, clearly miserable. "I mean, it's so easy for you in some ways to still be in school. At Walden, it was like, there you all were, at Harvard, and I just felt like such a loser."

"Well, no one else thought that . . . until you went off and disappeared by yourself."

For a few long moments, the only sound on the line was that of one or the other of us exhaling into the phone.

"Listen," I started, softly, suddenly feeling like I was beginning to submerge and had water in my ears. "Maybe we need a little time to think. I spent most of high school and college with a boyfriend three hours away, and it's hard for me to think of starting that all over again here. It's not your fault, but I wish we could just have a normal relationship."

He was quiet for a moment before answering, "Me, too. So what do you want to do?"

Though difficult, we agreed to think about what taking a break might mean. Neither of us was ready to let the relationship go completely, but the practicalities of maintaining it were daunting. I felt depressed, and probably a little angry, at the prospect of being tied to a long-distance boyfriend again, and he felt hurt (and angry) at my apparent ability to put the steel door of my heart on lockdown.

Perhaps it was inevitable, then, that one day I would pull out the scribbled scrap of paper that was tucked in my journal. When the day came, my heart pounded as I dialed the number. *What am I doing? What am I doing? What am I doing? What about Andy? And would Tomas even remember me? "Hi, I'm the barefoot girl you met on the street,"* I imagined myself saying. Or *"Hey, Tomas, it's me, Tomato Face."* Or maybe *"Hola, beautiful stranger—Furnace Girl here."* My mouth went dry at the first ring; then three ascending tones BB-gunned my ear. "*Bing, bing, bing.* The number you have reached is currently not in service. Please check the number and try again. *Bing, bing, bing.* The number you have reached . . ." *I am such a dope!* I let out the air that had been jammed all the way down into my stomach and shook my head. "Oh well," I said out loud, to no one. "That's the way it goes. Probably just as well."

I opened my Bible, not out of a need for inspiration but out of necessity. I had work to do for my class on 1 Corinthians, taught by Catholic scholar and sage George MacRae. Initially, I couldn't imagine how we would spend a whole semester on this slim Epistle, whose only claim to fame was the beautiful but overused passage on love found in chapter 13. The first time I read that passage, I was eight years old. My Vacation Bible School teacher had asked us to try to memorize it in its entirety; if we succeeded, we would get a prize. I remember thinking it was the most strange and beautiful thing I had ever read, next to Hamlet's famous "To be or not to be" soliloquy, part of which I had also memorized in the second grade. My second grade teacher and my Vacation Bible School teacher were one and the same, and she was very big on the art of memorizing. "It's good for your brain," she had told us, "and it's also handy to have a few things in your heart when you need them." When the day came for us to say the passage from memory, she had each student go into the room privately, so that no one would be embarrassed. After successfully reciting the chapter to her, she gave me a small plastic trophy. I couldn't have been more proud. It only occurred to me much later that perhaps the reason we did our recitation privately was because *every* student got a trophy, whether they successfully memorized the passage or not.

Hearing something for the first time can be a mystical experience. At eight, I was completely oblivious to the fact that this passage was trotted out at nearly every Christian wedding. I had new ears, and new ears marvel over phrases like "When I was a child, I spoke like a child, I thought like a child, I reasoned like a child; when I became a man, I gave up childish ways." And new ears do not snooze through the mystery of "For now we see in a mirror dimly, but then face to face. Now I know in part; then I shall understand fully, even as I have been fully understood." *What could this mean?* If the passage had a scent, it would be an exotic spice. It took years for me to stop marveling at this (and other passages), years for the words to lose some of their deep-purple, sacred mystique. Sometimes familiarity breeds, not contempt, as they say, but boredom.

As Professor MacRae slowly walked to the podium in the lecture hall on that first day of class, however, a reverent hush filled the room—and my ears became new again. It was immediately clear that we were in the presence of a great scholar and a master teacher. His aura was both commanding and gentle. Dressed in a suit and tie, his gray hair and spectacles gave him an old-school timelessness. He was broad and a bit round, with soft features and a rumbling, gentle voice; as he spoke, words seemed to tumble down the mountain of his chest. He set two books on the podium—a well-worn Revised Standard Version of the Bible and a Greek translation of 1 Corinthians. Then, without a note, he began to teach us. We spent the entire first two days of class solely on the first three verses of Paul's letter—you know, the introduction, the part that you always skip over because it's just like the heading on a memo, the "To" and "From" portion. I sat in amazement at the depth of his knowledge, his scholarly integrity, and at the way he spoke in seamless, articulate paragraphs. Someone in class asked the professor if the reason he never used notes was because he knew the material so well, to which MacRae responded, "Not at all. I don't use notes because, in doing so, I may overlook something that I haven't seen before. This way, I am always open to inspiration or a new understanding." I was blown away.

Now, back in the quiet of my room, I was staring at the scriptures, holding a Bible Scott had given me, thinking about Andy and using Tomas's scribbled number, absentmindedly, for a bookmark. *I have got to focus*, I thought, shaking my head like a wet dog's.

I had always believed that the scriptures held the hidden signposts for my life—I just had to be willing to look for (and be open to) God's guidance. If I was feeling sad or lonely, I'd often turn to the Psalms; if I needed courage, I'd find something in the Gospels. At the moment, I was feeling lost regarding relationships, and I prayed that something from 1 Corinthians might point me in the right direction.

We were on chapter 3 in class, and my eyes came to rest on one of my favorite passages:

> *Do you not know that you are God's temple and that God's Spirit dwells in you? If any one destroys God's temple, God will destroy him. For God's temple is holy, and that temple you are.*

"I am God's temple," I repeated to myself, "and God's Spirit dwells in me . . . I am God's temple and God's Spirit dwells in me . . ." I tried to honor the part about being God's temple by not polluting my body—I didn't smoke, drink, do drugs, or eat junk food. But I yearned to feel, in an ever-deeper way, the indwelling Spirit of God. If I stayed connected and in tune with God's Spirit, which was as close as my own heartbeat, then I was certain that my path would become clearer regarding all aspects of my life—including relationships. I shut my book, shut my eyes, and prayed: *Please, God, help me. Help me be who you want me to be. Show me the way.*

8

universal laws

It was bound to happen sooner or later. I could blame it on Sir Isaac Newton or on karma; both say essentially the same thing about the dance of action and reaction, cause and effect. Newton's laws of physics describe the relationship between the forces acting on a body and its motion due to those forces. Karma teaches that one's actions cause a ripple effect in the fabric of human life, which in turn determines destiny. Maybe it was science, maybe it was destiny, but something had been set in motion on the day I met Tomas, and our paths were meant to converge again, the gravitational pull silently nudging us along.

It was another pretty day in Cambridge, although cooler now. I was not barefoot or red-faced; I was wearing my cowboy boots and a jean jacket, and I was walking back from the laundromat with a pillowcase full of clean clothes. The air smelled of earth and dry leaves, leaves that crunched beneath my boots as if announcing my arrival (to no one in particular). I sounded like a marching band, an army of one—*crunch, crunch, crunch,*

crunch—my sack full of laundry held in front of me like a bass drum at rest. A neighborhood cat joined the parade, following me for about half a block before losing interest, deciding instead to sit down in the middle of the sidewalk and lick its paws. It was that kind of day, a relaxed, paw-licking day. I wasn't thinking about school or the work I had to do; I wasn't thinking about relationships, or even my buddies Stevie and Leo. I was in the moment, part of nature's comic improv, a moving body sending out waves of energy. *If an object experiences no net force, then its velocity is constant*, deduced Newton in his first law of motion. I was moving in a straight line, a constant flow, my course unhindered by any external force.

Leaves were falling like little flames, in oranges and reds, like sparks from the Divine—and I was walking through the fire unscathed. Occasionally I would extend my hand to catch one, then let it fall again, still burning. I could see a body moving toward me through the flames, this time on the same side of the road. I felt the energy, its force, its pull, and the smile that was causing me, again, to smile. Second law: *The acceleration of a body is parallel and directly proportional to the net force acting on the body . . .* I felt my forward motion change. My feet were walking at roughly the same pace, but my heart was skipping ahead to meet him.

"Andrea! Andie. It's me, Tomas." He came to rest in front of me, the gentle wave of his vibration washing over me like the wake rolling onto a beach. My laundry separated us; it was an inner tube, keeping me afloat and softening the forces. "I'm so happy to see you. I was hoping we would meet again."

"Well, you couldn't have been hoping too much because you gave me the wrong number," I said with a squint of my eyes, only half joking.

"I know, I know!" he moaned. "I was so nervous when I saw you that I reversed the last two numbers. I realized it later, but only after you'd disappeared."

"I was wondering what happened . . . I did try to call you, though. Well, I guess you know that since I just said you gave me the wrong number." Now it was I who felt nervous and shy.

I shifted my sack of laundry, trying to be inconspicuous about twisting the top closed so that my underwear was not front and center, then I threw it over one shoulder. Without the crunch of leaves, I was no longer an army—I was Santa Claus out of season. "Here, let me help you," he said, taking the pillowcase from my hands. He cradled it in his arms like a baby, which somehow made the gesture more natural and inti-mate, as if we were already a couple, although I think this was largely unconscious.

We walked back to my dorm, talking the way you do when you meet someone again for the first time. There was a familiarity about him, an instant trust and an ease of being that felt like spiritual déjà vu. We sat in front of Rockefeller on one of the stone benches on the patio. He leaned back on his hands and shut his eyes for a moment, face tilted toward the sky, and I took a secret snapshot of his image, an imprint of his spirit, and stashed it away in the pocket of my heart re-served for all things sacred. He told me about Bogotá and about his heritage, trying to explain the mixture of Spanish conquistador and Amerindian. He talked about how much he loved playing the cello and about music school. I liked the way he talked and the way that he had to *stop* talking, every now and then, to look at me with that same expression of wonder. I told him about Ohio and about HDS, about Pine Street and about not knowing what I ultimately wanted to do. I also told him about Andy, how we had met in college, and how difficult it was to keep the relationship together through the distance.

"Andrea"—he'd decided to call me that because he thought it was prettier and because he loved the sound of it—"I am not asking anything of you. I would only like to spend some time with you. I like you and would like to get to know you better."

How could I argue with that? I liked his company, liked the fact that he was not a divinity student, and I liked his face. The thought of spending time with someone who lived nearby, not hours away, was so refreshing. *Maybe we could just be friends*, I thought—though the attraction I felt toward him might make this difficult.

"Some friends are coming over on Saturday night," he explained. "I think you'd enjoy it. It's a very international crowd. We just hang out, we cook a lot of food—everyone brings something to share—then we sometimes play music or dance. I could teach you to salsa," he said with a flicker of playful mischief in his eyes. When I hesitated, he reassured me, saying, "If you're uncomfortable coming alone, bring some friends; everyone is welcome." We exchanged telephone numbers (this time the correct one for him), and he gave me directions to his apartment, which wasn't far from me. "Please try to come," he said with a smile. "It will be fun."

"Okay, I'll try" was my response, although I already knew I would. As per Newton's third law: *When a first body exerts a force on a second body, the second body simultaneously exerts a force on the first body.* Force 1 was pushing against force 2, action and reaction, karma and choice.

When Saturday night arrived, I decided to venture over to his place by myself. I had told Katherine where I was going, just in case he turned out to be an ax murderer, but, in reality, I had no fears. As I approached the building, I could hear the sound of laughter and happy chatter floating out the window of one of the apartments above. These voices, whose words I could not perceive, were set against the backdrop of Latin music; I knew I had arrived at the right place.

It wasn't necessary to ring a bell to get into the building, so I proceeded to walk up the steps to his second-floor apartment. As I got closer, the voices got louder, which put me at ease because they sounded warm and friendly. When I found the right apartment number, I knocked on the door and heard someone yell, "It's open!" Taking a little breath, I turned the handle and walked in. There was a short entryway, filled with shoes of various shapes and sizes, pointing in random directions, as if they were dancing or conversing on their own. Following their cue, I took my boots off and introduced them to a friendly looking pair of sneakers. I continued down the narrow hall, which had a bedroom on either side. It led to a small kitchen, where a number of people had congregated. A pretty girl with dark, wavy hair that hung just below her cheeks was sitting on the counter smoking a cigarette. She wore a long, loose skirt and a cotton shirt, both of which threatened to swallow her tiny frame. Dangling her feet, she was having an animated conversation in Spanish with a young guy leaning next to her in a Billy Jack hat and a leather vest. Another guy, who appeared to be in his early twenties, was standing at the stove, one hand on his hip, casually stirring something that smelled delicious. He had silky black hair that was swept behind his ears, and a graceful frame. He looked up when I walked in, smiled warmly, and nodded a hello.

Before I had a chance to ask for him, Tomas came walking into the kitchen from the living room, where other voices could be heard and from where the music seemed to be coming.

"You made it!" he said, clearly delighted. "I was really hoping you'd come. Here, let me introduce you to some people."

He took my arm and introduced me to the people in the kitchen. Most of them were from other countries—Colombia, Italy, Peru, Germany. All seemed to be between the ages of nineteen and thirty. Tomas, as it turned out, was seven years older than I; he was twenty-nine to my twenty-two, but it never seemed like there was a gap of years between us. He led me into the living room, where there were candles burning and people dancing. The smell of cigarettes and reefer comingled in the air, although I couldn't see where it was coming from.

"So now, would you like to learn how to salsa?" he asked. "Just follow me." He put his hands on my hips, and we began to move to the music, and I felt happy and free.

Such began the dance of Tomas in and out of my life. I would draw close, then pull away. I would feel myself falling deeper, then shut it down. Although Andy and I had talked about seeing other people while we were apart, the practical reality of this was confusing and hard. I argued (and justified within myself) that I was still at the start of my life, that I needed to learn about myself and about relationships, but I ended up feeling dishonest, and sometimes even resentful, when Andy would call or when he would want to come for a visit. His were open arms, trusting arms, and I was as quixotic and changing as the moon.

After the night at Tomas's apartment, we began to see each other fairly frequently. We were both busy with school and work but managed to find time to meet for coffee or to walk the streets holding hands. Most of the time, I was a mess. He knew this but was tender and present anyway. I liked being with him; I trusted him. I liked hanging out at his apartment. It was simple and comfortable, with a futon on the floor, plenty of cooking pots in the kitchen, and a lovely white cat named Femio. The cat was multilingual, of course, but tried hard not to be smug about this (though a flick of his tail at someone's stupidity would occasionally give him away).

Sometimes we would meet in Cambridge Commons, a small grassy park about halfway between HDS and Longy. On one of those occasions, he brought a book of poetry by Pablo Neruda.

"Do you know Neruda's work?" he asked, pulling the book from his bag. We were lounging on the grass, as children played around us and squirrels eyed us hopefully for a scrap of food.

"No," I replied. "Who is he?"

"He was a Chilean poet. He's gone now, but his poems are so beautiful." He shut his eyes as he said this and let out a little sigh, and I could feel the poet in him as well. "Would you like me to read one to you? This volume has the English translation alongside the Spanish."

"I would love that . . ." I lay down with my head in his lap, looking up at the sky and at his face, contemplating how lucky I was to have found him.

"Listen to this. It's from one of his sonnets," he began:

In my sky at twilight you are like a cloud
And your form and color are the way I love them.

En mi cielo al crespusculo eres como una nube
Y tu color y forma son como yo los quireo. *

We let the words hover in the air, like hummingbirds or perfume, before speaking.

"Could you read that again?" I asked, rolling onto my stomach, my head on my hands. Tomas stretched out, too, propping the book in front of us so that I could read along with the English as he read it in Spanish. And so we spent the afternoon reading Neruda, marveling over the beauty of a single line, savoring it, sharing it, until the sun began to fade.

Tomas walked me back to my dorm. When we got there, he said, "Before you go, I have something for you."

"What? You do?"

"Yes, it's something you inspired. It's a poem I wrote about you after the first time we met," he said shyly.

"You mean when I was walking through Harvard Yard barefoot?"

"Yes!"

Tomas opened his notebook, and there, in his lovely handwriting, was the poem.

Somewhere I have it; somewhere I have stashed it away, like buried treasure. I don't remember the exact words, but I remember him describing my feet like this: "*tus pies desnudos, como palomas besando la tierra . . .* your naked feet, like doves kissing the earth." It was so beautiful, I could barely take it in.

Tomas's roommate was a fellow Colombian named Nico, who was not a musician but was in graduate school somewhere

---

* Pablo Neruda, *100 Love Sonnets*, translated by Stephen Tapscott (Austin: University of Texas Press, 1986), 39.

in Boston. He had not been present the night of the party, and so, oddly enough, the first time I met him was at a march on Washington. I had taken the long bus ride from Cambridge Commons, with a handful of other divinity students, in the wee hours of a cold November morning. We were there to participate in a protest march against U.S. policies in Nicaragua. Katherine, Carla, and I were under the distinct impression that nearly everyone at HDS was going. It had been heavily advertised in flyers posted everywhere, with instructions in the Divinity School newsletter about transportation, and in impassioned discussions in the refectory. Word around campus: it was our sacred duty as divinity students to lead the charge and set an example for other parts of the university. As it turned out, there were a couple hundred students from all over Boston and Cambridge, but very few from HDS. We could not believe it. We joked that we had been duped, even though, at the end of the day, we were proud to be part of the march.

It was bitterly cold when we got off the bus in D.C. A sharp November wind cut right through my rather thin corduroy coat. Luckily I had a large wool scarf, which I wrapped snugly around my neck, practically up to my nose. Our bus had pulled over to the spot where numerous other buses were unloading hundreds of students. Katherine and I held on to each other's arm as we were absorbed into the massive herd of young people who were beginning to move along. We hadn't gone very far when someone tapped me on the shoulder. I turned to find a handsome young guy, with unruly black curls and a short, dark beard that framed his mouth like a work of art. His eyes were alive, a warm dark chocolate; I wanted to sip him.

"Andrea?" he asked with a sheepish smile.

"Yes," I answered, somewhat startled.

"I'm Nico. I live with Tomas. He told me that you would be here and to look for you."

"But how did you know it was me?" I asked, puzzled, and looking around at the growing crowd. "He doesn't have a picture and there are only about a million people here."

Nico smiled. "I know Tomas very well. I knew it was you."

I could never quite figure that out, how he just knew. I decided to file it in my brain under "mystery," a file that was growing increasingly fat. I liked Nico immediately, and I liked that he was close to Tomas. Somehow it validated my initial impression of Tomas: that he was a good soul. Nico joined my friends and me for the duration of the long, cold march. If I was underdressed, he was positively naked; so I took off my scarf and gave it to him. He gratefully accepted it, wrapping it around his neck, which still couldn't have been enough to keep him warm. And even though I was shivering, it made me happy to share it with him.

The next time I saw Tomas, I asked him how he had described me to Nico—so much so that Nico could pick me out of a crowd—but he only laughed and wouldn't tell me. Instead, he took my hand and walked me into Harvard Yard, to Sever Hall. It was an imposing, redbrick building, not particularly inviting (especially at night), but it held a secret. "Stand here," he said, gently positioning me face-first to the wall. "Don't move. Listen." Then he jogged over to the other side of the entryway, his back to me, and whispered into the bricks. His words were carried over the archway, as if he were whispering directly into my ear. I didn't know then that this is one of the architectural and acoustical wonders at Harvard, that countless others had stood in those same spots, faces pressed

into the archway, making late-night confessions or sharing secrets that might be difficult to say face-to-face. We stood like
that for a few minutes, whispering to each other; then he
crossed back over to me. Taking my face in both of his hands,
he looked into my eyes and said, "Andrea, I love you, just as
you are. It is that simple."

For a time, I tried to believe it was true—not that he loved
me, but that it was simple.

9

mitzvah, karma, blessing

The Inn was already a freeway of activity when I stepped through the doors at Pine Street. Bodies were colliding in the lobby, there was a traffic jam waiting for bed tickets, and voices cut the air in random intervals with the grating intensity of honking horns. It was going to be a long Saturday night.

As part of my field study, it was important that I experience all aspects of shelter life, including what happens overnight—and this was my night. I didn't really have to be there until 11:00 p.m., but the idea of stepping off the T at that late hour and walking to the shelter alone didn't thrill me. By November, I had learned enough about the dangers of the area to accept an escort when I left Pine Street; but there would be no one waiting to accompany me when I arrived at the station tonight, so I had decided to go early. Besides, I wanted to observe how the Inn transitioned from the bustle of dinner to the quiet of sleep. Walking down the alley around 6:30 p.m., it was strange to think that I wouldn't emerge again until seven the next morning.

Saturday nights were always busy and felt slightly un-hinged. The guests were restless. Many of the younger ones were frustrated by their lack of resources to party—or to be anywhere but here. The older men were wary. You could see it in their eyes, the way they were guarded and coiled like old scrapyard dogs. And then there were guests of all ages who were pleasantly numb, courtesy of their old buddies Jack Daniel's, Jim Beam, and Mary Jane.

The dip in the weather meant that it was going to be especially busy, so it was just as well that I had arrived early. I squeezed past the men in the doorway, apologizing for jostling them, and greeted the officer who was standing inside at his post (one that seemed to rotate too frequently to learn names). After stashing my coat in one of the locked offices, I said hello to some of the guests with whom I was becoming friendly, then returned to where it was most congested and chaotic—the front doors.

Men were still filing in by the dozens. They were hungry, they were tired, they were cold, and they just wanted to get settled. Tempers flared when one man who was intoxicated inadvertently stumbled into another who was schizophrenic. Before it could get ugly, Lauretta, who usually worked days, jumped from her stool behind the front desk, like a teacher about to break up a school-yard fight. Originally from New York, she was petite and tough, and I mostly tried to stay out of her way.

Spotting me, she yelled, "Grab those bed tickets and keep the line moving!" I hopped into action, grateful for a task.

Within a couple minutes, she was back on her stool, having squelched the problem without needing to involve the cop, and resumed her control of the flow of traffic. This was fine with me. I was learning by watching, by feeling, and by listening. I knew the routine by now, but it was always different. Anything could happen and nothing could be taken for granted. It was like watching an improvisational dance with similar music but different dancers every night. Men were shuffling through the small lobby, counselors were (respectfully) barking directions, and dishes were clanging in the next room. The dance was in full swing.

Suddenly, a commotion could be heard coming from stage right. The line of guests waiting for bed tickets parted as two police officers came through the door, dragging what looked to be an unconscious man.*

"Oh, geez," said Lauretta, pausing momentarily to look up from her work. "Whad'ya got for me, fellas?" She managed to sound both annoyed and concerned at the same time.

"Picked him up down the street," answered one of the men in a broad Boston accent. The officer was young and fresh faced, looking as if he'd just recently stepped off the local high school football field. "Poor bugger probably woulda froze himself to death."†

"ID?" she asked.

"Naw."

"Yer killin' me. Put him in that chair over there. Can he sit?"

They half dragged, half carried him over to a folding chair,

---

* I wrote about this in my first book, entitled *The Voice That Calls You Home* (New York: Atria Books, 2009).

† In the winter of 1986, just months after I graduated, a homeless man froze to death two blocks from the Pine Street Inn. After this, a street outreach program was started with a van that combed the streets of Boston each night. It continues to this day.

which was marginally out of the general path of the men streaming past, and poured him into it. That's what it looked like, anyway: like he wasn't made of solid material but rather of rubbery goo. He had obviously drunk himself into oblivion and was barely managing to balance his gelatinous frame on the chair.

"Thanks, guys," said Lauretta, compassion seeping out from behind her tough exterior.

"Just another day in paradise," said the other cop as they disappeared back into the night.

Lauretta exhaled loudly; then, as if suddenly remembering that I might actually be useful, she turned to me and said, "Try to get a name out of that guy, okay?" Before I could answer, she was back to work.

I zigzagged between the men, some of whom were headed to the dining hall, others to first aid, still others to destinations that existed only in their heads. When I reached the man in the metal folding chair, I squatted down next to him, trying to stay out of the way of the flowing traffic, which was easier said than done. He was an older gentleman, small and thin, with a weathered face and watery gray-blue eyes. He had a little navy-blue beanie on his head and a dirty jacket, which seemed to swallow him up without keeping him warm. As with others, it was impossible to tell his age—he could have been fifty but he looked seventy. Life on the street had obscured the details. He began to lurch to one side, and I reached up to steady him, trying to ignore the fact that he smelled like a mixture of urine and vomit. Men bumped into me as they filed past—and as I held on to the chair, it dawned on me that the man was providing an anchor for me, just as I was for him. I was keeping him from falling; he was keeping me from being swept away. I took his rough hand, which was still cold from the street, and felt only the faintest hint of his swollen fingers closing around mine. Perhaps the warmth of my hand registered somewhere because the man suddenly opened one squinty eye in my direction.

"Sir," I said gently, "can you tell me your name?"

He mumbled something unintelligible, while a long string of saliva began to spill over his lower lip like a slow-moving fountain.

I tried again, this time with some conviction. "Sir, what is your name? Can you tell me?"

Is someone looking for him? I wondered. *Does he have family?* He swayed again on his chair and we nearly knocked heads. He was coming dangerously close to tottering off the edge, so I had to steady him more firmly. This seemed to rouse him a bit, because he made some slurry sounds that could almost be construed as a name.

"I'm sorry, sir. What did you say? Was that George? John? Jim?"

Nothing. No response. *Please help me, God. You know who this is,* I prayed.

I was on my knees, literally and spiritually, looking up into the face of the stranger, and I didn't know what else to do. Just as I was about to give up, he opened his eyes and looked at me. His head was still bowed, his body slack, but his eyes were on fire and I was startled by their clarity. Before I could speak, he looked directly at me and whispered, in crystal-clear English, "Are you the one God sent to me? Are you the one?"

My heart stopped, my spirit gasped. His words went right through me. This one who could not pronounce his name was now speaking to my heart. What did he mean by this? What was I to say?

In a millisecond, which felt more like a millennium, he answered for me, saying, "Because, if you're the one God sent to me, then God sent me to you. Then God sent me to you."

After that, he was gone. Not physically, but gone in every other sense. He shut his eyes and resumed his incoherent mumbling; he did not speak again. I was still holding his hand, but I felt as if he had already flown away, as if I was only holding the birdcage, and not the bird.

My trance was broken by a voice behind me. It was Lauretta's. "Did you get a name?" she asked.

"No," I answered quietly.

"All right, that's okay. It happens."

"What happens?" I asked, as if she could explain the last few minutes.

"Huh?"

"What's going to happen to him, I mean?"

"I think we're gonna get him over to Mass General for detox. Who knows—maybe someone will recognize him."

With that, she yelled for Ernie to come and move him to a more stable place, and suggested I go into the big room to see who else needed help. I hesitated, not wanting to leave him, unable to understand or to process what had just happened, but I followed her directions. As I walked away, I looked at him over my shoulder, trying to see if the light had come back into his eyes, but he continued to sway and drool. When I came back a little later, he was gone.

I had no choice but to take what had just happened and to carefully tuck it away for later. Though I felt as if I'd been struck by lightning, the Inn was full and there was work to be done. The men with bed tickets had been ushered upstairs to shower, and the guests downstairs started staking out their territories.

The lucky ones (and the intimidating ones) stretched out on the long benches. Everyone else had to find a spot on the floor. I watched as one man carefully spread his newspaper, gently fluffing it in the air as if he were making a bed; another did so with the absorption of an artist stretching a canvas. I noticed that all of the guests kept their meager belongings close at hand, and few took off their shoes. If you had a good pair, it'd be a shame to wake up and find them gone.

My task during the night was, as usual, to just be on hand. Walking through the big room, I spotted Stevie leaning against a wall in the corner, his feet up on the bench. I was surprised to see him there, because I knew he always arrived early—certainly early enough to receive a bed ticket.

"Hi, Stevie," I said, sitting down next to him, being careful not to disturb the guest who was end to end with him on the bench. "Didn't you get a ticket?"

"Nah, I never take one," he replied with a wave of his gnarled hand. "It can get crazy up there. Fights break out, people get jumped. Believe it or not, I'd rather take my chances down here. It's safer. More staff around, not to mention the cop."

I put my hand on his arm and didn't say anything. What could be said? He gave it a little pat. "Don't worry, sweetheart. I'll be fine. I'm a tough old bird."

"Well, I'm here tonight," I offered, as if that was any reassurance. "I'll watch over you. Hope you sleep."

The dangers faced by those who took a bed had not occurred to me. Stevie made that real with just a few words. Downstairs, there was naturally some grumbling over space, but this was soon squelched. Everyone knew that an argument or a disturbance would mean a swift exit from the Inn. The authority of the staff was bolstered by the cop at the door—and no one wanted to be on the other side of that. But upstairs, there were rows of beds and not much staff presence once everyone was settled in. It made sense that men like Stevie would feel vulnerable—but I hated to see him slumped in the corner, with old bones that would ache in the morning.

As the night stretched into the wee hours, the Inn became quiet. Even the restless and the wary, the grumbling and the angry, surrendered to sleep. The smoke cleared, for the most part, and the only sound was that of soft voices and irregular snores. It was like a giant nursery for God's forgotten babies, an orphanage for the destitute and the lost, the addicted and the mentally ill. Watching them sleep, it struck me: every man here is loved. Each one is known by God, loved by God, created by God. Each man here is my brother; we have been sent to each other. When morning came, these brothers would receive a light breakfast before being ushered out the door and down the alley to survive another day.

The wee hours can go slowly, so around four in the morning, I found myself sitting next to Lauretta again by the front desk. She was smoking a cigarette and I was nursing my umpteenth cup of coffee. I knew Lauretta was not one for much small talk, so I didn't press her into conversation or ask her any questions. Doing so would have made me feel like a kid conducting an interview for the school paper. I was learning to just be in the moment, to tune in to the subtleties, and to trust where the Spirit was taking me.

Eventually, Phil, a tall man with a salt-and-pepper beard, emerged from one of the common rooms. He walked with halting steps and a bleary gaze. He stopped about twenty feet short of us, choosing instead to lean up against the wall, hands behind his back. With his wild hair, his graying beard, and his long wool coat, he could have been Colline, the philosopher from *La Bohème*. Instead of breaking into an ode to his old coat, however, he stood there silently, just swaying against the wall.

"See Phil over there," Lauretta said quietly, pausing to blow a bit of smoke over her shoulder, away from me. "Thorazine shuffle. You can see it a mile away."

"I'm not sure what that means," I replied. "I thought maybe he was drunk." I didn't mind admitting this; I was grateful to be learning something from her.

"Means he was probably deinstitutionalized with all the rest of the 'nonviolent' mentally ill." She made a gesture with her fingers, putting the word *nonviolent* into quotation marks. "He's schizophrenic but not dangerous. A little Thorazine, a little SSI, and he's out of the loony bin and onto the streets."

She glanced over at me and could tell that, even though I was nodding, I was not totally getting all that she was saying. Taking pity, her face softened as she continued her lesson in "Homelessness for Beginners." "Look," she said, her Long Island accent contributing to her tough-broad persona, "there was a big push about ten years ago to get people out of mental institutions. Not a bad idea, since they were mostly rotten places, but not practical either. It's almost impossible to track these guys, to follow up on them. They release them, but then what?" She paused, looking at Phil with compassion. Then she gestured toward him with her cigarette. "This is what. How the hell is Phil supposed to function in society? Answer is, he can't. And neither can ninety percent of these guys."

A few hours and a world later, I was exiting the T and thinking about the conversation with Lauretta—one that in the bright sunlight of Harvard Square now seemed like something from a dream. I was thinking about Phil shuffling down the hall, Stevie slumped on the bench, men dispersing and disappearing into the morning streets like undercover cops or angels incognito, and I was thinking about the man in the folding chair who had asked, "Are you the one?" I had the sensation of a bright light emanating from the center of my chest, and I could feel, even more than hear, the words from Matthew 25 washing over me, words long familiar but now accompanied by faces and names:

> *. . . for I was hungry and you gave me food, I was thirsty and you gave me drink, I was a stranger, and you welcomed me, I was naked and you clothed me, I was sick and you visited me, I was in prison and you came to me. . . . Truly, I say to you, as you did it to one of the least of these my brethren, you did it to me.** *

"Hey, Andie . . . Andie!" Within that deep blue sea of thought, in the sleepy Sunday morning–ness of the Square, I heard my name being called. The voice reached my ears like a Tibetan bell, soft and reverberating, fanning out across the expanse between us. I stopped in my tracks and looked around. There, sitting alone at one of the outdoor tables of Au Bon Pain, was Katherine with a giant coffee and the *New York Times*. She was wearing dark sunglasses and a teal sweater. A strand of pearls was peeking just below a purple scarf tossed casually around her neck. Her long legs were crossed, the loose jeans somehow making them look even longer and more slen-

---

* Revised Standard Version.

der than they already were. There was an elegance about Katherine that could not be denied. It emanated from her in the slope of her nose and chin, in the way that she spoke with a soft lisp, and in the thoughtful way that she listened.

I walked over to her table and sat down, happy for the chance encounter, which seemed both random and serendipitous. Although we lived right next door to each other in very close quarters and had a warm and friendly rapport, we hadn't really spent much time hanging out, just the two of us. I was slightly in awe of her brilliance and the way she collected friends so easily, like lost puppies. She probably thought that I collected men the same way.

Folding her paper, she offered to buy me a cup of coffee, but I told her, "If I have one more, I'm going to burn a hole right through my stomach."

"Where are you coming from so early on a Sunday?" she asked, sliding her sunglasses on top of her head. It gave her the look of a movie star relaxing off set. She leaned back in her chair, arms resting on the sides, appearing both relaxed and completely ready to listen, as if there was nothing in the world she would rather be doing.

"I'm coming from Pine Street," I answered, "the shelter where I'm doing my field study. I worked a night shift so that I could see what happens in a twenty-four-hour period. How about you? What are you doing up?"

"Nothing so noble as Pine Street," she said with a laugh. "I took an early run, then thought about going to hear Peter Gomes preach in the Chapel. Somehow I ended up with the *Times* and a coffee instead."

"Church in the Square." I smiled. "Makes sense to me."

I wanted to ask Katherine about her poetry. I often heard

her typing in the night and knew that it had nothing to do with writing a paper for class, but she insisted I tell her more about Pine Street. "This is really something that I need to hear," she said. "I'm fascinated. I'm in awe."

I proceeded to tell her about my night, about the guys whom I especially liked, and about the staff. I told her that I felt grounded when I was there, that it helped me balance the cool, cerebral study of God with the warm incarnation of God. I told her how scriptures that I had known all my life were now alive, fleshed out in the faces of these men.

"There are times I wonder what I'm doing at HDS," I confessed. "I love it, but I'm not sure where I'm going with it . . . and sometimes I don't feel intellectual enough. But when I'm at Pine Street, I'm not thinking about any of that. It's like I just surrender to the flow of the Spirit. When I get out of my own way, I can almost feel where God is leading me."

"I totally understand that," she said thoughtfully. "I don't know what I'm doing here either. What I'm really interested in is writing—writing and poetry. What that has got to do with divinity school is yet to be revealed," she said, laughing again.

We were on a path—and it was a good one—we just weren't sure where it was headed.

"And don't worry about whether you're intellectual enough," she added with a wave of her hand. "A lot of people can use big words. So what? I think you are about the first person I've met who does seem to have a purpose for being here."

"Really?" I asked, touched by her affirmation. "How do you mean?"

"I mean that here you are, coming from working all night in a shelter. You're doing the real thing. You're not living in the library; you're out there doing it."

I felt a rush of gratitude. "Thanks, Katherine. That's so kind of you." I felt myself relax into the outdoor chair. "You know, something surreal happened to me last night at the shelter. I haven't even been able to process it yet."

Katherine leaned in, her hand on her chin. "I'd love to hear about it, if you feel like telling." I knew she meant it and was not just being polite. Talking with her was beginning to feel like such an odd experience. Not odd as in unpleasant, but just the opposite. I was feeling a synchronicity of spirit, as if our roots were intricately connected somewhere in the deep.

Sitting there in Harvard Square, I told her the story of the man who was brought in by the police. How I had knelt by his chair and found silence in the middle of chaos, connection in the midst of the disconnected, purpose and meaning in the sea of despair. I had come there to learn and I had been taught; I had come to give and I had received. When I finished my story, I realized that the birds were chirping and cars were beginning to resume their endless loops.

"Wow," said Katherine, softly. "Wow."

I smiled and nodded my head. "I know."

"Do you think you'll ever find out what happened to him?"

"No, I really don't . . . but I will always think of him as an angel. It's like that passage from Hebrews, 'Do not neglect to show hospitality to strangers, for thereby some have entertained angels unawares.'"

With that, Katherine grabbed my hand. "I have got shivers from head to toe. Seriously, up and down my spine, from my head to my toes. That is an amazing story."

"Thanks," I said. "You know, that moment changed me— *is* changing me—in ways I can hardly articulate. It humbled me and it opened me up to something bigger than my meager efforts to be some sort of do-gooder in the world, bigger than my limited vision. I don't think it's about what we end up doing once we graduate; it's about how we're learning to live. On a deep cellular level, that moment taught me that we are sent to each other to learn from one another and to be present to one another; and that whatever we know of God lives in the circular flow of love between us. I don't know if I've ever seen God so clearly as I did in the eyes of that man, in that lightning moment of connection."

"I totally get it," she said quietly, her green eyes seeing through mine, her spirit honoring mine.

"I guess I've been hungering for an intelligent faith," I told her. "I want to learn, I want to study—but if I can't see Christ in 'the least of these,' then I might as well go home."

Katherine would tell me, years later, that this chance encounter also changed her. Something clicked into place, although she wasn't sure at that moment what it was. Maybe it was the vision of integrating the different parts of herself—the poet, the intellectual, the artist, the seeker—with her desire to be a healing presence in the world, in whatever shape that took.

We sat for a few minutes, picking up bits of the story like colored glass and holding them up to the light until there was nothing left to say. We hugged good-bye and, as I walked away, it was as if a long, shimmering cord was unspooling; one end was connected to my spirit, the other to hers. And in between there would be space enough for us to hang our sketches and our masterpieces, there would be space to put our toes in uncharted waters, to be with the brokenhearted, and to find our places in the world. The cord was long enough to throw each other a lifeline if necessary and strong enough to let go. We had not so much forged a friendship as unearthed one. It was as if the Divine had taken each of our hands, led us to the table, and said, "Here you are. I give you the gift of each other with my blessing. Have fun."

It took only a Saturday night with the homeless and a Sunday morning to share it with my emerging best friend to feel myself surrender, in a deeper way, to the journey. I knew now that I was on the right path, wherever that might lead. I learned that I needed to put myself in places where God was most present, that the road was not meant to be walked alone, and to rejoice in the mystery along the way.

10

oh henri

Thanksgiving was coming, and with it preparations. Most of the students living in Rockefeller were going home, going to friends', going somewhere. A few stragglers like myself, who were either too impoverished to travel or who were immersed in a research project, decided to share the meal together. I couldn't afford to fly to Ohio for both Thanksgiving and Christmas, so I had chosen Christmas. It was the first Thanksgiving with my family that I would miss, and I was a little down about it. Lucky for me, Katherine had also decided to stay at school, though I can't for the life of me remember why.

We spread the word that we were hosting an impromptu dinner and that anyone was welcome to join us on the second floor. Nine fellow orphans happily responded, making us a total of eleven. We divvied up the menu: Katherine would buy the turkey; Carla would cook it. I offered to make my mother's sweet potatoes and stuffing; someone else said they'd make mashed potatoes and beans. Paper goods, drinks, and desserts were assigned. Pam, who had been an art major in Colorado, offered to help Katherine make the table decorations. It was going to be a feast.

The day before Thanksgiving, Katherine and I were sitting in the refectory going over last-minute details when Father Henri Nouwen passed by. Henri was a Dutch priest—a writer, thinker, scholar—and one of the few professors who was quite open about his personal faith. His classes were always packed, despite being the source of not-so-subtle eye rolling among some of the other professors and whispers about the courses not being academic enough. Obviously, even the Divinity School community was not immune to petty jealousy. The fact that there was so much interest in his classes spoke volumes about the secret hunger for spirituality that existed among the student body. Henri's spiritual curiosity, his brilliant mind, and his comedic flair made each class an adventure. He was a scholar who also burned with a deep and compelling faith; he was humble and courageous, a leader and a fellow sojourner, a reluctant saint and a clown. He was beloved by his students and by spiritual seekers around the world.

When we saw him, it occurred to us that maybe we should invite Henri to our Thanksgiving dinner. Surely he had received numerous other invitations, we reasoned; why would he want to come to our ragtag little meal in the kitchen of a near-empty dorm? "Well, it never hurts to ask," I said. "Besides, it's always nice to get invited someplace, even if you can't come."

"Why don't we ask Jim to invite him?" suggested Katherine thoughtfully. "He's close to Henri. I'm sure he'd feel comfortable asking him—and Henri would be comfortable saying no."

Jim was a man who lived on our floor. He was about our age—in his early twenties—slim and rather shy, with perpetually disheveled blond hair. He had a unique way of walking, with his shoulders hunched slightly forward, his head down, and his hands in his pockets, as if he was deep in thought at all times. Perhaps he was, but this posture might also have served to stave off any unwanted conversation. He was intelligent and funny, but his face sometimes revealed one who was secretly tortured by demons he kept to himself. That he gravitated toward Henri made sense.

Perhaps Jim found comfort in sharing his inner struggles with someone who also knew what it was like to wrestle with demons. There is a loneliness that can be consuming when one thrashes about with unspoken things, things that evoke shame or uncertainty or self-hatred. I'm not saying that this was Jim's story, but Henri's friendship and compassion were clearly a balm for him. Henri had a deep capacity for empathy, for reaching out to those who were suffering; those who felt alienated from themselves, from others, or from God; those who lived on the fringe, banished by society or by their own self-loathing. Those of us who were lucky enough to intersect with him knew that we were blessed to have Henri there at the Divinity School at that moment in time—one which would never come again.

Henri had a gift for scooping up the outcast in his empathetic and loving arms. He had a tender place for them, feeling their bruises in his own bruised heart. He knew what it was to struggle spiritually, just as he knew the power of redemption, of aligning oneself with those who are suffering, and of receiving God's tsunami of love, forgiveness, and grace. When Harvard became untenable for him, he eventually joined his friend Jean Vanier, the Canadian theologian and humanitarian who founded the L'Arche community in

France. L'Arche, which has grown to include more than one hundred fifty communities in forty countries, was established as a place of love and acceptance for mentally and developmentally challenged people and their caregivers. Named after Noah's ark, it offers shelter and protection for those who might otherwise be languishing in institutions, suffering in silence from neglect or ill treatment. After two years in Cambridge, Henri left Harvard for L'Arche, where he spent a year writing. The following year, he accepted the position of pastor at Daybreak, the community north of Toronto. Although those of us who loved him were sad to see him go, it was at Daybreak that he was perhaps the happiest and where he experienced his deepest sense of calling and joy.

One day, Henri invited Vanier to speak to our Spirituality class. The tall Canadian with the striking white hair and the long, thin nose (the steep slope of which began with a prominent mogul) stood in front of the packed room. He began speaking without the aid of notes, a podium, or a microphone. It was strange how his soft voice could be heard even from the back of the class—and I thought of how Jesus spoke to the crowds in the same way. Vanier was fifty-five years old at the time but had the aura of one who was timeless or, more accurately, who had stepped out of time. His humble posture and the warmth that radiated from him like a fire deep in the earth gave me the goose-bumpy feeling of being in the presence of St. Peter.

For an hour (at least that's what the clock registered), we escaped *kronos* (chronological) time and were floating in *kairos*, the sacred moment that cannot be quantified or measured. You could hear a pin drop. He had been building the L'Arche community for almost twenty years by then and was sharing what it was like to live among those with severe physical and mental challenges. He later described it this way:

> *[It] is my belief that in our mad world, where there is so much pain, rivalry, hatred, violence, inequality, and oppression, it is people who are weak, rejected, marginalized, counted as useless, who can become a source of life and of salvation for us as individuals as well as for our world. And it is my hope that each one of you may experience the incredible gift of the friendship of people who are poor and weak, that you too, may receive life from them. For they call us to love, to communion, to compassion and to community.* *

When Vanier finished speaking, he said, "Thank you," and quietly walked out the door. There was a long pause, a moment of pure silence. His light still lingered in the room and it felt as if we were boats gently rocking in his wake. The room itself had become an ark, one where we were safe and dearly loved. Finally, the class erupted into soaring applause, standing applause, applause from the heart, which recognizes it has been in the presence of holiness. It was a moment I will never forget.

During Vanier's talk, Henri was positively glowing. There was no jealousy, no private critiquing of his lecture. He was totally present, receiving the Word along with the rest of us, his face animated like a child's. And I loved him for that, for his ability to be present, to be with us, among us, to share his experience of the Spirit, while being enthusiastically open to the

---

* Jean Vanier, *From Brokenness to Community* (Harold M. Wit Lectures) (Mahwah, NJ: Paulist Press, 1992), 9–10.

experience of others. This accessibility was part of why we felt we could invite Henri to Thanksgiving. We also wanted him there because he was genuinely fun to be around.

When Jim told us that Henri had happily accepted our invitation, we were ecstatic. We set the table, lit some candles, and the little kitchen became a banquet hall. Henri arrived with Jim, and we sat him at the middle of the table, so that we could all enjoy his presence. We told him how happy and surprised we were that he could join us. "But you see," said Henri with a little smile, "I had no other invitations." We were stunned. I suppose everyone had assumed that Henri Nouwen had a place to go, that he was so important and beloved a figure in our community that he would be dining with a much more prestigious crowd. It was hard to fathom that no one else had invited him, but even then he was teaching us the spiritual lesson of extending hospitality. Ours was not to assume who was important, or valued, or popular, but simply to invite others to the table with love and acceptance.

When everything was prepared, we took our seats. Henri thanked us again, profusely, for the hospitality and for the meal we were about to share. We asked him to offer the blessing. Before he did, however, someone said, "Look, Henri, you have made us twelve; you have made our table complete." And it was true. With his presence, and with ours, we invoked something greater than ourselves. He blessed the meal, broke the bread, and we feasted.

Strangely enough, I experienced the echo of this supper a few months later during Holy Week. It was during a Good Friday service in the Chapel, in which several professors and students participated. The service concluded with the enactment of Christ's foot washing. Those in attendance stood in line down the center aisle, waiting their turn to have their feet washed by someone at the altar. As I got closer to the front, I could feel my awkwardness and the shy horror at the idea of having someone wash my feet. It was like standing in line for a waterslide that you had changed your mind about but being too embarrassed to step out of it. I was reaching the top of the ladder and there was no turning back.

There were three foot-washing stations lined up across the altar and someone up front directing people. When it was my turn, I was directed, shoes in hand, to none other than Henri Nouwen. I froze for a moment. How could I let this man wash my feet? As I took a hesitant step forward, I grasped more than I ever had in my life the profundity of Jesus' act during that Last Supper, and (more directly) the struggle of the disciples as they extended their dirty feet. I could hardly bear it. But then I looked down at Henri's face as he placed my foot in the water, as he washed my toes like they were a baby's and gently dried them, and I wanted to cry—not with sadness or shame, but for the sheer beauty of it, for the effortless love I saw on his face and for the profound flow of divine energy.

This communion of spirit to Spirit and back again was something that Henri inspired time and again. Once, in the wood-paneled Sperry Room of the Divinity School, Henri had offered a simple meditation to about fifty students who had gathered there. We sat on the floor, crossed-legged and cozy, the lights low, a few candles burning. At the conclusion of his talk, Henri led us in an a cappella version of the hymn "*Dona Nobis Pacem*" (Latin for "Grant Us Peace"). After teaching the song to those of us who didn't know it, he divided us into two groups so that we could sing it as a round. Our voices began to resonate against the rich wood, tumbling and rising like waves

or like so many birds effortlessly ascending. Henri kept mo-
tioning with his hand for us to continue singing, his face rapt,
serene, open. We sang round after round, softly, gently, no one
wanting to stop the flow, until our singing had at last transported us to silence. It was one of the most ecstatic experiences
of my life.

We were twelve at the table, oddballs and goofballs, the
tortured and the shamed, the idealistic and the faithful. Henri
prayed; we shared our food. Loved, blessed, forgiven, be-
friended, the Spirit was present. And we gave thanks.

11

the catch

It was about eleven o'clock when I decided to pack it up at the Divinity School library and go back to my room. I'd been working on a paper for a class, Peace: Research, Education, and Action, but the only action I felt like taking was to put my head down and sleep. With a stretch, I closed my books and turned off the little study lamp. I still had a lot of studying to do before the night was over but I needed a cup of coffee and a change of venue. Taking my time, I started walking across the small span of parking lot between the library and Rockefeller Hall, filling my lungs with the fresh night air. The sky was an inky black and the moon was playing Salome, slipping in and out of the dark clouds like so many silken veils. A stillness had descended upon the evening, as if Night herself were in deep meditation.

The library was connected to Andover Hall, where most of our classes were held. Andover, impressive at any time of day, stood like a stone god against the black backdrop. It was a unique and beautiful building, completed in 1911 and described as Collegiate Gothic, the only building of its style at

Harvard. This was fitting somehow, the fact that it was different, for we were different. At least I'd like to think so. As in other buildings at Harvard, the halls reverberated with intellectual curiosity, with academic excellence, and with the countless brilliant minds who had gone before. But Andover, being home to the Divinity School, also bore witness to Mystery, to that which can never be fully known, solved by formula, autopsied. It had a powerful silent presence, like a mountain pointing toward the heavens, while hinting at things below. Pausing to admire it, I whispered, "Thank you, God. Thank you." No matter how much work I had, I was always wildly happy to be there, was grateful to be there. *This is a miracle*, I thought. *Life is strange and miraculous.*

I turned my gaze to Rockefeller Hall, where I could see a few people moving about through the large kitchen windows on each floor. The first floor of the building, the ground floor, was dark. This space held a few classrooms, including my Writer as Theologian class, and the refectory, which was open for breakfast and lunch. Occasionally some curious undergrads would pop in to eat there and to listen to the conversations at other tables. One day, while having lunch, I heard a couple of guys from the college talking. They were easy to pick out, not so much from how they looked as to how they were acting. While most people were blithely chomping away or happily engaged in conversation or both, these two were hunched over their trays, stealing sideways glances at the people around them. Though engaged in conversation myself, I caught a snippet of their exchange, which went like this:

"See, I told you," whispered one kid. "Don't they all sound stoned around here, talking about cosmology and phenomenology and ultimate meaning? What a freak show."

"Let's see how far that gets them in the real world," answered the other in a low voice. "What say we hit up the business school next?"

What they were saying was true to some extent. The language we used and the concepts we were discussing could sound like abstract ponderings, but this impression couldn't be further from the truth. What a majority of divinity students were thinking about, writing about, studying about, talking about involved the connection between the Unknowable and the created world; between holiness and human existence, scripture and politics, Buddhism and Christianity, Judaism and Islam. The question was not how to decipher some esoteric concept, but rather how to live authentically, how to explore one's own faith tradition while respecting another's, how to engage in genuine dialogue while striving for intellectual integrity.

In contrast, the last time I had been home, which had been over Christmas break, I'd exchanged some pretty terse words with the new pastor at our church. I was having lunch with him and a longtime church member, when the idea of biblical scholarship came up.

"Well, I'm not much for book learning," said the pastor rather slowly. "This is the only book you'll ever need." He held a Bible in his hand and gave it a little shake."

"But the Bible can be interpreted in so many different ways," I proffered.

"There's only one way, and that's Jesus' way," he countered, case closed. So much for dialogue.

The rectangular lights glowed from the windows of Rockefeller like flashlights in the dark, geometric signals to outer space, which said, "Hey, I'm here . . . and I'm pretty sure You're there. How are we doing?" I noticed a couple of people moving around the kitchen on the second floor, the floor where I lived, their movements silenced by the glass. I couldn't wait to get upstairs and rejoin that deep blue ocean of thought, that nightly ballet.

I felt tired but happy when I entered the dorm. Returning here was like plugging into an energy center, a humming vibration of thought and meditation, brain waves and soul searching. It was always quiet on the residential floors, but never more so than at night. Maybe that's why you could feel the energy so easily. Even those milling about in the kitchen spoke softly or maintained a respectful silence. It couldn't have been more different from what life had been like in my undergraduate dorms. At Rockefeller, we were like monks in our cells, bees in a hive, quietly working away on behalf of the planet.

I went upstairs and changed into my favorite cotton nightgown, a long, white, old-fashioned number, with full sleeves, a scoop neck, and three small buttons down the front. It might have been my mother's or grandmother's, I'm not sure, but it was soft and comfortable, and it made me happy for some reason when I wore it. Before settling in for the evening and starting on round 2 of my studies, I made a cup of tea and sat for a few minutes in silence. Life was an ongoing dialogue with God, a yearning for communion, for deeper connection, for direction. Prayer for me was often a wordless place, a time when I would empty myself like a hollow tube, get rid of all my sludge, and imagine the light of the Divine flowing through me like a brilliant, cleansing river. I yearned for God, I hungered for God; and I was certain that the less I talked and the more I listened, the better I could understand and make sense of my life.

In some ways, I was one of the more conventionally religious students at school. I was a Methodist from the Midwest,
for goodness' sake—enough said! For some students, talk of
Jesus or a personal relationship with God provoked a rather
embarrassed discomfort, a who-passed-gas backing away from
the conversation. We could have animated discussions about
the political implications of liberation theology or feminist theology; we could explore the history of religion or strive for religious and personal tolerance—but to yearn for God, to speak
of faith? This was largely left unspoken, the stuff of traditional
seminaries and church people, not academics.

I realized that my work at Pine Street and my studies with
Henri Nouwen were, in many ways, saving my soul. I was not
only there to study God, I was there to experience God and to
apply this living communion in my life and in the world
around me. Although a notorious night person, I would get up
early once a week to join Henri and a handful of other students for a prayer group. Sometimes Henri would direct our
prayers, other times we sat in silence, but always he would ask
if there were any concerns to share. As it turned out, my
mother had recently undergone a biopsy for breast cancer. I
shared this in the group—then Henri offered a prayer for her
that was so touching and heartfelt, tears streamed down my
face. A week later, she called to say the tumor was benign.
Such were the small miracles that happened during, and perhaps as a result of, that prayer group.

In Henri's Spirituality class, the Gospel of Luke was acting
as our springboard into the Deep. He asked us to keep a spiritual journal based on our reflections on the Gospel, to read a
passage and to meditate on it each day. Sometimes only five
minutes went by before I felt restless or anxious to get going,

but other times I would be so immersed in prayer that I would lose track of time altogether. When this happened, I knew I had been transported beyond my meager ability to get there, and I would emerge feeling refreshed and clear.

I turned to Luke 5:4, letting the words carry me: "Put out into the deep water and let down your nets for a catch." I felt myself floating, surrendering to the current, to those deep, mysterious waters and to the promise of life below the surface. I'm not sure how many minutes passed before I said "Amen" and stretched, but I had the sense of a continuous flow, an on-goingness of communion, unbroken by my moving around. The fact that there were no cell phones then, no messages to check, no texts to return, no emails or other fragments of dialogue to distract or to pull me away, certainly enhanced this flow. Simply put, there was no static.

Before opening my next book, I remembered to put some peanut butter on an old tin lid and stick it behind my refrigerator. A mouse had come to live there, a refugee of sorts. He was running from the hideous glue traps that had been set in various places in the dorm to control "the mouse problem." One could hear their screams as they struggled to escape, literally pulling themselves apart. All of us living there found this horrifying—shocking, even—especially for a divinity school. We voiced our protests until the administration removed the traps, replacing them with something more humane. My mouse had been hiding out for about a week now. During the worst of the trapping, I'd kept a towel under my door to discourage him from leaving and inadvertently getting stuck. And though it was safer now, he continued to hang around. "Here you go, little guy," I said, "midnight snack." He was in his spot, washing his little face, like a perfect gentleman cleaning up for dinner. We had an understanding, he and I—he could stay in my room as long as he didn't climb on my bed. That first night, I was a little jumpy, but he behaved himself. So far, so good.

It was almost two in the morning when Katherine returned to the dorm after celebrating her twenty-fifth birthday with some friends. As she opened the heavy outer door that led to the entryway where our mailboxes and intercom were, she was startled to find a young man standing there in the shadows. She didn't think too much of this at first, conditioned as we were to be friendly and welcoming, but then her heart started to pound a little.

"Oh, hello," she said, trying to sound casual and relaxed, like everything was okay, as if it made perfect sense for him to be hanging out there at that hour. "Can I help you?"

"Naw . . . I'm just lookin' for someone," he said nonchalantly, without looking at her directly. "I think I might have the wrong place." He proceeded to appear completely immersed in the study of names on the mailboxes, as if he really expected to find someone he knew.

"Okay . . . well, have a good night," she responded, in her most friendly, I-believe-you kind of tone. She unlocked the door to the stairs, while watching him out of the corner of her eye. Her mouth had gone dry as she considered the possibility of being shoved into the stairwell, and adrenaline surged through her limbs, turbocharging her body in preparation for fight or flight—but he just stood there staring at the wall, with his hands in his pockets. She sprinted up the stairs and began scolding herself. *Don't be so suspicious. Maybe he's just a college kid who really is looking for someone.*

I was immersed in a paper for Harvey Cox's class, Jesus

and the Moral Life, by then, when a tap at the door startled me. I opened it to find Katherine.

"Hi. Sorry to knock so late, but I saw your light and figured you'd be up."

"No problem," I said, waving her in. "What's up? You have a good birthday?"

"What? Oh, yes, my birthday—I almost forgot. It was really nice. But I just had the strangest experience. Do you mind if I run it by you?"

We sat down and she told me about the guy in the entryway, how it seemed rather strange for him to be there, how something seemed off about it. "Then, as I was walking up the stairs, it occurred to me that I didn't heard the door close behind me," she said. It was a heavy, metal door, one that usually swung closed with a distinct *cha-chink*.

"What if he's in the building?" she whispered, wide-eyed. My heart pole-vaulted into my throat, while shadowy images of some man creeping around our little sanctuary began running wild in my imagination. "Do you think we should call the police?"

I hesitated. "I don't know. You sure you didn't hear the door?"

"Positive."

"Then we've got to find out if he's here."

"Oh, dear God," sighed Katherine. "I'd feel so responsible if something happened, since I'm the one who let him in."

We cautiously poked our heads out of my door. Even on high alert, I was vaguely aware that we looked ridiculous, like a modern version of Lucy and Ethel. She was in festive, birthday purple; I was in my *Little House on the Prairie* nightgown. The hallway was quiet. "What do you think we should do?" she whispered. "If we call the police, and I'm wrong, I'd feel so stupid *and* biased. He was a young black guy—late teens, early twenties, maybe. I didn't get a *terrible* vibe but something wasn't right."

I hesitated for a moment. It was a moral dilemma. Here we were, earnestly trying (among other things) to purge ourselves of stereotyping, of racism, and of biases based on color, gender, sexual preference, gender identity. We were on a mission. We were champions of justice. Was this a test?

"Well, if this was a young white kid, would you be suspicious?"

"Yes."

"Then let's go."

It was a seminal moment in our friendship; together we were pulling Excalibur from the rock. If it had been a cheesy film, a choir of angels would have started singing and we would have been bathed in radiant light. But we were more Monty Python than Charlton Heston, bent more toward the absurd than the dramatic. We took our journeys seriously, but rarely ourselves.

We tiptoed out of our little suite and looked down the empty hall. "Maybe we can stop him before he does something wrong," offered Katherine, her hushed voice shimmering with possibility, "like an intervention."

"Maybe," I agreed. "Bottom line is there's no way I'm going to be able to sleep wondering if someone's creeping around in the building."

We stood for a moment, listening for footsteps, but it was as quiet as ever. "Look," I suggested, taking charge. "Why don't you find Al"—our resident advisor and fellow student—"tell him what happened: that you might have let someone in accidentally. That way he can decide whether to call the cops. I'll run up to the fourth floor and make my way down; you start here and go up. We'll meet in the middle."

"Right!"

With that, Katherine headed down to Al's room and I raced two flights up to the fourth floor. The kitchen was empty, so I quickly made my way down the long hallway, half expecting the stranger to leap from the doorway of one of the suites. Instead, I ran into Doug, who actually lived on my floor but was visiting someone upstairs. He was what one would accurately call a gentle soul. Doug gave me a puzzled look. "Did you lose something?" he asked, as if it were perfectly normal for me to be jogging the fourth floor in my nightgown.

"No, but did you see anyone strange in here?" I realized as soon as I said this that it could be perceived as a trick question.

We were all pretty strange, when it came down to it. There was Leslie, for instance, who used to be Lester. She was born a man but was in the process of becoming a woman. She was also a lesbian. I could never quite figure that out—although, to be honest, I didn't give it too much thought. Her physical transformation was basically complete, and she seemed genuinely happy and comfortable in her skin . . . happy, that is, until the feminist scholar and theologian Mary Daly refused to call on her in class. Daly was known to routinely ignore the raised hands of the men in class so that they could get a taste of what it was like to be ignored or marginalized. Leslie, she reasoned, had not been raised as a girl, so had not had the experience of being ignored. Her stance was quite controversial at the time and, eventually, the university intervened and put a stop to it. Then there was Muktar, a Peruvian man who'd served time in prison before turning his life around, and Cindy, the dimpled Episcopalian redhead who liked to tie her boyfriend up with his neckties.

How was Doug supposed to answer me, then, when I asked if he'd seen anyone strange? "I'm sorry?" he said with a quizzical look, cocking his head to one side, as if I had asked him for directions to the moon. "Never mind!" I called over my shoulder as I continued down the hall.

Meanwhile, Katherine had woken up Al, who emerged rather rumpled in a Yankees T-shirt and boxers. He placed his wire-rimmed glasses on his prominent nose, scratched his short beard, and promptly dialed the police. "Don't be chasing anyone!" he called as Katherine zoomed off. "It's dangerous!" Like any smart New Yorker, he knew when and where to draw the line.

Feeling understandably rattled, Katherine decided to get our friend Tim, more for a sense of security than anything else. Tim lived on the third floor, in the room directly above mine. He was a handsome, athletic-looking man, with stunning blue eyes and a broad smile. He was genuine and kind, with just the right amount of cynical, irreverent humor to make us laugh. He also happened to be gay, which kept my friendship with him pure and relaxed. Katherine and he, on the other hand, had a chemistry that defied easy categorizing. They were like brother and sister, husband and wife, soul mates and sparring partners. They loved each other without being lovers. Katherine knew he would be there if she needed him, and this was one of those times.

She bounded up the steps and headed toward Tim's room. Without knocking, she flung open the door and burst in. But it wasn't Tim who was sitting at the desk typing, his back to the door—it was David; nervous, intellectual, reclusive David. David, with his soft, melted-ice-cream-cone body, whose eyes were perpetually rimmed with dark circles, who studied ancient texts into the wee hours of the night, and who was well on his way to becoming a respected scholar. When the door suddenly flew open, David's hands came down on the typewriter with a slam. Then he turned in his seat to face the intruder, hands frantically clutching his head, as if to keep it from rolling off his shoulders.

"What are you doing here?" shouted Katherine.

"This is my room!" he answered, wild-eyed and terrified.

"What? Oh," said Katherine, standing in the doorway, her hand still on the knob. It was like yelling "surprise!" at a party before the guest of honor has arrived. "I'm so sorry. Wrong floor."

In her haste, Katherine had gone to the fourth floor instead of the third. Honest mistake. With no further explanation, she shut the door. She did not have time to process the terror that this sudden intrusion had prompted in David, or his faint cry of "It's two in the morning!" as she exited the suite. There was a stranger on the loose, and that took precedence. What we would do if we found him was an entirely different matter, one that we had not stopped to contemplate.

As I walked quickly down the fourth-floor hallway toward the stairwell door at the opposite end, I ran into Katherine coming out of the suite.

"See anyone?" I asked, hopefully.

"No, but I accidentally burst into David's room. Kind of a funny story, actually, which I'll tell you later."

Together we descended the stairs to the third floor. As we started walking past the kitchen, I saw him. In a flash, he darted out of one of the suites and started running down the hall in the opposite direction. He reminded me of a frightened deer, zigzagging this way and that, his long legs moving with impressive speed. "Hey!" I shouted, as I started running in pursuit. "Come back here!" He disappeared through the stairwell door at the other end of the hall. This presented him with two choices: to exit or to hide on another floor. By the time I got to the door, he was nowhere to be found.

I turned around and saw Katherine, striding toward me. My heart was racing and I was starting to tremble. "Wow, you were right," I said, looking into her wide, green eyes. "What now?"

"I think Al has already called security. We should let him know we saw the guy—then let's get back to our rooms."

We linked arms and went down the stairs together. It felt like we were exiting a thrill ride at an amusement park. Our eyes were in full saucer mode and our bodies were buzzing. It probably didn't help that both of us had consumed buckets of coffee earlier in the evening. *Note to self: caffeine and adrenaline are not to be taken together.* Al came by twenty minutes later to say that the police had caught the guy outside our building but didn't have enough evidence to hold him. Although the crisis was over, it didn't make us feel better to think of the police questioning him.

Before we went to sleep, we talked for a few minutes about privilege and need, about social justice and prejudice, about compassion and responsibility. We decided to pray for the young man, pray that he felt loved and cared for, and that life would be kind to him. We prayed that he would be safe that night, and that he might feel God's healing presence. He had come into a divinity dorm, and we hoped that he inadvertently carried something of that energy out with him. We prayed for our hearts to be opened, for our eyes to be opened to those who suffer; and we prayed to be forces of good in the world.

With that, we went back to our rooms, pulled out into deep waters, and let down our nets.

12

shapeshifting

Life in divinity school was challenging, stimulating, fun, and inspiring, but it was also exhausting. Besides my full load of classes and working at Pine Street, I was also babysitting the daughter of one of the school secretaries twice a week. Before she could stand on her own, little Rebecca would hold on to the windowsill watching for me, and would start bouncing excitedly when she saw me walking up the street. This always made me feel good, but it didn't leave me much extra time. Still, I needed the money. There were days when I would go through my pockets hoping to find enough change to buy a cup of coffee, and many days I went to bed with a pretty growly stomach. My parents would have helped me (in fact they would have been horrified had I told them), but I was determined to get through school by myself with the help of grants, loans, and jobs. It wasn't always easy.

I remember one night in particular, when I was coming home from the shelter. Big Derek had insisted on walking me to the T. One of the regular guests at the Inn, he was a young,

African American man, six feet four and about two hundred and eighty pounds. There had been news of a stabbing at the raised platform earlier in the evening, and he didn't want me walking alone. A rational person might have looked at Derek and thought, *This man could kill me; why would I want to have him walk me to a dark and dangerous station?* But I knew and trusted him. He was like my guardian angel at the shelter. He would not tolerate any disrespect or trash-talk leveled at me directly or whispered behind my back, and no one dared challenge him. I think seeing himself as my protector gave him a sense of pride and importance, which I always found moving. As we walked out the door of Pine Street, the cop on duty smiled, saying, "You're probably safer with Derek tonight than you are with me."

It was a bitter cold and rainy night, the kind of Boston cold that chills you to the bone with its wind and its sinister dampness. I was suddenly very grateful to have Derek there because the night felt wild and unpredictable, like something dangerous had gotten loose and was running amok. My guardian waited with me until the train came, trying to shelter me from the wind, his massive body on high alert, his eyes fierce. Once safely boarded, I smiled and waved at him—but he stood there, serious as a soldier, watching until the lights of the train disappeared.

The walk from Harvard Square had never seemed so long. I put my head down and pressed on as fast as I could. By the time I got back to my room, I was shaking. My hands were numb, my feet were like two frozen bricks, and someone had packed my organs in dry ice. I couldn't stop thinking about the men at the shelter and even more about those who remained outside.

The only thing I wanted to do was to stand in a hot shower. I would have fallen to my knees in gratitude when I found it unoccupied—but I was afraid they would crack off, like two broken icicles. The warm water made my hands and feet ache as they thawed out, but the worst part was that I could not stop shaking. After a few minutes, I turned up the water as hot as I could take it, filled the tub, and submerged myself, until only the tip of my nose was showing. If I'd had a straw to breathe through, like a makeshift snorkel, even that tip would have been submerged. It seemed to take forever for my body to defrost.

When I finally got out, I realized I was starving. It had been a busy night at Pine Street, which was to be expected with the extreme cold, and I hadn't had a chance to grab a snack. This was unfortunate because I knew the prospects of having something in my cabinet to eat were fairly grim. I was waiting on a check from Pine Street (I received a small stipend for my work there) and had already rifled through my pockets, my purse, and the bottom of my closet earlier in the day to scrounge up money for the T. With nothing in my cabinet and nothing in my pocket, I knew that nothing was all that I could do. I glanced halfheartedly at the floor outside my door, but Silvia had not left any offerings. It was too bad, because I would have wolfed down that banana boat.

Like one merely going through the motions in a hopeless situation, I opened my kitchen cabinet. As expected, it was empty, except for . . . could it be? Yes! A lone packet of Cup-a-Soup was hiding in the back, camouflaged in its white wrapper against the white linoleum shelf. I could not have been happier. I boiled some water, poured it into a cup, and carefully carried it to my room as if it were liquid gold. Then I sipped it slowly to make it last. I even remember exclaiming "meat!" as I savored the little acid-tab hits of chicken. I don't think anything ever tasted so good.

I didn't mind my poverty. In many ways, I thought of this as a time of austerity and spiritual discipline—but there were times I wished I could spend more hours on my studies and fewer on work. Recreation for me rarely involved spending money; instead it usually entailed a walk around Cambridge, a visit with Andrea in the North End, hanging out with Tomas, or the occasional dinner with Andy when he came to visit. Aside from that, there was always the pleasure of relaxing in my room. In many ways, it was a pretty quiet existence.

Until Mardi Gras rolled around, that is. One might think that divinity students would be more likely to host a Shrove Tuesday pancake supper than a Fat Tuesday party, but that's exactly why Katherine and I decided to throw one. It was February, it was cold, and we needed a little levity. In our experience so far, HDS did not host any real parties. There was the Dean's Tea, which happened once a week in the Sperry Room, but that consisted of sipping sherry and tea while rubbing elbows with the professors; it was very civilized and Ivy League. There was the occasional gathering of the Gay and Lesbian Caucus or a reception for a visiting scholar, but these didn't exactly amount to a party. Luckily, we had no problem getting permission to host one in Rockefeller, so we began planning. We figured that we needed to provide some music to make it festive. Our small boom boxes wouldn't really do the trick—and neither of us wanted to be sitting there flipping tapes, anyway—so I asked Andy if he and Bobo would consider driving up to play at the party with Tom. The three of them had been in a band called the Shuffle Kings at Denison, and we figured they could shuffle on up to Cambridge for our party.

I had only seen Andy a handful of times since September. He was busy working at the Love and Serve and writing for the local paper. In addition to doing obits, he was also covering some of the area's high school sports. This meant that he didn't have many free weekends, which was the only free time that I had. Before asking him if he wanted to play at our party, however, I had to decide if I *wanted* him to. Somehow, inexplicably, the answer was yes. Even when I thought that I wanted to let go, some unseen part always held on. I guess that part was hope.

We made flyers announcing, KATHERINE AND ANDIE PRESENT MARDI GRAS. The flyers also included a snapshot of Katherine and me in our Halloween costumes for some unknown reason. I suppose we were trying to emphasize the free-spirited intention of the party. In the picture, she was dressed as a friendly witch, in a tall black hat with bright red circles painted on her cheeks. I was supposed to be a blue fairy, but looked more like a life-sized Smurf. I wore a blue feathered mask and had dyed my hair a temporary shade of bright lapis. Luckily, the photocopy was in black and white. I'd also cut out pictures of Andy, Tom, and Bobo playing their instruments and included captions such as FEATURING THE SHUFFLE KINGS and LIVE BAND, not to mention DRESS WILD! But the real kicker, the real draw, might have been the two four-letter words that were written in bold: FREE BEER. Katherine, who never drank, offered to buy a keg of beer, and I, who never drank, said I'd supply the cups.

Even though it was a Fat Tuesday party, we were having it on a Friday night. When the day arrived, we made sure to remind anyone and everyone we saw to come. We scrambled around in the refectory, moving tables and chairs to create a dance floor, but realized it still didn't appear very festive. We had forgotten to get decorations and now it was too late. Undeterred, we ran to our rooms, retrieved some pants, shirts, socks, and scarves and started pinning these to the walls in various shapes. It actually looked quite funky.

On one of the runs upstairs to get more clothes, Katherine ran into Silvia, who was standing near her doorway holding a candle. "Silvia, I hope you're planning on coming to the party tonight," said Katherine. "I think it's going to be really fun." While they were chatting, Katherine bent her six-foot frame toward Silvia's five-foot-two and lit a cigarette off the candle. Silvia went silent. Then, without a hint of irony, she intoned, "Katherine. That's my holy Shabbat candle. You've just lit your cigarette off of my holy Shabbat candle."

"Oh, my goodness, Silvia! I'm so sorry," said Katherine with a nervous laugh. Without another word, Silvia turned around, walked into her room, and shut the door. "I hope you'll still come," offered Katherine before the lock clicked.

When she came downstairs and told me what had happened, she was genuinely horrified, but we could not stop laughing as she described Silvia's reaction to her gaffe. That's part of why we adored her.

The party was a big success—and Silvia did end up coming *and* dancing like a wild woman. The keg got emptied, primarily because quite a few fellow Denison grads living in the Boston area decided to come hear their old friends play. Rumor had it that it was the first time a keg had been emptied at HDS. I don't know if this was true, but it was a funny addendum to the night. The band sounded great, really making the party, and I was proud of Andy, who looked happy again to be in his element, back in his skin, and not so freaked out.

This did not mean, necessarily, that I was sad to see him go. I liked my life at HDS, liked my freedom, and liked keeping my options open. He was also casually seeing a girl he'd met in Greenwich. We didn't have much chance to talk about this, or anything, really, over the weekend. This time it was all about the band and the party. Maybe it was just as well. We were able to enjoy each other almost the way you enjoy looking through old pictures. I still had at least another year of school ahead of me, possibly two, and he had no plans to move to Cambridge. So, for the moment, we agreed to hold each other loosely, through phone calls, letters, and the occasional visit.

When the party was over, Lent began in earnest for me. It was back to work, back to school, back to trying to figure out where God was leading me. About the only thing I was certain of was that I wasn't ready to leave school after the coming year. Although I still maintained that I was not interested in ordination, and I definitely had not heard "the call," I was planning on talking to Rusty about switching to the three-year master of divinity program. If nothing else, I wanted to extend my time at HDS.

"What do you want me to do, Lord?" I prayed, nearly every day. It was my mantra. And it was applicable to almost every area of my life. "What do you want me to do regarding relationships; what do you want with me professionally?" I had a running dialogue with God, as constant as the tide rolling in and out. Consciously and unconsciously, I yearned for an answer, reaching upward with my heart like a green shoot straining toward the sun. I loved being at Pine Street but wasn't sure I wanted to work in a shelter when I graduated. When asked whether I was considering the ministry, I always answered "No" and wanted to run the other way.

Being a minister still seemed a rather grim profession. To me, it was the equivalent of voluntarily stretching out your beautiful wings and agreeing to have them permanently clipped. It came with a boatload of projections, assumptions, and expectations, and didn't seem like any place for a free spirit. Besides, I felt as if I would be a walking mixed signal if I were to be ordained, like a traffic light that flashes both green and red: *Look! Don't look! Normal! Not normal! Holy! Sinful!* I just didn't want it.

On the other hand, it never occurred to me that I *couldn't* be ordained if I wanted to be. After all, the ordination of women in the Methodist church began before I was born. The idea that only men should be ordained seemed archaic and ridiculous, and I had no interest in arguing with people who believed this. I was familiar with the scriptures used to justify the exclusion of women, verses such as "Women should remain silent in the churches" (thanks, Paul) and "The head of every man is the Christ, the head of woman is man" (thanks again, Paul), but I also understood fully how scripture could be used to justify all sorts of evil and oppression. My not wanting to be ordained had nothing to do with church politics or conservative naysayers; in fact, those views were almost reason enough for me to get ordained just to prove a point. I didn't want to be a minister because I couldn't see myself in the role. It was not the kind of job I wanted; it was not how I wanted to live.

To complicate things, I still had an unrequited desire to be a doctor. Perhaps to satiate this curiosity, I decided to take a class at Harvard Medical School. It was a rather bold move, but an opportunity that I knew would never come again. Graduate students at Harvard were allowed to take courses from any of the schools within the university; divinity students could also choose an offering from any of the ten divinity schools in the Boston Theological Institute. Although the course that I had enrolled in at the med school was not Organic Chemistry but rather Psychiatric and Physical Problems of the Aged, I was the only non–medical student in the class.

That first day, I was rather nervous, to say the least. The medical school was not easy for me to get to. Instead of being near Harvard Yard, it was set apart in an entirely different area of Boston, more than five miles away from the Divinity School. It wasn't near a T stop and I didn't have a car. To get there, I had to take the T as well as a bus, which wasn't too pleasant in the cold and often slushy weather. To make matters worse, I wasn't familiar with the buses and their schedules—I had just barely mastered the T. But somehow, I managed to get off at the right stop. I found the correct classroom in the correct building, and took my seat. I was wearing a black cotton pinstriped dress that I had bought at a flea market in Vienna. It had a little white collar, three-quarter-length sleeves, and a drop waist. I wore it with black tights and my little Chinese slippers, which looked great (at least to me) but were ridiculously inappropriate given the weather. UGGs were still a phenomenon of the future—not that I could have afforded them anyway—and I didn't have anything else that would match.

Feeling a bit self-conscious, as if I were a poseur or a spy, I looked around the room. *These are the best of the best, the biggest brains in medicine*, I thought. *Who here might one day discover the cure for cancer? Who will become a brilliant surgeon, saving people's lives? Whose will be the hands that bring life into the world? And who is that beautiful man sitting by the window?* My eyes had come to rest on the profile of a young man with light-brown curly hair, a beard, and a large, beautiful nose. The sun had cast a halo around his silhouette, and I tried not to stare but I couldn't stop myself from looking. In that light, he reminded me of Mandy Patinkin in *Yentl*. The movie, starring and directed by Barbra Streisand, had just come out and was already a huge hit—and Mandy Patinkin, in my opinion, was absolutely gorgeous in it. When the student at the window caught me looking at him, I immediately became very immersed in the syllabus that had been handed out, even if I wasn't registering a word of it.

I snapped out of it when the professor, who was distinguished as well as cordial and relaxed, asked all of us to introduce ourselves and say what our field of interest was. I found this rather surprising because I had envisioned the medical school as a scary, no-nonsense, cutthroat place—but that was perhaps more fitting for the law school or the business school. Instead, the students I encountered were serious but friendly, even if few seemed to have much use for the Divinity School. Later I learned that one of the traditions at the med school was to have a resident speak to the first-year students. "Congratulations on the hardest thing you have ever done, which is getting into Harvard," he or she would say. "Now the only thing you have to remember is"—and here they would take a piece of chalk and draw on the blackboard in large letters—"P = MD." In other words, "pass" equals "doctor." I believe all the classes at the med school were pass/fail in order to ease the pressure and to encourage collaboration. Of course, anything below a B– was considered failing.

When it was Mandy Patinkin's turn to introduce himself, I
learned that his name was John. He already had a PhD in psy-
chobiology from Harvard University and was now interested
in psychiatry. He was clearly brilliant, with the kindest eyes
and a sweet smile that only half hid the feeling that he had a
private joke going on in his head. When it was my turn, I
could feel him looking at me, an amused expression on his
face. I soldiered on. *Maybe it's the dress.* I winced. *What was I
thinking?* I felt a few heads turn when I announced that I was
from the Divinity School—*charlatan*—but the professor
seemed pleased to have someone in class who might be able to
offer a different perspective.

Class ended. I gathered my books without sneaking another look at John, and I headed out to the bus stop. A rather
brutal sleet was beginning to fall, and (of course) I had not
brought an umbrella. *Oh, great,* I thought, *I can look forward
to another freezing walk home.* Just then, a small sports car
pulled up and a hand was reaching over to the passenger's side,
unrolling the window. It was John. "Hey, you want a ride? I
don't think that bus is coming for a while . . . and I live just
around the corner from the Div School." My stomach flipped
a little. "Sure! I'd love one. Thanks," I said as I got in. There
was a momentary awkwardness from suddenly being thrown
into tight quarters after having just met. It was like finding
oneself stuck in a rolling elevator with a stranger—albeit one
who was handsome and who had just rescued me from the
rain.

"Hmmm . . . interesting choice of shoes for a day like
today," he said, a smile twitching at his lips.

"I know. I don't know what I was thinking. I guess I wasn't
thinking!" *This guy is a genius and I sound like a moron. Great.*

But instead of treating me as if I were an idiot, John seemed genuinely interested and friendly. We chatted as he drove, exchanging the usual information—where we were from, what we were doing. I liked him immediately. As he pulled up to Rockefeller, he said, "You know, I've seen you walking around here before."

"You have?" I asked, surprised. "When?"

"You cut through my street sometimes. I suppose it's on the way back from the laundromat or Mass Ave, since you're usually carrying something."

"And you recognized me?"

"I would know that hideous coat of yours anywhere!" He laughed.

This was not intended to be mean, and I didn't take it that way.

"You think it's hideous?"

"Yes."

"Good thing you don't have to wear it, then. Thanks for the ride. See you next week."

I found myself thinking about John more than I would have liked to as the week passed. The last thing I needed was another complication regarding a man—then again, I was getting ahead of myself. He could have a girlfriend, for all I knew; that's what I told myself anyway. He was charming and clearly smart, and he had a dry sense of humor, which I liked. I nonchalantly thumbed through my closet, putting a little extra thought into what I would wear to the next class, and I took a hard look at my brown jacket. Maybe it *was* hideous. In some ways, I was too distracted thinking about John to be nervous about the reality of taking a class at Harvard Medical School. Hidden blessing, I guess.

Each week, I looked forward to seeing him—not just because I was attracted to him, but because it was so nice to see a
friendly face when I got there; knowing him made me feel like
less of an outsider and a misfit. We often rode home together
after class, unless he had another commitment at the med
school. I enjoyed the opportunity to squeeze into his little car,
where I could look at him with unabashed interest or not look
at him at all. We would chat about our class or about what was
going on in our lives. He was easy to be around, and one of
the sanest people I had met. Once in a while, he would join
me at Rockefeller to study—although I sometimes found it
hard to concentrate with him there. I would get fidgety, or
want to talk, and he would respond by firmly reminding me of
the intense nature of his workload. In retrospect, I can't believe
how calm he always was or how easily he seemed to handle the
stress of medical school.

One of the highlights of our Problems of the Aged class
was a team presentation we gave on a fictional character, Rose
Blumberg, an elderly woman with multiple health and family
problems. John presented the psychiatric and medical issues,
while I elaborated on the field of spiritual counseling and its
benefits. It was well received by the professor, who seemed to
appreciate what my theological perspective added to the discussion, and "Rose" became a favorite running joke between
John and me.

Because we only lived a couple of blocks apart, it was easy to
stop by for a quick hello. But if I was busy, John was busier, and
in some ways this was a blessing. We didn't have a lot of time to
spend with each other, and so we chose to keep things loose. We
had an easy rapport and a mutual affection, but we played our
feelings a little too close to the vest, and both of us put school

before any kind of relationship. "If we ever lose touch," I teased, "I'm going to dig up my old corduroy coat and send it to you as a present." Too bad I have lost track of that coat.

Taking the class at the med school did in some ways clarify things for me—and it brought me the gift of John's presence in my life. I knew, more than ever, that medical school was not where I belonged. I had no desire to study the things required of doctors, even if I felt awed by the power of medicine and the skills that these brilliant future healers were learning. I belonged at the Divinity School, where we were learning to be healers, too, but of a different sort. Still, it's fascinating to think how my path would continue to intersect with medicine. Little did I know that I would be helping people like "Rose Blumberg" every day.

When I told Rusty Martin about my experiences at the medical school, he asked if this had impacted my thoughts about the future. I was moving toward the end of my first year at HDS, and we were discussing my desire to transfer into the MDiv program. I was now certain that my path would never be medicine, and I was pretty sure it wouldn't be ministry, either. Rusty didn't seem alarmed that I'd been there for a year and still had no idea of what I wanted to do. This was part of why I liked him so much. Rusty had guided me from Denison to Harvard, had wisely advised me to complete a field education, and had pointed me in the direction of Pine Street. Now he was trying to help me find the next rock across the pond, the next sure footing.

"Are you completely ruling out ordination?" he asked gently.

I hesitated. "Well, pretty much, although I do think more women should be ordained. I just don't think I want to work in a church."

"Listen," he suggested, leaning toward me, his hands clasped around his knee, "you have to complete another year of field education for the MDiv. Why not do it in a church? That way you will have a better idea of how you feel about it."

This made some sense. I had to do my fieldwork somewhere, and a church was as good a place as any. Rusty promised that the pastor he would recommend for my placement was someone I would like. He had graduated from the Divinity School only five years earlier, his theology and politics were very much in keeping with mine, and he was known to be a gifted speaker.

"You should try to set up an interview as soon as you return in the fall," he said thoughtfully. "If it's not going to work, then we'll have to figure something else out."

I left his office with a strange feeling. It was not foreboding, exactly, but it was close. It was that eerie sense that life was about to change, like the split second before the sun breaks free of the clouds. The image of Moses suddenly came to mind. Not that I thought I was Moses, but rather that God was eyeing me with a purpose in mind. There was Moses, walking along, minding his own business, tending to his flock, when out of nowhere a bush bursts into flames. Next thing you know, God calls his name and, without thinking, he answers, "Here I am." A similar thing happened to the prophet Isaiah, as a matter of fact. *Note to self: think before you speak.* I don't think those guys read the fine print. Then again, it was written in the language of angels.

I had successfully found my way into another year at HDS, but I was not ready to answer the call of ministry. I hadn't heard it; didn't want to hear it. It was hard enough just thinking about answering the call of some minister trying to set up an interview. An unseen force was rearranging the shape of my life, rearranging who I was or, rather, who I thought I was. I felt like I was one of the decorations that Katherine and I had tacked on the wall for our party. I was comfortable in one configuration, the one who went to school and worked at Pine Street. Hadn't God called me there, and hadn't I happily answered "Here I am"? But shaping me for church work? *Please, God—send someone else.*

13

follow your gnosis

I was running late for class, when I dashed out of the rain and into Andover Hall, my books pressed against my sweater to keep them from getting too wet. Students were shuffling in and out of classrooms, each trying to get to where they needed to be. I called a friendly hello to a couple of people I knew before involuntarily launching myself into the air. I should have figured the halls would be slick from dripping umbrellas and soggy shoes, raincoats and hats, but this reality just hadn't registered. And so, as I rounded the corner in my cowboy boots and a skirt—of course I couldn't do this wearing something as modest as a pair of jeans—I found myself horizontal in midair. Books went flying, I went flying—in full cartoon mode. I was Charlie Brown, and an invisible Lucy had just pulled the football out from under me. A few people stopped to make sure I was okay and to help gather my books while I tried to gather my dignity. I didn't blame them for the giggles that they were clearly trying to suppress. It was genuinely hilarious, but I was still late for class.

Quickly (but more carefully), I walked into the classroom; then my face flushed red again. There was a soft rumble of laughter. *Oh, great. They've all seen my not-so-graceful leap of faith.* I slinked into a seat next to Katherine and asked her if she had seen my spill.

"No! I didn't," she said, turning to me with genuine concern. "Are you okay?"

"Yes, I'm fine. Just mortified, is all. What are people laughing about?"

Katherine directed my attention to the chalkboard in the front of the room, which, in my embarrassment, I had walked past without noticing. There, beautifully drawn in colored chalk, were a series of giant noses with descriptions such as ROMAN GNOSIS, UPTURNED GNOSIS, STUFFY GNOSIS, and the phrase NOBODY GNOSIS THE TROUBLE I'VE SEEN. The drawings were a playful ode to Professor Dieter Georgi, who was a few minutes late himself. We were taking New Testament Theology with Dieter, and the current topic was Gnosticism, the mystical knowledge of the Divine, and how it was experienced and expressed in the early Christian communities. Knowing that he had a good sense of humor, someone (ahem . . . Katherine) had taken it upon herself to offer an illustration to accompany the lecture of the day.

Dieter walked confidently into the packed classroom, exuding a striking, athletic vitality, even at fifty-five. Maybe this was because, in addition to being a professor, he was an avid soccer player and coach. His physical presence, coupled with his pastoral sensibilities and his academic pedigree, made him a huge draw at the Divinity School. He and Helmut Koester (another German-born New Testament professor) had studied under Rudolf Bultmann, the renowned German theologian and one of the twentieth century's most important biblical scholars. I had encountered Bultmann's work as an undergrad, and I had found it challenging and even life changing in some ways. The fact that Dieter Georgi was but a step away from this giant in the field of biblical studies was quite amazing. I imagined, however, that Dieter was a lot more approachable and less intimidating as a professor. He insisted on being called by his first name, which garnered him no less respect; rather, it fostered a sense of camaraderie with his students, as if we were all on the journey together.

One day during lunch, he happened to join Katherine and me in the refectory. We had noticed him come in. Not too many professors ate there with the students, and so we were rather startled to find him standing at our table holding his lunch tray like a schoolboy. "Do you mind if I join you?" he asked in his polite German accent. *Gulp.* We were a little nervous, but mostly we felt honored. His presence had that kind of effect. In contrast to us, he seemed completely at ease and genuinely interested in making conversation. We chatted about this and that, but not about the class we were taking from him, and we were managing not to say anything ridiculous—until the topic of speaking German came up somehow. My conversational German was decent at that time, and Dieter and I were exchanging a few pleasantries. Then Katherine chimed in. "I only know one phrase in German."

"Oh," said Dieter with a smile. "Let's hear it."

"Ich liebe dich," she proudly proclaimed, with the earnestness of a child. As soon as the words left her lips, there was an awkward pause. She had just told Professor Dieter Georgi that she loved him.

"I see," he said, his face and hairless pate turning a bit red.

"Oh, what I mean is . . ." she began, trying to ignore my barely suppressed giggle. "Well, actually, what would be the response to that? I mean, if someone said, 'I love you,' how would you answer in German?"

This didn't help. I bit my lip and she stepped on my foot under the table.

Dieter smiled. I don't remember whether he offered the German response. All I remember is the warmth of his presence and the kindness of his eyes.

He also had a depth of spirit, born out of his life experiences, that was profoundly compelling. In 1945, when he was sixteen years old, Dieter happened to be in the city of Dresden when British and American forces firebombed the city. Four raids over a three-day period left fifteen square miles of the city center in ruins and an estimated twenty-five thousand civilians and refugees dead.* Dieter escaped by jumping into a sewer, while fireballs ravaged the city above and the screams of the dying could be heard from below. This was something that could never be unheard or unseen but would stay with him for the rest of his life. It was a seminal moment. Who was good? Who was bad? When he went on to become a pastor and then a professor, Dieter searched for the connections between politics and religion, imperialism and injustice, the Roman Empire and early Christian writings, the all-encompassing humanity of Christ and the challenge of living one's faith in the world.

---

* For many years, the estimated number of fatalities varied wildly. Some claimed it was in the hundreds of thousands. A recent report has estimated the fatalities at 18,000–25,000 (http://www.spiegel.de/international/germany/death-toll-debate-how -many-died-in-the-bombing-of-dresden-a-581992.html)

Katherine and I both loved Dieter Georgi, loved him for his humor and his brilliance and his life—but we often could not make heads or tails out of what he was saying. This wasn't because of his accent, and it wasn't because he intentionally tried to baffle us. Dieter just seemed to operate on a different plane. Because of this, his was one of the most stressful but enjoyable classes I took at the Divinity School. During his lectures, I filled my notebook with cries for help, with notes to Katherine, with doodles, and with the occasional nugget of meaning. Sometimes Jennifer, another one of our friends, would quietly distract us with her growing belly. She was expecting her third child, who accompanied her to class like a stowaway, and whose hiding place was becoming increasingly obvious. When the baby would move, she would sometimes nudge me and point to her stomach with a knowing smile, or place my hand upon her belly so that I could feel the kicks and squirms. *This is the meaning beneath all meanings,* I thought, *the a priori awareness of God's incarnated love for us.*

One definition of *Gnosticism* is revealed knowledge, experienced knowledge. It cannot be understood through the cool lens of analytical thought; rather, it is the intuitive understanding of the mysteries of the universe. One of the difficulties I was having with Dieter's class was that I was panicking. I felt as if I just wasn't *getting* it, which perhaps blocked my ability to *experience* it.

Strangely enough, this was not the case a year later when he happened to speak at the church where I was doing my field study. He came as a favor to the pastor, who had been a student of his a few years earlier. My role on that Sunday was to offer the pastoral prayer before the sermon, one that Dieter had agreed to preach. Even though I felt a little nervous about him being there, I decided to forgo any written notes and just pray from the heart. I have no recollection of the words that came out of my mouth, but when I said "Amen," Dieter had tears in his eyes. He walked to the pulpit, looked at me, and said, "I really have nothing more to add to that." Something had happened. Perhaps I had finally been receptive to the inner wisdom of the Spirit, which pierced the fog of my intellect and ego.

This is part of what I learned in Dieter Georgi's class—to open myself to the treasure buried within the very fabric of our lives, our spirits, our identities as God's created children, and to understand ourselves in relation to those who went before and those who will come after us. It's funny . . . I can't remember, really, the specifics of what he said, and if I could, I probably still wouldn't understand it. But I carry with me this spark of his wisdom: our faith has a history, stretching back through the centuries and extending into the future, and it should be lived out and made manifest in the context of this needy world. Truth, guidance, spiritual understanding—these are close at hand, he seemed to be saying, ready to be revealed and experienced. And when we experience the power of God's revelation, we will see ourselves differently; we will see the world differently. For Dieter, the writings of the early Christian community, with its politics and people, its culture and its struggles, were inherently relevant. By looking through the lens of history, he suggested, we might recognize the Holy hidden in our humanity, as It has been from the beginning of time, and live in such a way as to bring the Kingdom closer.

I believe we all hope for clarity, for revelation, for our paths to be illuminated, for purpose, and for direction. We look back, trying to make sense of our lives, but we can't see ahead. It's almost as if we get in the way of ourselves, trying to think our way onto the path instead of allowing it to emerge. The more we listen for that still, small voice within us, however, the more well lit our paths will be.

Sometimes this comes in small sparks, little eureka moments that guide the next step of our journeys. One of these came for Andy, and it happened to be at our pregnant friend Jennifer's house. She had invited us to spend Easter with her and her family, which provided a lovely break from school. Her two young children were friendly and loving, and her husband, who was an artist, was mellow and hip. Spending time with them gave us an unspoken glimpse of what it might be like to have a family and children of our own.

I was happy that Andy had agreed to go with me. We were reaching for each other, even though our future was uncertain. He was still the person with whom I could most easily talk, the one I found endlessly interesting in his uniqueness and intelligence, and to whom my heart kept holding on, even when I tried to shake it loose. This was an unusual experience for me. Whether I quickly darted or merely tiptoed off the other way, I was more likely to run *from* a relationship than *to* it—and this holding on surprised me. I could only think that maybe some inner wisdom was at work.

Jennifer happened to have a piano at the house. Andy, who was a self-taught electric-bass player, loved music but couldn't read it, and he had never noodled around on the piano. I, on the other hand, had taken piano lessons for five painful years as a child—painful, that is, for my teacher, since I rarely practiced. The same could be said for my sister Jennie. Our lessons consisted of long pauses and wrong notes as we tried, mostly without success, to bluff our way through the music. Our teacher, who was also the organist at our church, was incredibly patient. When at last I would reach the end of a piece, after having limped along like a three-legged dog, she would just smile and say, "Why don't we try that one more week?" It usually sounded no better the following week but she would still give me a sticker anyway, and we would move on.

Once in a while, I was lucky enough to have her doze off during the lesson (which I can't blame her for, since it was the afternoon and those pauses were *so* long). When this happened, I would sit very still, trying not to make a sound. The clock would tick slowly, my sister would give me dirty looks, and I would manage to escape most of the horror of those thirty minutes. I regret it now, of course, wasting that opportunity to really learn how to play the piano, but I have fond memories of those afternoons in the sunlit living room of Mrs. Stiling, who could have lost her patience with me but didn't. With her, there was always another opportunity, like a musical repeat, always hope that the next time would be better.

I was telling Andy about my lessons when I noticed that he was looking at the piano as if he had just stumbled upon the Holy Grail. "Wow, do you know where the notes are?" he asked, placing his hands lightly on the keys. I told him that I did, adding, "But don't ask me to play anything! All I remember is 'Chopsticks' and the right hand of 'Heart and Soul.'" Laughing, I showed him middle C. I was being lighthearted, but something had been ignited in him; his path suddenly began to unfurl, each note a streetlight marking the way. It was as if his spirit, which had been living in only one part of the house, had suddenly found the hidden door to a whole new wing—and it was a sanctuary, a spiritual playground, a banquet hall for his soul. Easter had come to him through an unusual channel; his deepest experience of the Divine would be through music, especially through the piano.

When he returned home from that trip, he knew his path. Perhaps, like me, he wasn't completely sure where it would lead, but he was on it. He rented a piano, found a teacher, and started (at the age of twenty-three) with *Teaching Little Fingers to Play*. The tension we had experienced in the fall during our visit to Walden Pond vanished (to a large degree) with his discovery of the piano. Now he had a calling, and he was pursuing it with discipline and determination, passion and love. By unearthing his destiny, maybe we had a chance. He was doing his part anyway.

If only I could have kept from rushing around the corners and landing on my rear. Relationships can be a slippery slope, especially if you are running from one to the other. Even though Andy had found his path, his sacred gift, and was still hanging in there with me, I was not ready to commit. I was still on a fact-finding mission. Yes, that's it! I was doing research. Like a spiritual archeologist, I was excavating the ancient ruins of my psyche; I was trying to figure out what my spirit needed in order to learn and to grow and to (please, God) be happy. This would lead me down paths that were lovely and some that were rather dark. Sometimes I still feel as if I am a remedial student of the Way. Gnostics (and romantics) believe there are things that you just *know*, and that this knowledge is innate, inherent, and revealed through experience. I felt as close to a gnostic at that point as the chalk nose on the board—but I believed such knowledge was available to me. I believed that if I listened closely enough, listened with my spirit open, I could hear the voice of God coming from within and without, like celestial surround sound. Who knows, I might even be able to understand what Dieter Georgi was saying.

On the day of the rain and my embarrassing fall, when life was confusing but an adventure, when I always went too fast and hardly looked before I leaped, I found a seat and some comfort next to my best friend. Bruised or broken, it didn't matter. If I was having trouble hearing God's voice, I trusted her as the next best thing. With Dieter's entrance, the classroom went silent. Stopping short of the podium, he took a look at the chalkboard. "Nicely done," he said slowly, with a nod. Then, turning sideways, he presented his profile to the class—and with a sly smile, asked, "How's my gnosis?"

14

---

the call

As our first year was winding down, everyone in Rockefeller had to find another place to live. The Divinity School dorms were primarily for first-year students, to help them get settled and acquainted with the area. Katherine had found an apartment in Central Square, but I had no idea what I was going to do. Close as we were, Katherine and I rarely saw each other outside of class. She had a separate set of friends, and her writing, of course, which kept her busy, and I was usually bogged down with work or some romantic entanglement. So I was happy when Carla told me about two positions that were opening across the street at Jewett House.

Jewett House was a beautiful redbrick building opposite Andover Hall. In addition to being the home of the Divinity School dean, it offered overnight accommodations for visiting scholars and was the site of numerous faculty dinners and receptions. On the left side of the house was a small wing reserved for three students; two served as maids (or nannies, if need be) and one worked as a cook. In exchange for twelve hours of work per week, the students received free housing in the servants' wing, but would be on their own for meals. This was not a problem, because there was a small kitchen for them to share on the third floor, where one of the bedrooms was also located; the bathroom was on the second, near the other two rooms. The students who lived there were asked to enter and exit through the side door of the main house. This meant passing through the dean's kitchen before ascending the steps that led up to their rooms.

"What do you think?" asked Carla, showing me the small notice in the *Nave*, the Divinity School newsletter. "Two out of the three students who have been living there are graduating. I'm going to try for the cook's position. Why don't you interview for the maid's? It could be fun, and would really help financially."

She had a point. Not only would it save us the expense and hassle of renting an apartment, but it was right on campus; this obviously meant no commute, which would be an additional savings of time and money. The fact that Carla wanted to cook was a relief because there was no way I could have fulfilled that position. And, contrary to how my room usually looked, I was certain I could do the cleaning. "Let's do it," I answered without hesitating. "Sounds like a godsend." We called the dean's wife immediately, as she was the one who was doing the hiring, and we set up an interview. Before most people had even read the notice, we were hired—and, just like that, our housing was secured for the next two years.

I will always be grateful to Carla for telling me about that ad, even though we had some rather tense times in the end at Jewett House. For the moment, however, I was immensely relieved that I didn't have to find an apartment, find a roommate, or figure out how I was going to pay for it. The main challenge I faced was the time commitment. Fieldwork also required twelve hours a week—and if the position that Rusty had told me about worked out, this would entail a thirty- to forty-five-minute commute each way on top of that. The grim reality was that I would be working almost thirty hours a week in addition to going to school full-time. The way things were looking, I could eat, but I might not be able to sleep.

We moved into our new rooms at the end of the school year, making trip after trip with a handful of belongings down the stairs of Rockefeller, across the street, and back up the stairs of Jewett House. Luckily, I really didn't have too much to move. My old room could hold only a limited amount, and my new room was about the same size. What we brought to school was vastly different from the warehouse of clothes, appliances, and equipment that college students bring with them today. I had a typewriter and a small cassette player, a couple pairs of shoes, a box of clothes, a jean jacket, and my old brown coat. Add to that my tiny refrigerator, and I was all set. My mouse had long ago moved on to greener pastures.

Carla and I were given the rooms across from each other on the second floor; Kim, the one returning student, had the room on the third floor next to the kitchen. Kim did not seem overly enthusiastic about us, but I really couldn't blame her. She was disappointed that one of her friends, who had expressed interest in a position, had been late in applying and had missed out. The dean's wife, a thin, rather pale woman with a sweet smile but a stiff New England vibe, seemed to genuinely like Carla and me. Not only were we the first to respond to the ad, but she also saw us as a unit. It made sense to her to hire two people who already knew and liked each other, because we would be working closely together for the next two years. In addition to the dean and his wife, the only other person in the house was their twelve-year-old daughter. Their older daughter was in boarding school somewhere.

With our rooms secured for the following school year, I went home for the summer and took a job working at one of Procter & Gamble's research-and-development plants in Cincinnati. There I spent the better part of the summer, eight hours a day, five days a week, in an eight-by-twelve-foot windowless room with three other college-aged girls. We sat on a long table facing the wall, with our feet dangling and a white bucket centered below each of us on the floor. In front of us were pairs of soap dispensers with pull handles, the kind that are common in public restrooms. Our job was to dispense the soap into the bucket at our feet until the handle on the dispenser broke. Then we recorded how many cartridges of soap we had gone through before this happened.

It was truly the most monotonous job I have ever done. We were nicknamed "the milkmaids" and would sometimes attract curious onlookers who had heard about "the girls in the closet." To make the time go by, we would listen to the radio or talk about school, boys, pop culture, whatever came into our heads. By the end of the summer, my forearms were so strong, I could have passed for Popeye's little sister. When this job was finished and enough data had been collected, I was sent to the orange-juice line with another girl about my age named Sam. Our supervisor was a friendly middle-aged man, who slapped his hand to his balding head and rubbed his brow when he saw us. "I hope my wife never comes here. When I tell her that my two new workers are Sam and Andie, she's not going to be picturing the two of you!"

By the end of the summer, I was excited to return to Cambridge. It already felt like home and smelled like freedom. Harvard Square, now beloved and familiar to me, was packed again with students—and my room was waiting for me at Jewett House. I felt so lucky; lucky and happy and blessed. I hadn't seen Andy all summer, although we had written some letters and had spoken on the phone at least once a week. He had been working steadily at the piano and was making enormous progress. It was quite staggering, really. I loved hearing the excitement in his voice when he talked about it. "I know this may sound crazy," he told me, "but Kevin, my teacher, thinks I may have a shot at getting into a music school in a couple years. Wouldn't that be wild?" Yes, I thought it would be, I told him. But the wildest part was not the fact that this was his goal but that two years later he would land at the music school from which Tomas had just graduated—Longy School of Music in Cambridge. You can't make this stuff up—and if you did, no one would believe you. There's a reason we can't see into the future; it would make the present so much more nerve-wracking or, at the very least, less interesting.

I called Andrea to let her know that I was back, but I didn't have a number for Katherine; I'd never needed one. I would have to wait till I ran into her at school. Carla had been at Jewett House for more than a week by the time I got there. She filled me in on the workings of the house, but it was clear that Kim was the student in charge. She showed me where everything was—the vacuum, the cleaning products, the nine bathrooms that were my responsibility, the sheets, towels, and guest rooms—but she deferred to the dean's wife when it came to the family's private quarters. I would also be cleaning their rooms and bathrooms once a week. How odd to have my head in the dean's toilet, I thought.

With those responsibilities sorted out, I contacted the pastor from the Cliftondale United Methodist Church, where Rusty had suggested I do my field placement. We had spoken by phone but had not managed to arrange a meeting in person before I'd left for the summer. Now it could be avoided no longer. We agreed to meet in the lounge at Rockefeller for an interview, which was basically a formality. Michael Curry, the pastor, knew that Rusty would not be sending him anyone he wouldn't like, and I felt the same way. What I neglected to tell the pastor over the phone, however, was that I had been dreading this meeting. It didn't sound at all fun or particularly compelling (as Pine Street had); in fact, it sounded positively awful. *I'd much rather be hanging out with a couple of drunk, crazy homeless guys than sitting in church*, I thought. But hearing his warm voice, with his West Virginia accent—and I mean *southern* West Virginia—was reassuring. He sounded young and hip, and it gave me hope that this was not going to be a disaster.

When I walked into Rockefeller for our meeting, I saw a burly man in a short-sleeved clergy collar, with hairy arms, a full beard, and long brown hair that was styled in a curly mullet. Think Adam Sandler in *The Wedding Singer*. He'd made a paper sign, upon which was written ANDRIA in magic marker, and he was having trouble getting it to stand up. I found this both humorous and slightly alarming. *What person cannot spell Andrea?* I wondered. Thank goodness he didn't have a go at my last name, Ruehrwein. My first thought when I saw him was *What a friendly-looking goofball; at least he's not some uptight religious stiff.* His first impression of me, he later admitted, when I came through the door in my cowboy boots, jean skirt, and a men's paisley vest over a white T-shirt, was *Oh, Lord, I've got myself a hippie.* In some ways, we were both right.

I couldn't help but like Michael. He was clearly very bright, very outgoing, and full of energy. We quickly discovered that we had some things in common, both theologically and personally. He, too, had gone to HDS on scholarship and knew, even more than I did, about what it was like to struggle financially. He had grown up in rural West Virginia, with very little money but a lot of love. For Michael, faith was both personal and political; he embraced liberation theology, which emphasizes God's concern for political, economic, and social justice, especially for the poor and marginalized, and he considered himself a feminist. His wife, Ella, who was from northern West Virginia, was a brilliant critical-care nurse working in Boston. If I had to do a field study in a church, this would be my guy. Rusty had not let me down.

We shook hands and agreed on when I would start—then I headed back over to Jewett House. My second year at HDS was beginning to take shape. It was exciting, but I was going to have my work cut out for me. I was taking another course from Professor MacRae, this time on the Gospel of John, as well as an Old Testament class, which had the reputation of being incredibly hard. I was taking Feminist Perspectives in Ministry and a class on Hindu dharma. In addition, I had promised the director at Pine Street that I would continue working there when I could, although I couldn't imagine making it more than once a week. This did not leave a lot of time for existential angst, much less romance, but I managed to fit in a little of both . . . well, actually, a lot of angst and enough romance to keep it going.

When the time came to start my field placement at Cliftondale United Methodist in Saugus, I was feeling a little less anxious about it. Michael and I had met several times to discuss how the year might take shape, what I hoped to learn, and what he thought was important to teach. He had boundless energy and a passion for ministry—but he was also a real person. Those closest to him knew that he had a talent for dropping the occasional swear word to punctuate his point, and he understood the difficulty of bridging the generations in his congregation. What might be a draw for the younger people—a young, cool minister—might be a turnoff for the older ones. Michael managed this by being entirely attentive and accessible to all members of his flock. It also helped that he had Ella by his side, a woman who was beautiful and brilliant in her own right. Michael was incredibly smart, a gifted preacher, and a wonderful pastoral counselor. He had come from the Bible Belt, so he understood conservative ideology, but he was courageously progressive. He and Ella both had lovely voices; she sang in the choir and he was known to break into song from the pulpit. The congregation loved him, even if they didn't always agree with his politics.

This was entirely new to me. I had grown up in the church, attending nearly every Sunday since the day I was baptized, but I had never known a minister quite like Michael. He could reference scholars such as Tillich and Heidegger with the animated and dramatic flair of a Gospel church preacher, all while rocking that mullet in his pink Harvard robe. With his southern accent and gregarious presence, he could have been mistaken for a country rock star—an association that I think, to some humorous extent, he enjoyed. That being said, it was all well and good to hang out with Michael and Ella—I already felt as if I had known them for years—but I was still slightly queasy about the work itself.

The first Sunday came. It happened to fall on a Communion Sunday (Methodists take Communion only once a month). I was assigned the Call to Worship and the Gospel reading, and I was to assist Michael during Communion. There are many ways that Communion can be served in the Methodist church. When I was growing up, the ushers, like celestial waiters, would bring the elements to everyone seated in the pews. We did not stand and walk forward to receive them at the altar—maybe this was thought to be "too Catholic." The ushers, who were almost always men at that time, would carry round trays with tiny glass cups of grape juice, thimblefuls of Christ's blood. We would pass the tray down the pew, family-style, handing it off to the usher on the opposite side. Then they would bring the bread, which was cut into perfect half-inch cubes by women I knew—my mom and her friends, my Sunday-school teachers—the behind-the-scenes women who were the workers and backbone of the church.

I was not allowed to receive Communion until I was confirmed at age twelve. There is no hard-and-fast church ruling on this, but it was the practice in my family. Perhaps having to wait lent more of an air of mystery to it. It certainly felt this way when the tray was passed under my nose; it looked like Wonder Bread and Welch's, and yet I was not allowed to have it. I watched the adults take the tiny cups and the squares with no crusts, waiting for something to happen, but they didn't look any different afterward. My mother and father were still there, sitting with their heads bowed. Sometimes my dad would reach over and squeeze her hand. The bread was a part of them, the juice was a part of them; they had ingested holiness and lived to tell about it.

Perhaps this is how atheists and agnostics see those of us who believe in Mystery. What looks like a case of the Emperor's New Clothes is really God's sleight of hand; the mundane becomes the holy, people sitting in pews become one family at the table. The important things happen below the surface, often in that which cannot be seen with the naked eye; only the spiritual eye will do. I did not begin to comprehend this until I was able to partake of Communion myself. Then I began to intuit the ancientness of it, the connection, the significance. As time went on, this wonder did not diminish in me—it grew. The sacrament did not become more mundane with familiarity but, rather, more profound. This is difficult to explain to those who only see Wonder Bread and Welch's. Rituals can be powerful, symbols can be powerful, and participating in symbolic acts in the right spirit can launch one into a deeper spiritual experience.

When I became a mother, I chose not to put an age restriction on my children regarding Communion, although I can see the merit in both approaches. Theologically, I couldn't quite imagine Jesus denying children the bread or the wine (juice for us Methodists); they are part of the Body, I reasoned, and would grow in their understanding. And, let's be honest, what adult fully grasps the meaning of it? For me, Communion is an ongoing process of learning and growing spiritually, and of dipping my bucket a little deeper into the well each time. That being said, I did see my parents' point years later when my six-year-old son turned to me in church one Sunday and asked, rather loudly, "Are we having snack today?" Snacking on the body and blood of Christ—maybe I needed to rethink things;

or maybe he had something. Maybe we do just nibble on the mystery. He was either a heretic or a pint-sized guru.

As Michael was explaining how we were going to serve Communion on that morning, it was clear that he had a whole host of other things on his mind. He was putting his arms through his clergy robe, grabbing his sermon notes, making sure he knew who was in the hospital and who needed to be mentioned in prayer. His warm brown eyes scanned the office for one last check before curtain call.

"So, do you use individual cups?" I asked, refocusing his attention. I didn't want to get up there without knowing what I was doing. I was nervous enough over the idea of being introduced to the congregation.

Pushing the Pause button on his whirlwind, he stopped and looked at me with a conspiratorial smile. "Naw," he said, "we're just gonna do the old rip-'n'-dip."

I burst out laughing. Intinction had never sounded so friendly and accessible. Maybe this wasn't going to be such a nightmare after all. As we walked toward the back of the sanctuary, I ventured one more question.

"So, do you have a good sermon prepared?" I asked politely.

"Are you kidding?" he whispered, giving me a playful nudge. "I'm gonna knock their effing socks off!"

Michael's friendly humor had relaxed and distracted me. By the time we were walking down the aisle behind the choir, I was feeling less nervous and more centered. Everyone rose to sing the processional hymn, which filled the small sanctuary with warm, round voices. The singular power of this simple act struck me: when else do people ever sing together anymore, old and young, off-key and pitch-perfect? Individual voices could be heard as we walked past, but these were woven together by the time we reached the front. Singing in church is about the only time I ever heard my mother or grandmother sing. I loved to stand next to my mom because of this, her soft, earnest voice somehow shy and yet infused with faith. My father sang, too, but this was less unusual. He would also sing at home sometimes, entertaining us with his Mario Lanza impression. This was usually done at the kitchen table at full volume. He would belt out songs like "Because You're Mine" (by Sammy Cahn and Nicholas Brodszky) until his face turned red and he burst into laughter. Though he would argue with me, he actually had quite a set of pipes. He had sung in his high school chorus and in some community-theater productions. By the time we kids were born, he just sang to make us laugh.

I was carrying all this with me as we made our way toward the altar—carrying the voices of my parents, the safe haven of my childhood church, and the genetic stamp of generations of spiritual seekers and faithful Christians that make up my heritage. I had grown up in the church, had played in the church, had sung and had spoken in the church from the time I was a baby; but this didn't mean I wanted to work in the church. Clearly that was for someone far holier than I, someone who had it more together, even someone who looked like Michael. Members of his humble congregation, which was made up of working- and middle-class people, smiled kindly at me as I passed. Once we reached the steps of the altar, the choir took their places in the choir loft, while Michael and I paused to bow our heads in silent prayer. After he said "Amen," he shot me a sideways look. "Ready, kid?" he whispered. I nodded. Ready or not, the wheels were in motion.

When the hymn had been sung, he took a seat across the span that separated the pulpit from the lectern, his face beaming. Without introduction, I climbed the lectern steps and opened my bulletin to read the Call to Worship. I have no idea what the words were, or even their ballpark meaning. Something was happening. It was as if the congregation were in freeze-frame and I was able to take my time looking out at them, or as if I had stepped outside of myself and could see the whole picture as a stunning mosaic of light. For a moment, we were a living stained-glass window, each person a different hue. The hairs on my arms stood on end. My mouth was moving, but a voice inside was saying *This is it. This is what you are supposed to be doing.*

I took my seat, head spinning. I had that feeling you get when you're about to faint. The room tipped on its axis, and I had an overwhelming urge to go with it, to fall into the deepest sleep and wake up to the relief that it had all been a dream, that I had not heard that Voice. Michael was introducing me to the congregation, telling them that I would be with them for the next year, giving them some information on my background. I sat there smiling, but it was a mock-up of myself. I had quietly propped a very good replica of my body in that chair, while my spirit retraced its steps up to the lectern. I was looking for the secret to the magic trick. Where was the hidden microphone, where was the illusion? But, of course, there was none. I had heard a voice, and it had come from Somewhere Else. Someone or Something had picked me out of the lineup—surely there had been some kind of mistake.

The service ended, Michael had indeed knocked their socks off, and now people were coming up to greet me. I stepped back into my body, trying to snap out of it. During the bus ride back to Cambridge, I reviewed what had happened in the sanctuary. I saw myself standing at the lectern looking out at the congregation, and I could *feel* the words that had run through my head: *This is what you are supposed to be doing.* My first response had been an almost simultaneous *Oh no!* followed by all the reasons that I would make a terrible minister: I was too funky, I didn't fit the part, I would never be able to be myself, I wasn't holy enough. I just didn't want to do that kind of work. What a nightmare.

When I got back to Jewett House, I tried to shake it off. *No one is forcing you into a collar*, I reminded myself. I needed to exhale. Maybe it had been temporary insanity. I went about my business scrubbing toilets and dusting furniture. I walked baby Rebecca into Harvard Square in a backpack, pretending I was a single mother; I immersed myself in my studies. In short, I tried to forget about it. *That call must have been a wrong number*, I reasoned, *a prank call from above. Good one, God, very funny!* I'd say next time we talked. *Now, if you'll just excuse me, I'd like to go back to my life.*

There were so many reasons that this church thing was not a good idea. As I was thinking about this, Moses surfaced again. He was fresh in my mind from the Old Testament class I was currently taking. How ironic that I was reading about the moment God called him. How many reasons did he give to say that he wasn't the right man for the job? Five? I shuffled through Exodus till I found the passages in the third and fourth chapters (thank you, Professor Hanson). It might sound bold to say, but I related to him. When God calls him from within that flaming bush to go to Egypt, Moses argues, "Who am I to do this job?" Then he asks, with some desperation, "What would I say?" When this argument doesn't seem to make a difference, he tries a third one: "What if they don't believe me?" Fourth: "I'm not a good speaker." Finally, his fifth and final plea is one most of us can relate to. He simply cries out, "O Lord, please send someone else to do it." You have to love him for that. If Moses had five reasons to question his call, then I must've had five hundred.

I managed to place that call on hold temporarily (sorry, God) while going about my work. This included traveling to Cliftondale twice a week in addition to Sunday services. During the week, Michael was teaching me about pastoral care, about church administration and the responsibilities of a pastor. We went on hospital visits together, and sometimes (with the permission of the congregant), I would sit in on a counseling session. We also discussed the challenge of being a "normal" person who happened to be a minister. On Sundays, we settled into a routine where I would offer the prayer at the end of his sermon. Michael's sermons were almost always engrossing, challenging, and enjoyable. I had no problem giving them my full attention, and I developed a flair for continuing his themes in the pastoral prayer. Unconsciously, this evolved into a mini-meditation on the sermon—a spontaneous encapsulation of the message, where I would tie up any loose ends for the congregation, reshaping this into prayer. It was our one-two punch, something we attributed to our growing friendship and mutual trust.

After a long day at the church, I would be relieved to get back to the Divinity School. I felt like myself there. I felt young and alive. At the church, I often felt out of body, tight, strange. It was one thing to be sitting in the pew, as I had done all my life; it was quite another to be standing in the pulpit. As much as I loved and trusted Michael and Ella, I didn't quite know how to show my true face regarding the institution. Could I be myself—not a fraction, but the totality, of me? And what about relationships? It was hard enough trying to navigate the waters of being young and single in Cambridge; what would this be like if I were a minister? Would every sweet granny try to fix me up with her grandson? (The answer is yes, by the way.) It made me feel panicky to think about living under the curious and potentially judgmental microscope of the church. I had a deep faith, but it was on safari at the moment. I was exploring uncharted territory. I was with my man Moses—who was I to do this work?

It's not that I was afraid to get up in front of people. I had been in leadership roles since I was a teenager and had spoken both in church and in school on numerous occasions. I could give a speech to my peers, I could read scripture in church; I could even sing while taking off my clothes on stage. (Don't panic—I played Gypsy Rose Lee in my high school production of *Gypsy*.) I knew how to pray, both silently and aloud. But could my voice be heard as a minister? Should it be heard? Sermons made me squeamish. I was uncomfortable with the idea of telling people what to do (my misconception). I didn't even like climbing the steps into the pulpit—that act alone spoke volumes. It seemed to set the pastor apart, above, supposedly closer to God. Who was I to tell anyone *anything*? I didn't feel qualified, on any level, to get up in the pulpit and advise others on how to live. What would I say?

Church was one of the few places that made me squeamish and tongue-tied. I had no trouble speaking up in my classes, venturing ideas or risking the wrong answer to a question. Through Pine Street, I was learning how to be an advocate for the poor and the needy, the sick and the lame. I could stand up for what I believed in and could even stand up for myself if need be. But I was afraid that the church would put me in a box, would clip my wings and require me to be someone I was not. I enjoyed going to church and participating in the services but I also loved returning to the freedom of being just another young person walking around Harvard Square. Sometimes it seemed these two worlds, these two parts of myself, just did not mesh.

Case in point: one Sunday, returning from church, I had gotten off the bus and was walking through Cambridge. It was an early spring day, one that was unusually warm, the kind of day that brings people out of hibernation to squint at the sun like a long-lost friend. The air carried the promise of more such days to come, which lent an unmistakable lightheartedness to the atmosphere. I was feeling particularly buoyant, lifted perhaps by that same warm sun, the returning friend of heaven and earth. To top it off, I was wearing one of my favorite dresses. It was made of a soft jersey material, in pink and gray floral, with three-quarter sleeves, a scoop neck, and a fitted bodice that laced up the front like a Renaissance princess's. The lower half was full and flouncy, hanging just below my knees, and I had on a purple version of my Chinese slippers. *Happy, happy, happy,* I thought. *I am happy to be alive.* Maybe there was a chance that I could take that call from God. Maybe I had not been wrong about the Voice. These were the thoughts that were cushioning my feet, making the sidewalk feel like a trampoline, springy and fun, like anything was possible. I was a princess in my own movie—and I was accompanied by angels.

I decided to take the long way back to the Div School in order to enjoy the weather for a few extra minutes. Instead of walking through Harvard Yard as I usually did, I walked down the street along its western border, Mass Ave. I was smiling to myself as I walked along. *Life is good and glorious* were the words that ran through my head like a song. But suddenly different words reached my ears—ugly words, embarrassing words. A group of undergraduates had just come out of Harvard Yard through one of its side gates, like animals escaped from a cage. They were walking on the opposite side of the street, in a large moving clump, and they were starting to shout things to the women they passed. No one seemed to be immune.

"Hey, baby, nice boobs. Why don't you come over and join us?" they shouted to one young woman. Laugh, laugh, laugh, hoot, hoot, hoot. *It's the middle of the afternoon*, I thought, *what a bunch of morons*. People gave her sympathetic looks; others shook their heads. "Idiots," said one woman as she passed. But the talking clump wouldn't stop. The girl managed to escape onto a waiting bus, leaving me next in the line of fire. *Just keep walking*, I told myself. But it was hard; their shouts were escalating, growing louder and more crass. When I ignored them, showing no signs of distress, they took this as a challenge, clearly wanting to rattle me. Finally, one of them yelled (at the top of his lungs), "Suck my——!" And without thinking, without flinching, I shot back (with equal volume), "It's not big enough!" This prompted everyone on the sidewalk to break into applause. I kept walking, head held high. The one who shouted this tried unsuccessfully to toss something back, but his friends shut him down, guffawing. "No, man, she burned you! You got nothin' after that!"

I don't think this is what Moses was going for when he asked God, "What do I say?" At that moment, I was like a balloon that had been popped. I was back on the sidewalk, which was no longer a trampoline but was made of hard cement. And I was no longer a princess; I was a poor man's Cinderella back in her cheap rags. Had those Harvard boys sensed this, that I was not one of them? My face was still hot with embarrassment and fury, and my defiant spirit, which had cracked a whip across the street to school those boys in manners, felt deflated. *This is why I can't be a minister*, I decided. *I don't look like one, I don't act like one, and I don't know what to say.*

Luckily, God has a tender heart and a sense of humor. God kept calling, sometimes, it seemed, on speed dial, sometimes in the middle of the night when I was trying to sleep. The Voice I had heard on that first Sunday at Cliftondale did not go away. If anything, it was growing stronger. Sometimes this made me shudder and want to plug my ears. Sometimes it still does! But one cannot run from God. Wherever I went, that Voice accompanied me, breathing courage into my body, strength into my spirit. It whispered again and again, "I have made you, I have formed you, and I have loved you since the beginning of time. You are mine. Trust me."

15

prisoner of love

On Sundays, I might be standing in the pulpit, but on Mondays, I was on my hands and knees scrubbing floors. Living and working at Jewett House proved to be an interesting experience. As part of the staff, Carla, Kim, and I were expected to fulfill our usual duties as well as serve at official functions. Dinners were formal when a scholar was visiting, and our serving skills had to be spot-on. It was one of the few arenas where the Harvard-ness of the Divinity School was front and center. Usually things felt pretty relaxed in terms of formalities at HDS, but not during those dinners. We wore white blouses and black skirts, and we moved silently and smoothly, as if we were not there. Some of the professors were clearly uncomfortable with being served and waited on by us in this way; others (even those we knew well) simply disregarded us. If I hadn't felt bad for him, it would have been comical to watch how uncomfortable Father Henri Nouwen was during these events—not with the dinners, but with being waited on. Without fail, he would come into the kitchen and thank us profusely at the end of the meal. It was painfully clear that he would have been more comfortable eating with us in the kitchen than in the dining room with the distinguished guests.

In contrast, during one dinner, a rather well-known visiting scholar could not stop peeking down our blouses each time Carla and I leaned over to refill his or someone else's water glass. It was awkward and embarrassing. Carla and I wondered if anyone had noticed. We were cracking up and rolling our eyes in the kitchen every time we made a trip back to retrieve something. How much water could one man drink during the course of a meal? Apparently, a lot, and I mean *a lot.* This didn't stop me from running up to my room and getting one of his books at the end of the dinner. I had studied this man's body of work, and now he was studying mine. Oh well. Whether despite or because of his ogling, I couldn't resist the urge to have him sign my book. The inscription reads, "In fond remembrance."

The student servants were in a rather unique position living in such intimate proximity to the dean and his family. It made sense that we were friendly and informal with one another, but it was also, naturally, awkward at times. He was never overtly inappropriate (and I feel compelled to say here that he was an excellent dean and a decent man), but there were times I felt a bit uncomfortable. For example, after a scholar had stayed at the house, it was my job to clean the room and get it ready for the next person. On one occasion, while I was bending over making the bed, I caught his reflection in the mirror looking at me. Maybe it was an honest mistake or just bad timing, but I jumped up reflexively, saying, "Oh, hi! Do you need me for something?" When there was an awkward pause, my face turned red, and he shuffled off, mumbling something about looking for a book. Even a girl from Ohio was smart enough to know he was not going to find that book in my back pocket.

Despite my questionable run-ins at Jewett House, I was enjoying my apprenticeship with Michael. He was teaching me volumes about ministry, pastoral counseling, and preaching. He was also becoming my friend, and someone who never made me feel uncomfortable or gave off an inappropriate vibe. I felt safe with Michael; I trusted him. If any issues arose in the church, he mentored and protected me, and when things started heating up in the national political arena, he began teaching me about civil disobedience.

It was 1985, and Ronald Reagan had just declared a crippling embargo on Nicaragua. Many people, including Michael, felt this was unjust and should not be passively accepted by the American people, at least not without voicing some outrage. A large community group had planned a demonstration. Protesters were to peacefully occupy the Federal Building in downtown Boston, which would most certainly lead to arrests. Michael encouraged me to join him in the protest and tried to prepare me for what it would be like.

"Remember," he said, "our main objective is to call attention to the issue, not to engage in any sort of violence or disrespect with the police. They are doing their jobs and we are doing ours. If they decide to arrest us, just go peacefully and cooperatively. Some people will make a point of being dragged away for dramatic impact, but that's really not necessary." I listened carefully. Although I had participated in various marches before, I had never taken part in an act of civil disobedience, and I certainly had never been arrested. "We'll be okay," he reassured me. "Oh, and remember to wear a clergy collar. I'll lend you one. It's important that the world knows the church cares."

"But I'm not ordained."

"It's okay," he reassured me. "For this purpose, it's symbolic."

Oddly enough, I wasn't all that nervous when the day came. A few other divinity students were participating as "supports," but I'm not sure if anyone else was planning on getting arrested. Michael and I entered the Federal Building with a few hundred other people and took a seat on the floor. When it came time for the building to close, we were all asked to leave. No one budged. Instead, a few rounds of "We Shall Overcome" started to swell in that slightly off-key and wobbly way common to crowds. Then the police started moving in.

As Michael had said, a number of people chose the you-have-to-drag-me-away method of exiting the building, but we were prepared to go quietly. An officer came for Michael, who smiled and gave me a thumbs-up; then another one came for me. When we were taken from the building, we had to walk through a gauntlet of reporters and TV cameras. It was starting to get dark by then, making their lights and flashing bulbs all the more dramatic. We were loaded onto school buses, because there were too many of us for police wagons, and people were sticking their arms out the windows flashing peace signs or pumping their fists. The atmosphere was joyous; triumphant, even. One would have thought we were all going to celebrate a Red Sox win over the Yankees; instead, we were headed toward the county jail.

At the jailhouse, the men and women were separated, so I lost track of Michael temporarily. We were shuffled into elevators going *down*, which is never a good sign. I was there with about fifteen other protestors and cops when a woman at my side said that her plastic handcuffs were hurting her, which they obviously were when I looked at her wrists. Apparently she was one of the draggers, and the draggers got cuffed because they were technically resisting arrest. Like an innocent but well-prepared Buckeye, I pulled out the Swiss Army knife that I had gotten in Europe and that I almost always carried with me—more for the tools than the blade. "Here," I offered, like a helpful Girl Scout, "I've got a knife that you can cut them off with." I was smiling when I started to hand it to the officer next to me so that he could relieve her pain. Instead, he grabbed it away with a growl.

"You can't have weapons here. What's wrong with you?"

"Oh, I'm sorry," I stammered, still in shock. "I wasn't thinking. I was just going to—"

"I know what you were going to do."

"—have you cut those plastic handcuffs off of this poor woman. She's in pain."

"We'll get them off as soon as we're downstairs," he said, without looking at me.

"What about my knife?"

"It's mine now."

"So sitting in a building is illegal but stealing isn't?" (I couldn't help myself.) Then I felt my eyes tear a little, although I really fought this.

He didn't answer me, nor did I ever get my knife back.

When we got downstairs, we were fingerprinted and photographed. Somewhere there is a mug shot of me (that you can probably get off the Internet for a small fee). I spent the night in jail with about a hundred fifty women, in a couple of large holding pens. There were no chairs, so we just sat on the floor, continuing our singing and chatting until we were too tired or bored to continue. The next day, we were released on our own recognizance and told we would be notified when to show up in court for the arraignment. When that day came, we arrived en masse. In the end, the charges were dropped because more than three hundred of us had gotten arrested and it would have been too costly to prosecute.

I was exhausted and dirty when I got back to my room, and there was still work to be done. A visiting scholar was leaving Jewett House today and his room would have to be cleaned. But before I took a shower or went to lie down, I called my parents.

"Hi, Mom," I said cheerfully. "Did you happen to watch the news last night?"

Mom, without missing a beat: "Andrea . . . are you in jail?"

"No, I just got out. Did you see me?"

She let out a groan, but it was loving and supportive. I hadn't even told her what I was doing, but she knew it immediately. My parents and I rarely agreed on politics, but they were proud of me for standing up for what I believed in.

As I was talking to her, there was a knock on my door. I figured it was probably one of my friends coming to check on me after the protest. Instead, I opened the door to find the scholar. He was standing there, sheepishly, with his hands in his jeans pockets, and no explanation for why he had knocked on my door. I became aware of several things at once. It's funny how lightning fast the mind is, even when exhausted. In a flash, I realized that the house was completely empty except for the two of us. I also realized, with some embarrassment, that my room was a wreck and I looked completely shot. If I was going to have an awkward encounter, I might as well look my best. And finally, I realized that my mother was still on the phone, hanging there like an invisible witness.

Startled, I said hello, waiting for him to say something. He stood there for a minute, shuffling around. It was pretty clear that he expected me to invite him in—but it would be presumptuous and perhaps unfair of me to say I knew this for certain. I had my mother's voice in my hand—I had *her*—suspended in midair as I pulled the phone from my head. I wasn't about to let her go. She was there, protecting me, even over a curly phone cord. It was such a vivid moment. I felt like I was holding on to her hand, as I had as a child when a hideous man in a discount store had touched me inappropriately. I was seven years old then, and I had been bending down to pick up a toy, when suddenly someone ran their hand between my legs and up the crack of my behind. I jumped and turned around. There he was, laughing at me, a smelly man with about four teeth in his head. I took off running and found my mom—my five-foot-tall, 105-pound mom—and told her what had happened. She took my hand, squeezing it hard, as if someone were threatening to rip it away, as if she were saying out loud, "No one is going to mess with my baby." Then she proceeded to march down every single aisle looking for him, with me in tow because she didn't want to let me go, but he was nowhere to be found. *Good thing for him*, I thought, *because it would not have been pretty.*

So here I was with a professor at my door and my mom on the phone, and no logical reason to explain it. Finally I said, "Oh, hey, I've got my mom on the phone. Did you forget something from your room?" From the look on his face, it was clear that he had not, but he mumbled something about thanking me for my work. I shut the door and locked it, even though he just looked to me like an overgrown prep school boy who didn't know much about women.

A week later, I received a letter from my mom. It contained only two lines in large cursive handwriting:

> *Andie,*
> *I told your dad that you were in jail and needed $500 to bail you out.*
> *He said, "Oh no!" but started balancing his checkbook!*
>
>   *Love,*
>   *Mom*

I still have that letter—in part because I still think it's very funny and telling about my family, and in part because it reminds me of that experience. But the deeper reason behind keeping it is that it is a talisman, a window into my father's immediate and wholehearted responsiveness, the way he would spring into action (and still does) when I am in need, and of my mother's fierce love, for the way she takes my hand, protects me, makes me laugh, and reminds me that, wherever I am and whatever I do, I am loved.

16

---

lost and found

My year with Michael at Cliftondale had some real highs and lows. I continued to question my call, at least outwardly, even though in the depths of my spirit I knew it was real and inevitable, my path, and my destiny. Michael and Ella were not only my friends, they had also become like family. We spent a great deal of time together (as much as my schedule would allow) hanging out at the parsonage with their big tabby cat, Kierkegaard, sharing meals and talking about life. Individually and together, they provided wise counsel, a shoulder to lean on, and steady support.

Ella was like a sister to me. She had shoulder-length raven hair and bright blue eyes, which sparkled when she laughed. Her deep dimples made her look girlish and approachable, which in many ways she was, but her staggering intelligence was revealed quickly in conversation, making her a formidable combination of beauty and strength. Though I spent more time with Michael, Ella was equally important to me. She understood the difficulties of being a young woman trying to navigate the church and relationships. She shared some of her own experiences of being a nurse, which also has its stereotypes, and was my sounding board and confidante.

Michael, too, was wholeheartedly supportive and encouraging. The only blind spot he seemed to have was on how vulnerable I really was to the projections and fantasies of certain male members of the congregation. This wasn't his fault. He did not objectify or view me in this way, which I loved about him—we were comrades, spiritual Vikings, kin—but it probably made him a bit naïve or, at the very least, caught him off guard. He was always looking out for me when it came to the institutional church, and he had full confidence in my ability to handle myself—but one cannot anticipate every scenario.

For example, there was a lovely young couple, Bobby and Donna, who came to church regularly with their three small children. The woman was vibrant and pretty, with wavy auburn hair and a curvy figure; the man was fit and handsome. They seemed to be very happy—they came to church together, they worked out together, their children were cute and well behaved. They got involved in the activities of the church and attended almost every week. In short, they were two of my favorite people.

Then Donna injured her knee. It wasn't a severe injury, but she couldn't go to the gym anymore with her husband, so he wasn't going either and was becoming grouchy. "Why don't you go with Bobby to the gym?" suggested Michael. "I think he could use the support."

"Michael, I don't know about that," I said slowly. "I'm not really comfortable with the idea. And what would Donna think? Feels weird to me."

"No, I've talked to her and she thinks it'd be a great idea.

In fact, she said for you to just come over so you and Bobby can ride together."

I had a bad feeling about this—but I trusted Michael's judgment, trusted that he wouldn't be sending me into the lions' den. *Maybe I'm paranoid*, I reasoned. Funny thing is, I didn't even *want* to go to the gym. I barely had time to study, much less to work out. I hardly had time to eat, which showed in my thin frame. Once in a while, Carla and I would exercise in the hallway between our rooms to a tape recording of Jane Fonda's 1982 workout. She had memorized the moves and I just followed along, while Jane's voice pushed us like a drill sergeant's: "And one, two, three, four. Stretch it out, two, three, four . . ." This was fun. Going to the gym with Bobby? Not so fun.

When the day came, I felt nervous and bizarre. "Are you sure, Michael?" I asked one more time. He was sure. I went to the couple's house, where Bobby's wife bustled around with the kids. As she put their dinner on the table, she made a point of telling me what a relief it was to get her husband out of the house for a bit, and how bad she felt about not being able to go to the gym with him because of her knee. Bobby just smiled and said we'd better get going.

We made small talk in the car. When we got to the gym, I went into the ladies' locker room to change into my full '80s regalia, including leggings, my high-waisted and high-cut spandex bottoms, a matching cropped top, sneakers, and (I admit it) the requisite white sweatband around my head. I walked out of the locker room feeling self-conscious—not about my body, but about the way Bobby was looking at it. His delighted smile was more unsettling than reassuring. We worked our way around the large gym, doing the reps that he showed me. My body still had its athlete's memory. I was flexible and strong and determined to keep up. Bobby was sweet and appropriate—until it came to the hot tub. Why in the world would a coed hot tub be allowed at any gym? I knew nothing good would come of that, but I could not seem to get out of it. My midwestern manners inhibited me from jumping off the train and hightailing it out of there. Besides, I didn't have a car; I was stuck. I tried to convince myself that I was being foolish and that my instincts were off. We changed into our bathing suits; I was now fully mortified. I felt, and was, stripped down and vulnerable. Quickly stepping into the foaming water, I kept reminding myself that I was supposed to be there to offer support—but it was absurd to think this qualified as a pastoral visit.

In retrospect, it was a disaster waiting to happen. I felt like the mouse who's been thrown into the python's glass home but told that it's safe because people are watching. Anyone could see the danger in this, anyone—except for Michael. Maybe he was too trusting to see it, or maybe it was so out of his experience as a man that he couldn't fathom it. This realization did not help me in that hot tub. Once in the steamy water, Bobby offered to give me a little massage on my shoulders. That's when I knew I had to get out of there. Instead of the proverbial cat on a hot tin roof, I was the cat in the hot tub. I jumped out, telling him that I had a lot of work to do and needed to get back to school.

On the car ride back to his house, he told me how much he liked me, how attracted he was to me, and how he couldn't take his eyes off me during the service. I was starting to feel totally trapped and horrified. If he could just take me away, if he could just keep on driving with me, he'd be happy. Next thing

I knew, he was pulling the car over, saying he wanted to talk to me. *Oh, no. Gulp.* Then he tried to kiss me.

"Bobby, listen," I stammered, putting my hand up. "This isn't about me; it's about you feeling unhappy. I think you and Donna should try to talk to someone, maybe go to counseling with Michael. I'm flattered, I really am, but this is not going to happen."

He slumped back into his seat. "I'm sorry, Andie. I'm so embarrassed—please forgive me. Why don't I take you to the bus stop?" I told him that would be great.

The whole way home, I was replaying the evening in my mind. I was mad at myself for not trusting my instincts, mad at Michael for being naïve and setting me up, and I was haunted by the thought that I now had to keep this a secret from Donna. I felt totally bizarre. I also felt like a failure as a future minister. It was reason number 425 why I did not *ever* want to work in a church.

I got back to Jewett House and tried to immerse myself in my Hindu dharma work but I was too distracted; I was also tired from the workout and the hot tub and the stress. *Maybe I'll go to bed early for once.* By 11:45, my teeth were brushed, my face washed. Just as I was pulling the covers over my head, the phone rang. (Carla and I had our own lines by then.) When I picked it up, it was Katherine calling me from Harvard Square.

"Hi. Did I wake you up?" she asked, the sound of the lively Square filling the space behind her voice.

"No, of course not," I answered, "although I was just getting into bed, believe it or not."

"Shoot. I was going to ask if you, by any chance, would want to meet me at the Harvard Square Theatre. There's a midnight showing of *Stop Making Sense*, the Talking Heads movie."

"Sure," I said without hesitation. "I'd love to. Be there in a few."

"I love it—you always rally. I'll get the tickets. Meet me inside."

With that, I pulled my jacket over my nightgown, slipped my bare feet into my boots, and walk-ran into the Square. I got there just as David Byrne came on the screen. He was walking onto the stage with a cassette player and guitar in hand. I snuggled down into the worn theater seat next to Katherine, my feet up on the seat in front of me. The first song was "Psycho Killer." *How ironic*, I thought.

Psycho killer, *qu'est-ce que c'est?* . . .
Run run run run run run away

That's exactly what I had felt like doing an hour before when I was trapped in the car with Bobby: run run run, run run run away. As the movie went on, I relaxed, and it brought me back into my own skin. Well, not the movie exactly, although it was mesmerizing, but the joy of being myself, of having my best friend call fifteen minutes before a midnight showing of a movie, and jumping out of bed to run a mile in my nightgown to meet her.

We walked out of the theater and sat on some steps across the street from it. The Square was quiet, although there were a few people still walking around, as well as a lone guitarist singing in a darkened doorway. I told Katherine about my bizarre experience earlier in the evening. She listened attentively; then she shook her head. "Michael should have known better. God help him, he meant well, but *really*, Andie."

"I know." I grimaced. "What do you think I should do now? I'm going to feel so weird around the guy and his wife."

"Tell Michael what happened, for one thing," she offered. "Immediately. Let him take it from there. They're his people." *Wise words*, I thought.

Katherine gave me a lift back to Jewett House. The next day, I phoned Michael and told him what had happened. Instead of saying he was sorry and that he would handle it, however, Michael suggested I go with Bobby to the gym one more time. *What?* He reasoned that it would be a learning experience for me to handle this, that Bobby was, at heart, really a nice guy and that I should try more directly to offer a pastoral presence. I told him that I didn't think this was possible in a bikini. "Okay," he agreed, "skip the hot tub." *Gee, thanks.*

I was dreading the next week. I felt so awkward and nervous, and I could have killed Michael for suggesting I go with Bobby again. Michael did his best to pump me up, to try to strengthen my sense of identity as a pastor and a legitimate counselor. The only problem was that I was neither of these. I wasn't a pastor yet, and I wasn't a trained counselor. Michael's optimism and his faith in me were touching, but this situation should never have been laid on my bare shoulders. In retrospect, Michael was also young at the time. I doubt he would give the same advice today that he did then. We were trying to figure it out as we went along.

The next week, when I got on the bus that would take me to Saugus, I was miserable; I was dreading the conversation that I knew I needed to have with Bobby. Michael picked me up at the bus stop, gave me a pep talk, and told me to be compassionate but strong and direct; then he dropped me off at the couple's house. Maybe it was my imagination, but I sensed that Donna was slightly cool to me this time. I felt suddenly queasy and guilty, although I hadn't done anything wrong. Who was the genius behind this plan? It was just so ridiculous. When we got to the gym, I told Bobby we needed to talk before we changed into our workout clothes, so we took a seat on one of the bench presses.

"We need to talk," I started. "About last week—"

"I know," he interrupted. "I'm really sorry to have put you in that position. It was wrong of me. It's just that Donna and I have been having problems ever since she hurt her knee. I really love her but something's been missing for a while. I don't want to lose her . . . I don't know what I want. I'm forty years old and I'm feeling so lost."

He rested his head in his hands, his elbows on his knees. When he looked up at me, there were tears in his eyes. What was I supposed to do with that? I felt like yelling "Michael!" or "Beam me up, Scotty!" Instead, I sat with him for about half an hour, listening and talking. We never did change into our gym clothes, never exercised or (thank God) approached the hot tub. Because Michael had offered to give me a ride back to Cambridge that night (in order for us to process how things went), Bobby drove me to the church. Regardless of his apology at the gym, I still felt on edge in the car. As he drove, he kept looking over at me, finally asking in a mock joking way, "So, you sure you don't want to just drive away with me?" I was sure.

During our drive, Michael and I reviewed what had happened that evening. In some ways, he was right when he said that I would have to learn how to handle myself. People in the public eye, including ministers, are often the objects of projection, fantasy, and unwelcome advances, and there are some who take advantage of this power. When it comes to clergy, a very strange thing happens with some (but not all) people. Some think they own you because you are a servant of God, and therefore a servant of every member who pays your salary with each lonely dollar that is dropped into the collection plate; others put you on a pedestal. You're either seen as holy or as an object of sexual curiosity. For some, sleeping with the minister, the priest, or the rabbi is almost like sleeping with God, and therefore can't be wrong, and some clergy unfortunately buy into this. These projections were not something I was looking forward to dealing with on an ongoing basis. Who needs that?

"It is such an odd profession," I said to Michael with a sigh. "How do you stay yourself? How do you deal with people's strange expectations or keep from getting knocked off course? I don't want to pretend to be holy; I'm not ready to have that mantle laid on me."

"You just do your best," he said. His voice was soft and sincere. "Remember, Jesus chose some pretty rough characters to hang out with. I'm sure the disciples were no angels. You got fishermen and a rotten tax collector, and at least one Zealot—regular, flawed people—but Jesus chose them, warts and all."

What he said helped, but the idea of actually doing it, of actually being ordained, was still daunting. Just as a highway can be dangerously pocked with potholes, causing tires to go flat and alignments to go off, this road to ministry was no less perilous. To travel it safely, one would have to navigate around projections and temptations and countless future hot tubs. I was trying to read the road signs—CAUTION, U-TURN, REST STOP AHEAD, ONE WAY—but it was confusing because my spiritual GPS was rebooting. I had changed the destination on the day I read that Call to Worship, but I was still hoping for an alternate route.

17

dark side of the moon

By the end of my second year, I was exhausted, completely and utterly exhausted, but several things had been accomplished. I'd finished both of my field placements, had passed my German proficiency exam, and had decided on a thesis topic for the next year. It'd been a tough few months, both academically and personally. Not only had it been difficult to keep up with my academic work and my various jobs, but it'd been a challenge to keep up with Andy as well. We had not seen much of each other over the past six months, and the stress of the distance was finally taking its toll. He was busy, I was busy, and our phone calls were often flecked with misunderstandings, misread comments, and the sea of imaginings that drown you in silence on the other end of the line. Without the benefit of being face-to-face when we talked, the nuances of expression and meaning were often lost—we'd take things wrong; we'd want to hang up too quickly.

When he came to Boston in the spring for a friend's wedding, Andy did not ask me to accompany him, nor did I see him; what relationship we still had was hanging by a thread. Oddly enough, it turned out to be made of spider silk—outwardly fragile but strong against all odds. And I found myself wanting to hold on, perhaps for the first time in my life, instead of happily letting it go. I observed what was going on within myself, almost from a distance, as if I were my own therapist. It was curious to me, this new desire to hold fast, and I tried to follow its origin by rappeling down into the cavern of my psyche and past experiences. Was it the fear of not having him in my life that caused me to hold on, or was it simply the pain of letting go? As I hung up the phone after our last conversation, the one where he said he was coming to Boston but didn't want to see me, the one where we decided to take a more decisive break from each other, I felt myself doing something relatively unfamiliar—reaching for him. How interesting. It was like cracking open a rock and discovering an amethyst buried inside. I had thought my heart was a stone when all along it was a geode. Go figure.

I went back to Cincinnati for the summer. The days went slowly at first—then sped up, as they always seem to do, like water moving toward the falls. One minute you're floating along, getting stuck in the shallows, going nowhere fast, and the next minute you're rushing toward a vertical drop. Scientists claim that waterfalls are formed when a river is young. A river is born as water begins to flow through a deep but narrow channel. Over time, it begins to cut through the bedrock, carrying sediment, gathering strength. Rocks eventually give way beneath the force, creating a plunge pool—and the river thunders forward. What we cannot see with the naked eye is how, with time, the waterfall will eventually recede, becoming a quiet pool, a rushing waterfall no more.

This explains a lot. The intensity of youth, of experiencing certain emotions for the first time, of self-exploration, often feels as if we are careening down uncharted waters—will we survive? Will we go over the edge? These years are no tranquil pool; they can be as exciting as a ride down the rapids or as frustrating as getting caught in a whirlpool. Even when the latter happens, we will eventually break free and keep moving, despite the frantic waves of those who've traveled these waters before. Regardless of their warnings, it is a singular journey. We move toward our own futures with limited sight; we cannot see around the bend. Maybe we're not supposed to. These are the days that we begin to explore the river, begin to understand the currents and hone our navigational skills. Even if we sense turbulence ahead, we do not stop. We cannot stop. We have to learn the falls before we can appreciate the calm. At twenty-four, I was still a young river, and young rivers form waterfalls.

My father was twenty-four when he married my mother— but he was so much older than I was then. He had already been carved by experience, by the death of his mother when he was a child, by the army. He had gone over some pretty steep drops, had been banged up, and had found the strength not only to rise but to wholeheartedly jump into the river again. That is courage—to know the waters can be dangerous but to risk it all anyway, to open your heart knowing there are no guarantees in love. My mother, too, was a deep and mysterious reservoir by the time she was my age—in fact, she still is! As a mother, a working professional, a wife, she did not have the luxury of a thrill ride when she was young. Instead, she became the safe harbor we all turned to for rest, the rock upon which we clung when the waters were rushing too fast.

Sitting at home, in the house I grew up in, in the room that changed colors with my years—apple-green Raggedy Anns and Andys as a little girl, fire engine red and white (my school colors) as a teen—I felt too old to be there and yet unable to be anywhere else. My sisters were married and my nineteen-year-old brother was working at a camp outside of Dayton. I had filled out an application for a temp agency but wasn't having much luck, and I really didn't want to go back to waitressing at Denny's or working at the Procter & Gamble plant. Seems I was stuck in an eddy for the summer.

Only in retrospect did it occur to me what a mixed blessing my presence must have been to my parents. Of course they were happy to have me home, but they had their own routines, their own life together. I was their child and they were my parents, but I wasn't a child anymore. Sometimes this felt awkward. They eyed me curiously, perhaps trying to find the little girl they knew and loved within the woman I was becoming, a blossoming that was happening, for the most part, at a distance. Perhaps I was looking for the connecting thread, too. Sometimes I felt like I was Frankenstein's monster—like I was a mishmash of different people, stitched rather haphazardly together, heart and soul and limbs all askew. Other times, I was Goldilocks—home, but not really. My bed felt too small, I felt too big, and only life at HDS seemed to be *just right.*

I returned to Boston a couple weeks before school started, excited to begin another year of study. The dean and his family had moved out of Jewett House while I was home for the summer; he had accepted a position as president of a large university. In the interim, my New Testament professor, Father George MacRae, was appointed acting dean, but would not be moving into the house. This left Jewett House to Carla and me. A temporary house manager was soon hired, taking a room in the main part of the house, and another student, a man named Chris, moved in to take the place of Kim, who had graduated. We were still expected to do our jobs and to stay within the basic boundaries of the servants' quarters, but there was a little suite on the third floor near the kitchen that the dean's youngest daughter had lived in—with a sitting room, a bedroom, and a bathroom—that was now vacant. I assumed that Carla and I would share the sitting room and that we would mutually decide who would inherit the bedroom with the private bath. This was not to be the case. While I was in Ohio, she simply moved into the suite, taking both rooms.

I moved into the room on the other side of the kitchen, which was light and airy and plenty big enough. I adopted a black and white kitten, named him Isaac, and we lived quite happily there together in our room with a mattress on the floor and a beat-up blue denim couch that was going to get kicked to the curb anyway. Chris moved into Carla's old room on the second floor, using mine across the hall as a study. As for Carla and me, our once warm friendship was reduced to cool cordiality.

My friend Andrea had spent the past few months managing a little shop in Faneuil Hall called Boston Brownies. Faneuil Hall is a historic marketplace and a favorite tourist destination in the center of Boston. Built in 1742, it had been a meeting hall, where men such as Samuel Adams and James Otis had given speeches, igniting the hope for independence and freedom. The façade of the building was still beautiful, though it was now used for less lofty purposes. Over the years, it had evolved into a marketplace, with shops set up like booths, one after the other; where food and souvenirs, and just about anything else, could be purchased. It was frequented by businesspeople during the day, who were grabbing a bite for lunch, and by tourists at all times, especially on the weekends.

Andrea had stumbled on the job quite by accident—or, more accurately, the job stumbled upon her. One evening, while walking through Faneuil Hall with some friends, she stopped at the Boston Brownies stand. As was often the case, it was a madhouse, with a crowd of people waiting in line. The smell of brownies cooking on site was like an invisible Pied Piper leading people to the booth. The line moved slowly because there were so many flavors to choose from and because the counter was understaffed. When Andrea and her friends got to the front, they were in a festive mood despite the wait. After ordering her brownie, Andrea boldly informed the harried owner that she needed a manager. The boss told her to name her salary and hired her on the spot. Most of the employees that Andrea managed were college students. When they began returning to their own schools at the end of the summer, she asked me if I wanted to fill in until she hired someone. While I was no baker, and basically had no idea what I was doing, the work wasn't difficult and it was fun spending the time together. Basically, I felt as if I were getting paid to hang out with my old friend. What could be better?

To the left of Boston Brownies was Colombo Yogurt. Mr. Colombo (real name Colombosian) would stop by on occasion. The first time I met him, I thought he was kidding when he introduced himself. I could not believe that there actually was a "Mr. Colombo." When I told him this, he merely laughed, seeming to relish the opportunity to talk about the family business, which was the first in the United States to produce yogurt commercially. Managing his shop was an intriguing-looking guy with an English accent. His hair was clearly tucked up into his hat, which was part of the uniform, but a long blond braid would occasionally slip out the back. He had almond-shaped hazel eyes, a beautiful profile, and that darned accent. Whenever we made eye contact, which was almost unavoidable given the close proximity of our booths, he would smile rather shyly at me. Curious, I asked Andrea about him, assuming she would know something because they had been working virtually side by side all summer, but she just rolled her eyes and told me she had no idea. "He's the manager of Colombo, that's who he is," she said with a wave of her oven mitt. "I do not feel compelled to learn every person's name in the world like you do." I wasn't sure whether she was irritated or just pretending to be (sometimes it was hard to tell the difference), but I felt awkward not introducing myself. Only a flimsy half wall divided our open-air shops. We were like neighbors separated by a hedge, and it seemed un-neighborly not to say hello. Before the day was over, I turned to Andrea (clearly proud of myself) and announced, "By the way, his name is Rupert."

"You are an ass," she replied with a laugh.

It turned out that Rupert was an artist and musician from London. He managed Colombo by day but was lead guitarist in a rock band called Siren by night. They played in bars and clubs throughout the Boston area and were gathering quite a following with their mixture of hard-edged rock-and-roll and '80s grunge. The club scene was lively and happening in Boston. New bands were being discovered (without the advantage of YouTube), giving hope to those who were still sweating it out in front of a handful of drunken college students. The success of area legends such as Aerosmith, Boston, and the Cars fueled the imaginations of other up-and-coming groups like the Pixies, Girls Night Out, the Del Fuegos, and Aimee Mann's fledgling band, 'Til Tuesday. A group that you saw at the Channel on Friday night might be the next big thing on Saturday. Such was the feeling then, that anything was possible.

A few months earlier, I had been walking around Harvard Square on a Saturday night with Andrea. A large crowd had gathered around a busker who was playing a guitar and singing. The voice was rich and textured, the acoustic guitar silvery and steady. "Is that a guy or a girl singing?" I asked, trying to see through the crowd. "A girl," she replied. "I think she goes to Tufts. Someone told me that she just signed a record deal." Turns out it was a young Tracy Chapman. Even then, her distinctive voice made people stop and listen. Legend has it that a fellow Tufts student, whose father ran a record label, happened to hear her singing one night on the street. He introduced her to his father, and the rest, as they say, is history.

When Rupert told me, then, that he was in a band, it was exciting, and it seemed quite possible that they could be "discovered" at any minute. Later, as I got to know him, he also mentioned that he'd appeared in a British film with Malcolm McDowell. He was very humble about it and seemed almost hesitant to reveal this to me. When I confessed that I hadn't seen the movie, he laughed and said, "Good!" As we became closer, however, he would sometimes tell me what it was like on the set, how naturally shy he was, and how difficult some of the scenes were. His mother was a rather well-known British actress, something he seemed proud of but might have added to the pressure. When we would start talking about this part of his life, he would often deflect the conversation with his dry, distinctly British humor. He was a complex but gentle person, a virtual Pandora's box of contradictions.

After a week of working next door to each other, he told me that he and his bandmates were meeting at a club downtown later in the evening. They were going there to hear a drummer whom they hoped to snag for their band, and he invited me to join them. Despite the fact that I had been living in the area for a couple of years, I had never been to any of the clubs. This was so outside the realm of my experience that it had never occurred to me to go. My day-to-days centered around school and church and the homeless. Rupert and his invitation were intriguing to me. My relationship with Andy was in neutral, and the future didn't look promising. I had pulled back from Tomas, probably more out of fear of commitment than anything else (what would I do if he moved back to Colombia?), and John was incredibly busy with medical school. Rupert offered yet another new world to explore, one that sounded interesting and adventurous. "I'll try to come," I heard myself saying, even as I was thinking *Here I go again*. When I told Andrea about his invitation, she shrugged her shoulders and didn't look impressed. "Just be careful," she said.

It was a perfect summer evening when I got off the T in Kenmore Square later that night. The air was warm and balmy—electrified, even. I was wildly happy to be back in Boston, back among the sea of students, especially since I was not yet bogged down with work. As I approached the club, I was surprised to find that it was basically just a large bar. I don't know what I was picturing, but the word *club* seemed to evoke something slightly more mysterious, something for which you'd need to know the secret password, or the correct knock, before you entered—something exclusive and daring, like a speakeasy during Prohibition. Instead of an unmarked and shadowy building, however, the place had a neon sign in the window and a door that was propped wide open. The summer air was blowing in and an overflow of friendly noise was tumbling out.

I paused for a moment before entering the club, a little flutter of nervousness rising like a startled sparrow in my belly. On a small, lit stage at the far end of the darkened room, one that was full without being crowded, a band was playing. There were people dancing near the stage, their bodies silhouetted, with heads bouncing and arms rising and falling like black flames licking at the light. Others were standing along the outer edges, spilling beer as they leaned in to shout into one another's ears. A long wooden bar stretched along the right side of the room from the door to the dance floor, like a conveyer belt constantly moving people along, and a few sticky tables were scattered in the middle.

After a quick scan, I spotted Rupert sitting on a stool with his back to the bar so that he could watch the band. He was leaning casually on his elbows, which were propped on the smooth wood like two wings folded behind him. He had on black skinny jeans and a black T-shirt emblazoned with the logo of some band I hadn't heard of, his blond hair framing his face like a lion's mane. Internally, I stumbled a little because he looked quite different than he did at Colombo's. It was the first time I'd seen him with his hair down, the first time that the rock guitarist beneath the hat was revealed. It suddenly occurred to me that he, too, spent much of his day incognito. To some degree, we are—all of us—a mystery to the other. Sometimes we present select parts of ourselves, sometimes we hide ourselves completely; rarely do we reveal the totality of who we are. It is the push-pull of human relationships. As we become more comfortable in our own skins, more self-accepting and certain of who we are, we reveal a little more. Maybe I related to Rupert because of what was hidden. At first glance, he was the guy in the Colombo hat serving frozen yogurt—but there was something both noble and wild resting beneath the surface. *At first glance, who was I to him or to anyone else?* I wondered. Imagining myself in a clergy collar someday, I shuddered involuntarily. It was the billboard equivalent of the Colombo hat. How would others see me? As an oxymoron, a joke, the eternal vestal virgin, a charlatan? Would I be able to reveal the self beneath the collar, my true self, the deep-down part that loved God but craved freedom? Were they mutually exclusive? Rupert clearly didn't have a clue about what he was getting himself into when he tossed that casual invitation my way—and, I guess, neither did I.

Standing next to him at the bar was a pretty girl with dark, heavy bangs that came to rest on her eyelashes, and an abundance of shoulder-length hair framing her thin face like a half-closed curtain. This had the effect of accentuating her cheekbones and full lips, lips that were moving dangerously close to Rupert's face in an intimate way. She was mouthing words that I could not hear, her straight white teeth occasionally flashing like lightning. I hesitated, feeling suddenly out of place—what was I doing here, anyway? Before I could change my mind, Rupert turned his head to gaze in the direction of the door and spotted me. His face lit up in the sweetest way, and his warm smile disarmed me. Clearly he'd been watching the door, hoping that I would show. Looking around, I realized that I stuck out like Sandra Dee at an Alice Cooper concert. I wasn't wearing black—black clothes, black eyeliner, black anything; I had on a pair of Levi's and a turquoise tank top. If that wasn't enough, I was about to order a seltzer, and of course I didn't smoke—two more red flags pointing to the fact that I was a neophyte and an interloper.

As I approached him, the breeze blew through the open door and fluttered the large peacock-feather earrings that I was wearing. It was as if the Spirit was suddenly whispering in my ears, my private annunciation, centering me, lifting me, and reminding me of who I was. I unconsciously reached for the silver moon in my right ear, a small earring hovering just above the feather. I had gotten the second piercing two years before as a favor to Katherine. She had asked me to accompany her to get her ears pierced for the first time—but when she got to the jewelry shop in the Square, she began to have second thoughts.

"Will you go first?" she asked nervously.

"But I already have my ears pierced," I explained.

"Can't you just get another one? It would really help."

Since then, I've always thought of that second piercing as a touchstone of our friendship. Whenever I put an earring in that hole, I think of Katherine.

That was about the only funky thing I had going for me— that and perhaps my long hippie hair and my own incongruities. Rupert stood up as I approached them and greeted me with a little kiss on the cheek. The dark-haired girl eyed me warily for a moment, behind the shelter of her bangs, scanning me for trouble, but I realized pretty quickly that it was not competitive on her part but, rather, protective. She was screening me for Rupert. Before I could assimilate the myriad of impressions, he introduced me to her—to Karen. As it turned out, she was also a guitarist and the lead singer in the band. Although the nature of their relationship wasn't clear at first glance, I soon understood that the obvious intimacy they shared was from being bandmates and friends and nothing more. Karen was confident and cool and a little intimidating. She had the clothes and the look of a rock star, a killer body, and the attitude to go with it. She was also a talented musician and singer who had graduated from Berklee College of Music. Karen had a commanding presence, onstage and off, and a powerful voice that erupted from her lithe frame like fireworks shot from a straw. From the look in her eyes, I realized that *I* was now the curious specimen to be studied and observed, and I felt certain that she was not impressed.

As we sat at the bar listening to the band, she and Rupert would occasionally put their faces together to share their impressions of the drummer, known as Boby Bear. On one of those cheek-to-cheek encounters, I overheard her shout-whisper into Rupert's ear, "I like her, Rupe." Almost instantly, I liked her, too—not because of what she said, but rather why she said it. She had observed me out of concern for her friend, had reserved judgment, and had come to the conclusion that I was okay. Obviously, she had impeccable taste. With that, I rested my paddle and rushed heedlessly toward the falls.

18

winding cloths
and changing winds

The school year began with an ending. A few days before orientation for new students was to begin, Father George MacRae, my incredible New Testament professor and newly appointed acting dean of the Divinity School, died of a sudden heart attack. He was fifty-seven years old. It's strange—looking back, I thought of him as so much older. Maybe fifty-seven always seems old to those in their twenties. It happened while he was lecturing to a group of fellow priests on retreat. After George finished his lecture, he sat down in a chair, and died. He simply died. There, surrounded by love, held in prayer, treasured, blessed, he left this world, and the world was left without his singularly intelligent and compassionate voice, his learned, priestly presence, his gentle spirit.

Word of his death quietly seeped into the communal consciousness of the Divinity School. Students arriving for orientation were met with a simple note posted on the door of Andover Hall announcing the date and time of Professor Mac-Rae's funeral service. Many returning students learned of his death only after he was already buried. The community was in shock—and many of us who knew him, faculty and students alike, were in mourning. The halls were heavy with hushed voices, and the usual excitement that accompanied a new year was appropriately muted. I found it difficult to accept the reality of his passing, when his voice was still vividly accessible in my ears and the vibration of his presence was still palpable on campus. If only the vibration could be harnessed, then maybe he would appear again as hologram, as spirit; but, alas, he had left us—and I can't imagine that he ever looked back.

Sitting under a tree in front of Jewett House, I looked across at Andover and was overwhelmed with feelings of gratitude for having intersected with the professor's life, be it ever so briefly. His sudden death highlighted the fact that nothing could be taken for granted. These days would not come again; this opportunity would not come again. There may not be a "next semester" to study with a great scholar, to pray with a priest, or to run through the halls with a best friend. George MacRae was gone; Henri Nouwen, although alive, had left Harvard for L'Arche, and this was my last year at HDS. It also occurred to me that it might be my last year as a "normal" person, an unordained person—how was I to live it? One way, as it turned out, was going to be in a pair of black leather pants and some spiky hair.

We made ready at Jewett House for a faculty reception to begin the new academic year. It should have included a welcome for George; instead we honored his life. Professor John Carman, director of Harvard's Center for the Study of World Religions, assumed the position that George's death had left vacant. I had taken his course on Hindu dharma and knew him to be a brilliant scholar, a quiet leader, and an unassuming man. The Divinity School would be in good hands while the community healed and the search for the new dean continued.

So much about the start of this year felt different. Jewett House was empty, save for the student servants. We were slightly unhinged, loose limbed and wild, as we began the year—thoughtful revolutionaries without a leader, reverent marauders, respectful squatters. We had only passing contact with the house manager, whose job came down to overseeing the formal functions, and we were still trying to figure out what it would mean to live there without a dean. None of us could quite believe that the house would be unoccupied for the year, that there would be no more awkward entrances through the kitchen, no concern that we would be interrupting a private conversation. I guess it's fair to say that we all exhaled a little, and that the house was a bit less work to maintain. Because my two years of field study had been completed, my time was freed considerably. This was a tremendous relief, but I still needed income. To help, Michael found me a housecleaning gig for someone who lived near the church, and he paid me a small stipend to continue participating in Sunday services. Between those jobs and my occasional work at Pine Street, I would manage to survive.

Katherine and I had exchanged letters over the summer but had not talked very much. This added to the excitement of coming back together in September. Apart, it seemed as if we had so much to catch up on; together, we couldn't for the life of us remember what was so pressing. Being back at HDS trumped anything that might have happened in the months between spring and fall. Nothing was as exciting or as vibrant as the present moment. While I was in Ohio, she had moved from Central Square to an apartment in Allston. My parents had generously bought a friend's old Dodge Omni for me, which made it easier to visit her (and to get to the church in Saugus). I had driven the little burgundy bomb from Cincinnati to Cambridge, almost without a hitch. The only problem came somewhere in the middle of Pennsylvania, about eight hours into my fourteen-hour drive. The muffler had come loose and was dragging to the tune of hideous. I pulled the car over on the shoulder as far as I could get it, surveyed the problem, considered flagging down a car or a truck but thought better of it. Inexplicably, I found a piece of strong twine in the backseat (minor miracle), crawled under the car, lay on my back like I was a piece of bacon pressed onto a hot griddle, and tied it up. I was quite proud of myself for that. Dusting myself off, I waved to the truckers who honked without stopping, and made it to Cambridge unscathed. The car looked rather sweet resting there in the driveway of Jewett House—it would have pinched itself if it could have (*The old blue van is never going to believe this!*)—and I was happy to have some wheels.

Everything seemed to be in motion, galloping toward a checkered-flag finish line that still remained a mystery. With Michael's help, I had started my "process" with the Southern New England Conference of the United Methodist Church, which included taking a Methodist polity class, writing a statement of faith, and preparing for interviews with the Board of Ordained Ministry. There would be many hoops to jump through before the possibility of ordination, with built-in waiting periods during which one could re-evaluate the decision.

Although I had considered exploring the Unitarian church because it seemed more spiritually open, I was a Methodist at heart. I knew the church, I was aware of its strengths and weaknesses, and my Methodist roots went back practically to

John Wesley. I was wise enough to know that any institutional church would have its challenges, and I trusted the way in which the Methodist church was structured. It came into being at the same time that our new nation was forming, reflecting much of the same democratic process of decision making. I was proud of this history, but I still had an immediate allergic reaction to all terms relating to official church boards and procedures; the mere mention of them made my eyes glaze over, my mouth go dry, and my mind go blank. Among other things, I was afraid the process would be going along just fine until someone had the nerve to point out the obvious—that I was clearly the wrong person for the job.

Perhaps to counter this fear, I enrolled in a course entitled Thinking and Doing the Sacraments and Offices. It was one of the few practical classes I would take in divinity school, the other two being Thematic Preaching and Methodist Polity (a course on the governance and structure of the church). The latter was taught by a professor from Boston University, because no one at HDS offered it. Luckily, he was a fun and personable man, a Methodist minister himself, and he managed to keep it from being a snooze fest.

I was thankful that Katherine had also decided to enroll in the Sacraments class, even though she was not tottering as close to the edge of ordination as I was. One would think that learning about the sacraments would be a big draw for divinity students—a natural and practical introduction to what would become part of one's daily work—but the course was more of a novelty at HDS. We weren't surprised to find that it was not a packed house.

On the first day of class, which was held in the chapel, Katherine and I were semi-giddy. From the outset, this course had a very different feel to it. Taking a seat in one of the pews, I glanced around at my fellow classmates. To the naked eye, most of them filled the bill of future minister and priest more closely than we did. Were it not for Katherine and our friend Terry, a handsome gay man, who surprised us by sliding into the same pew, I might have changed my mind and snuck out of there. Instead, we sat like three baby birds on a branch, with necks craned and mouths open to accept whatever spiritual nourishment might be coming our way. Nothing was ever masticated and jammed down our throats, but it was our nature to be open—open to receive the wisdom, insight, and guidance that was offered. If we were going to be exposed as round pegs trying to squeeze into square holes, we might as well do it wholeheartedly. We looked at each other with raised eyebrows and smiles that said, "We're in."

A slim, slightly graying man in blue jeans and a button-down shirt quietly slipped from the front pew and glided up to the front of the chapel without making a sound. Before he opened his mouth, we were hooked. Hooked on the sacraments, hooked on God, hooked on whatever it was this man deemed worthy to impart. It was that immediate. There was something about our teacher Mick, a Congregational minister, that was both mesmerizing and comforting. Perhaps it was the clear-eyed integrity that emanated from him or his genuine faith. Whatever it was, Katherine and I found ourselves talking almost as much about him as we did about the course. If this thoughtful, hip man could be a minister, maybe there was room for the likes of us. Mick had an easy presence that was like sitting in the shade of a great oak tree with a gentle breeze blowing; there was no need to be afraid, no need to be anything other than ourselves. He was eminently present and yet respectfully detached, interested and yet not invasive. In a sense, he became a screen for our own projections of a future that might include ordination.

The only slight problem with the class was a level of silliness that could not be ignored. There was something inherently funny about putting on mock weddings and funerals in front of each other—although I'm not sure everyone felt this way. A few students performed their assignments without a hint of irony. For example, a woman who was in the process of becoming an Episcopal priest donned a red raincoat (in lieu of vestments) to officiate at her pretend wedding. With an air of solemnity and a sweet southern accent, she led the acting bride and groom through a traditional wedding ceremony, one that was uninteresting but flawless. She was brave to go first . . . but that raincoat! Well, it was hard to get past it without giggling.

Katherine and I, of course, paired up for both the wedding and the funeral ceremonies. Inspired to do something different, we decided that our wedding ceremony would be a lesbian wedding. This may not sound so groundbreaking now, but in 1985 it was fairly risky. In the spirit of progressivism, we decided not to have a stand-in minister; the couple (played by us) would just officiate themselves. We put quite a bit of work into crafting the ceremony, writing our own vows, choosing Ruth 1:16–17 as our scripture passage ("where you go I will go . . .") and exchanging lines from an Adrienne Rich poem, lines such as

> *I dreamed you were a poem,*
> *I say, a poem I wanted to show someone . . .**

---

* Adrienne Rich, "Twenty-One Love Poems," from *Dream of a Common Language: Poems, 1974–77* (New York: W. W. Norton, 1978).

At the end of the ceremony, we pronounced ourselves "Married!" and danced back down the aisle to the tune of the Talking Heads song "And She Was."

We felt quite elated by the experience, but the class responded with uncomfortable politeness. Stunned silence would probably be more accurate, come to think of it. Mick nodded and smiled, but he looked a little dazed. It occurred to us (only after the fact) that many people in the class clearly thought that Katherine and I were a couple, such was the obvious love between us. I found this rather funny, given the abundance of men in my life and the fact that Katherine was also involved with a man. No one asked us, however, as we stood in front of the class, ready to field questions. In some ways, it was the best wedding I have ever been a part of. It was creative, honest, and artistic. In the years to come, whenever either of us was having man trouble, the other would say, "Just remember, you're married to me first!"

If our wedding made people uncomfortable, the tables were turned when it came to our funeral, which was a shocker. Our assignment was simply to create a fictional deceased person and to design a service for him or her. This time Terry joined us in the planning and performing of the ceremony. We decided that our deceased man was a dancer who had died of AIDS. Terry would play his grieving partner; Katherine and I would officiate, as well as take on the role of liturgical dancers. The AIDS epidemic was only a few years old at the time and still largely referred to as "the gay disease." Rock Hudson had just died, the first celebrity to publicly admit having AIDS, and Ricky Wilson, guitarist for the B-52s, soon followed. It seemed important to raise the issue in a liturgical setting—but there were several glitches that we hadn't anticipated.

Some things look good on paper but not so good in person. Terry played his part very well in his black turtleneck and jeans. His fake eulogy was moving and sincere—almost making us forget that the deceased was not a real person. The words that Katherine and I offered went over well enough, although I detected a small roll of the eyes from a few classmates. The problem was mainly in our liturgical dance. The idea was to engage the congregation in a dance as a way to honor the deceased. We imagined this as something fun, something that the class would go for, something experiential and different. Looking back, one could say we were a tad naïve. We'd brought a boom box to the chapel, with a tape of Native American flute music queued up and ready to go. After finishing his eulogy, Terry pushed Play on the boom box, and Katherine and I started moving around the chapel, doing our best to approximate liturgical dance—something that neither of us really knew anything about. In addition to this small oversight, no one in the class would participate. There was nary a sway nor the slightest hint of a rocking motion among them, despite our best efforts. It was like a weird dream where you realize you've stumbled into the wrong party—naked—or like trying to keep six balls in the air when you don't know how to juggle. Beginning to panic, and feeling increasingly self-conscious, we danced our way, not so inconspicuously, to the back of the chapel, where we had a quick conference. It went something like this:

"Oh no! Oh no! This isn't working!"

"You'd better go to the front . . ."

"No, you!"

"Someone's got to. We can't stay here!"

"Oh no, oh no, oh no!"

Meanwhile, Terry was a prisoner in the pulpit. He was keeping his eyes downcast and his arms crossed, trying to look somber as he swayed like a lone reed in the wind. The service had become a runaway train. Realizing that we couldn't leave him stranded forever, we came up with a brilliant idea: "Let's cut it short." The music was awkwardly faded out, the benediction was offered, and the deceased rolled in his imaginary grave. I never could have fathomed then how many funerals I would eventually do as a hospice chaplain—none of which has included liturgical dance.

This was not the only mishap involving a funeral (another included singing in German—long story for another time), but it was one that was immortalized. Katherine had recently bumped into a journalist from the *New York Times* who happened to be spending a year at HDS. After chatting with him, she casually invited him to attend our class sometime. As luck would have it, he showed up the day of our funeral. While we pranced uncomfortably up and down the aisles and Terry swayed, Ari Goldman was taking notes. This became part of his 1991 book, *The Search for God at Harvard*. When we found out six years later that this moment had been captured in his book, we burst out laughing. Our funeral was admittedly a disaster but we were still proud of it. We had raised an important issue, stuck our necks out, and tried something different. We might have fallen on our faces, but we got up smiling.

Through the course of the semester we learned about the sacraments, yes, but we also learned that a minister does not have to fit into a starched white collar, with eyes glued to a crisp blue prayer book. Mick gave us hope that there was room for people like us, people who didn't necessarily fit the mold, whatever that means. He patiently observed us, with either an open mind or a poker face (I didn't know him well enough to tell the difference), and encouraged us to think about what we were doing and why. He was just as kind to the future Episcopal priest in the red raincoat as he was to the man acting out the death of a fictional lover. He shared his wisdom without an agenda, which I always felt was a mark of his innate compassion.

In the end, perhaps the most important thing we experienced was that of a permeable church. Moving in and out of the role of minister within the safety of our class was like trying on clothes. Would the collar fit? Would we fit the collar? In Mick, we glimpsed a blue-jean Jesus; in the Episcopalian, yet another expression of the Divine. We were dipping our toes in and out of the water, trying to determine whether it was a baptismal font or a tank filled with sharks, whether we would sink or swim, emerge feeling refreshed or be eaten alive. The only thing I was sure of was that the world was in desperate need of light—all kinds of light—even ours. If our intention, our aspiration, was genuine, if we followed God's direction, then nothing else really mattered. We could be "fools for Christ," as the saying goes; we could dare to be ourselves. And I was beginning to intuit the slim and surprising possibility that being a minister could actually be fun.

19

does this collar
make me look fat?

Outside of a church or a divinity school, nothing kills a funny conversation or a playful flirtation faster than revealing you are a minister or a minister-in-training. At a party, it is the quintessential turd in the punch bowl (as we used to say in Ohio). Suddenly people stop telling jokes, they apologize for swearing; they excuse themselves rather quickly, as if being religious is contagious. So far, in my experience, it is not. Being a minister is perhaps unique among professions because, well, first of all, people assume you work for God (and therefore work for free). Who needs a decent salary with all those heavenly rewards? And second of all, being a minister is not only what you do, it is who you are—or at least who people think you are. So much is superimposed on this identity. To be sure, every profession conjures certain images and stereotypes. Say the words *secretary, doctor, lawyer*. Each evokes a visual or visceral reaction, but I doubt any come with the universal assumptions that accompany being a minister, a priest, or a rabbi—who, by many accounts, all walked into a bar and . . .

Maybe I'm just traumatized. After my hot tub fiasco, Michael had suggested that I invest in a clergy collar—in part to make my role and my presence clear to the congregation, and in part to make it clear to me. I'm not sure how much this would have helped me in a bikini, but it was worth a shot. I was in the home stretch academically, and I was moving toward ordination (albeit still somewhat kicking and screaming and dragging my feet). Because I hadn't started the process until well into my second year of divinity school, I wouldn't even be eligible for ordination until a year after graduation. This built-in waiting period was one for which I was grateful. I needed more time to think about it.

When Michael suggested that I get a collar, I felt immediately stressed and uncomfortable. The obvious reason was that I wasn't yet ordained, and the hidden reason was that I was still ambivalent about it. I already felt like I was an imposter at times; the thought of wearing a collar before being ordained only heightened my anxiety and self-consciousness. But Michael saw no problem with bending the margins for a good cause—and helping me acclimate to the role of pastor qualified. When I argued with him about this, he was firm and convincing.

"It will be good for you," he reasoned. "Just get one. Put it on. See how it feels. Start getting used to the idea. Besides, it's important for people to see women in collars, especially young women. Come on, kid. The church is changing, the world is changing, and you are a part of this. You should be proud."

It was hard to argue with him. Michael was my teacher and mentor, my friend, and my ally. I relied on his guidance and I trusted him, even (at times) against my better judgment. I knew he was genuinely trying to help me, and I appreciated

the support, but there was that nagging reality of not being ordained, which compounded my feelings of illegitimacy. To
make matters worse, I wasn't used to Methodist ministers in
collars. None of my ministers wore them when I was growing
up—this was reserved for Catholic priests, Lutherans, and
Episcopalians—so there was a double dose of discomfort built
into the transaction. They also didn't drink wine, shop at Vic-
toria's Secret, or drop the occasional swear word (at least to my
knowledge). It was hard enough to wrap my head around the
idea of ordination, much less wrap my body in the unfamiliar
garb. What's more, wearing a collar would be akin to "outing"
myself—outing myself as what, I wasn't sure. I was still trying
to figure that out. All I knew was that going to divinity school
was one thing; wearing a collar was a whole different ball
game. Divinity school was interesting to people. It sparked
good conversations. The fact that it was *Harvard* Divinity
made it that much more intriguing. But the prospect of a
clergy collar, at least on me, had the exact opposite effect.
When I imagined myself wearing one, I did not feel interesting—I felt like a freak.

It was October when Michael sent me off on my quest.
"And don't come back until you get one," he joked, clearly enjoying my pained expression. When it was obvious that my
misery was genuine, he softened, giving my shoulder a little
squeeze. His eyes were both warm and intense as he gave me
one more pep talk about how women needed to claim their
authority as clergy, how I offered a prophetic witness by wearing one, etc., etc. As with many ideas at the time, I bought it.
It appealed to me intellectually and theologically. But when I
found myself at Sheehan's, the oldest and most traditional
Catholic religious supplies store in Boston, I began to lose my

nerve. Turns out I went to exactly the right kind of shop for everything about me to be just plain *wrong*. Suddenly I was not the modern feminist from Harvard, I was the unsure hippie girl from Ohio. My bravado quickly did a U-turn and took the T back to Harvard Square, leaving me standing in the doorway like Eve without her fig leaf. My immediate impulse was to run for cover. Instead I stepped inside, trying to act natural and hoping no one would notice me.

And so I strolled up and down the aisles. I dawdled. I browsed. I observed the rosy-cheeked clerks in their jackets and ties, mostly older gentlemen with Old World Boston manners. Although I could have been imagining things, they seemed to be watching me with measured hospitality. Trying to look nonchalant, I sidled over to a table full of books, where I surreptitiously observed the other customers in the store. By anyone's account, I stuck out like a sore thumb. There was a middle-aged priest checking out chalices and another trying on stoles. A few elderly women were browsing the candles and crucifixes. They lingered over framed images of St. Francis and Jesus and tenderly caressed the ceramic Mother Marys. I felt as if I had a giant *P* stamped on the front of my forehead for *Protestant*. It could also have been for *Poseur*. For a moment I seriously considered leaving, but I took a deep breath, determined not to come away empty-handed. Michael had sent me on a spiritual scavenger hunt. I was searching for my identity, scavenging for my calling, amidst the relics of the Christian faith.

I continued to meander through the store until I came upon a pile of folded shirts stacked neatly in a tall case. Bingo. The shirts were in a variety of colors, from basic black to white or gray, to a more adventurous deep purple, soft blue, or pale yellow. The plastic tabs that formed the iconic white square in the collars were perfectly placed. They were like tiny blank slates waiting to flash me warnings such as *Don't touch. Go back. Not for you.* Amazing, the power of that little plastic square. Trying not to dwell on it, I ran my fingers lightly over the shirt on top—but it was as if I had set off an invisible alarm. Immediately I became aware of the fact that I was being watched, that people in the store were beginning to stare at me, and I felt my face flush. I avoided the raised eyebrows of the women cradling Mary. I ignored the fact that all the shirts were in men's sizes. I soldiered on. As I squatted down to riffle through the shirts on the bottom shelf, I no longer held out hope for purple; I hoped only for something close to my size.

Then I saw his feet. Wingtips. Brown. Respectably shiny without being fussy. The socks? Almost certainly GoldToe. I followed the vertical crease up the pleated pants to the bow tie that topped him off like a giant gift for the altar. He was hovering so close to me I was practically looking up his nose. Staring down, he asked (in an arch voice), "May I help you, Miss?" So much was said in those five words and by the tone in which they were delivered. I suddenly felt flustered and off-balance, and I popped to my feet like a kid caught in the act of stealing. "Well, yes, actually," I began, feigning a confidence that I didn't actually possess at that moment. "I'm looking for a clergy collar and there don't seem to be any in my size." The words and the image hung for a moment in the air—then they collided, creating a ripple of dissonance. I could see his brain working quickly. One plus one did not equal three; me plus a clergy collar did not equal a priest. Now it was his turn to flush and stand up straight. Unlike me, however, he didn't look embarrassed—he looked indignant. "I'm sorry, Miss," he sniffed, "but we don't sell clergy collars for Halloween."

Halloween. I'd forgotten that it was but a week or so away. Of course! I started to laugh, but caught myself. He wasn't joking, which was too bad, because it would have been a good one. "I'm not buying this for Halloween," I said with a smile. "I'm a Methodist minister (well, almost) and I need it for my work." Then something happened. I can't quite explain it—call it the Holy Spirit, Something Greater, the Goddess, the Calling—but something came over me and I was no longer embarrassed; instead, I felt grounded. *I have been called to ordination in the church. Of course I deserve to wear this shirt! Of course these doors should be open to me!* I looked into his startled, well-meaning face and knew that he was not trying to be rude—he just hadn't seen the likes of me before. The church was obviously important to him; it wasn't something to be mocked, and I appreciated that. Working there at Sheehan's, for probably more years than I'd been alive, he'd surely seen it all . . . until now.

"Did you know that Methodists have been ordaining women since 1956?" I asked, blinking up at him with the innocence of a baby genius. I watched his face change from indignant to embarrassed, to composed and mannerly again.

"Well, no, I didn't know that," he said. "I'm terribly sorry. It's just that we have a lot of young people coming in this time of year thinking they can buy clergy apparel for costumes, and we try to discourage it. Forgive me. How can I help you?"

The air had changed between us. I had changed. His willingness to accept the reality of me, of what I symbolized for the church, was both startling and touching. What's more, *I* began to accept the reality of me, and this took me by surprise.

Maybe it *had* been like Halloween to me at first; maybe I *had* seen it as a costume, something uncomfortable and absurd. The seasoned clerk had smelled this from across the room, like an animal smells fear. But, when confronted, I discovered there was nothing to be afraid of. It was as if the dust had cleared and I realized I'd been standing on home base all along.

"It's okay," I said with a laugh. "I know I don't exactly look the part. On the other hand, where has Sheehan's been for the past thirty years?" With that, we both turned and started riffling through the pile of shirts, a rainbow of holiness waiting to be incarnated.

20

sackcloth and ashes
vs. leather and lace

U p in my room on the third floor of Jewett House, I was
hunched over my desk reading a book about medieval women,
which suddenly seemed painfully uninteresting. The only
reason I had taken Clarissa Atkinson's class, The Family and
the Church, 1300–1700, was because of the professor herself.
But now, at eleven thirty on a Thursday night, engulfed in silence and reading the same sentence over again three times, I
was kicking myself. I was having trouble focusing, not only because the book was somewhat dry, but also because I had decided to allow myself one evening to cut loose a little—and it
was this one. I leaned back in my chair and looked at Isaac,
who was sleeping on a cushion on my desk. He was wedged
between a stack of books and my typewriter and was directly
under a desk lamp, giving him the appearance of an incubat-
ing chick. I gently laid my cupped hand on his back; his fur
was warm from the light. Instantly he began to purr, sounding
as if he'd swallowed a tiny ticker-tape machine. Then he
stretched and yawned, blinking at me with sleepy, but star-

tlingly intelligent, green eyes. "I'm gonna go out for a while, little guy," I said softly. "But don't worry, I won't be late."

I still couldn't quite believe that he was with me. Because things were looser now at Jewett House in the absence of a dean, I'd been able to adopt him from a local shelter. To say that I loved having him would be a gross understatement. Isaac kept me company through long hours of solitary studying and gave me someone to return to after class. Sometimes Katherine would bring over her orange tabby, Lorna, to play. She was about the same age as Isaac, although we had gotten them independently of each other. We had not yet imagined that we would be sharing an apartment after graduation, and that these playdates would make the transition for the two of them effortless. I took Isaac with me wherever I could—out for a walk or to the grocery store in my cloth shoulder bag, his little head popping out of the top to survey the terrain.

Isaac was the crown prince in the long succession of animals that I had loved, and to whom I had felt a deep and abiding connection. They had accompanied me throughout my life as silent friends, trusted confidants, and bearers of deep, humming joy. Perhaps my animal companions helped to stave off the inherent loneliness of childhood. Don't get me wrong—I had a very happy childhood. It was replete with a house full of siblings, loving parents, close-knit friends and extended family, but at some point (and for me this came fairly early on) most of us become acutely aware that we are essentially alone in the world, an individual soul embarking upon an individual journey. Perhaps this is what prompts our first yearning for the Divine—when we begin to see ourselves as separate from our mothers. Trying to understand ourselves in relation to the outside world, we search for connections that will tether us, comfort us, inspire us; connections that will remind us of what it is to be one with our life source, one with God. Some find a path toward God in music, others in art, still others in dance or yoga or running or meditation. I always felt connected to God through animals, and eventually through the drawings and the poetry that I would create, either for them or in their company.

In almost every candid picture of me as a child, there is an animal. Our family didn't take that many pictures—film, and developing it, was expensive—which makes this fact more poignant. There I am at three, sitting on the front porch holding a kitten, and then at four, with my arm around our boxer, Jingles. At eight or ten or fifteen, I invariably had some creature in my arms or nearby. This also speaks to the nature of our family. My father has a compassionate heart and he could never turn an animal away—whether a stray, pregnant cat, an orphaned squirrel, an abandoned dog, or even an ornery pony. Luckily, my mother was patient (and loved my father), because she often became the caretaker of the four-legged family members that he brought home. In our little house, there was always room—for humans and animals alike. Tuning in to the vibration of the dogs and cats in my life invoked a stillness that allowed me to listen for, and occasionally hear, God's voice.

Isaac was the first animal companion I had gotten as an adult, the first for whom I would be solely responsible. It was never easy for me to leave him for any length of time—and sometimes he was my excuse to cut an evening short when I wanted to go home. But tonight Rupert's band was playing at Jack's, a bar not far from me, and I needed the mental break. *It will be fun to be out*, I reasoned, *fun to let off some steam.* These evenings, though rare, always provided an interesting contrast to my life at HDS. They gave me an excuse to pack up my books, rest my brain, leave the world of theology and academia, and enter an entirely different realm. For a couple of hours, I was Dante, exploring the various levels of heaven and hell. An observer more than a participant, I was in the scene, but a step removed. Before passing through the gates of purgatory (or Jack's, or Bunratty's, or Spit, or the Rat), that realm between divinity school and oblivion, between curiosity and damnation, I would try to find my inner compass. This was not somewhere I wanted to get lost.

If I went alone, I might sit with whoever was running the lights for the show. Once when the light guy didn't show up, Rupert asked me to run them, which we soon learned was not my forte. Although the band members were kind about it, they didn't ask me again. Just because I could exegete a difficult biblical passage, write a sermon, or translate something from German did not mean I knew what buttons to push on a light board (which was more intuition than rocket science at that point in the dark ages). I never drank; in fact, I can't recall ever having a single beer. I wasn't particularly against it, but it simply wasn't my thing, wasn't what I did. Sometimes, if I was standing by myself in the crowd and a guy approached to chat me up, I would politely decline by pointing out that I was with the guitarist. This connection to Rupert protected me from any persistent solicitations and gave me instant props. If he happened to notice such an interaction while he was playing, he'd look at me with a raised eyebrow and a knowing smile. There was an easy affection and a trust between us, despite the fact that we spent most of our time in very different worlds.

"What should I wear, Isaac?" I asked as I got up from my desk. At the moment, I was in a large T-shirt and a pair of white knee-high athletic socks, with my hair on top of my head and no makeup on. I walked over to my closet to survey the limited options. "Can't go wrong with leather," I said aloud again, reaching for my high-waisted black leather pants, inspired by Joan Jett. Although they looked expensive, I had gotten a great deal on them at a factory warehouse store over the summer. They were soft and supple and fit my long legs like a glove. I pulled on a simple black tank top and set out my black jean jacket. Surveying myself in the mirror, I shook out my ponytail and rumpled my hair; then I took a little styling paste, spiked the top, and scrunched the rest of it into a messy avalanche down my shoulders à la Nancy Wilson of Heart. I was a virtual one-person girl band. I couldn't be bothered too much with makeup, aside from a little mascara, but I did take the time to put on a pair of large, leaf-shaped earrings made of a light silvery tin. It was like getting ready for a costume party, where dressing up was half the fun and you could decide whom you wanted to be for the evening. I pulled on my jacket and gave myself a final once-over in the mirror; then I gazed over at Isaac, who had resumed his nap under the light. He was curled in a tight baby's fist, his pipe-cleaner tail wrapped around his little body as if to hold himself together. I picked him up and pressed my face into his warm coat, inhaling him like a scent hound, in case I got lost and needed to find my way home. He was limp and relaxed as I tossed him on my shoulder while I hunted for my keys. We walked around for a few minutes like that before I retrieved them from the pocket of a sweatshirt hanging on the back of my door. "Be back soon," I promised, returning him to his throne under the light. Hesitating, I turned it off, rested my hand on his back for an-other moment, and headed out into the night.

It was an easy drive to Jack's. The place was respectably crowded and the band was already playing. As I slid onto a stool, Rupert spotted me, and I gave him a little wave. He had on a white ruffled shirt with full, billowy sleeves; this gave him the look of a prince or a pirate, depending on your point of view. We didn't know each other all that well, but I was sure that he was an inherently good person, more prince than pirate. It was interesting to be able to observe him this way. It reminded me of watching Andy play the electric bass in college. I was aware that this brought out a particular part of his personality, an important part but not the totality of who he was. In both instances, I was also very aware of the girls who were trying, coyly or desperately, to get the musicians' attention. I rarely felt threatened—in part, I suppose, because they were both good men and in part because I trusted how they felt about me. In addition, I never lost sight of the person behind the stage persona; this was the one with whom I was making eye contact. If I had not met Rupert first at Colombo's, I'm not sure this would have been the case. I, like the other girls, would have been seeing only the public expression of personality and creativity; I would not have had access to the whole person. As I looked around, watching the girls watching him, I knew they were only seeing the surface, the fantasy cutout of a rock musician. But when the guitar was put away and the sweaty clothes were thrown in the hamper, I had the privilege of encountering the real person, the private person, who was searching for connection and love as much as I was.

When the set ended, we chatted for a while before I helped him pack up. This was usually my favorite part of the evening—especially if the gig had gone well. The band would be in a good mood, everyone would be sitting around talking and laughing, and I would leave with his arm around me. Then I would drive home, and darkness would begin to descend on my spirit. It was like clockwork. The uncertainty of who and what I wanted in life would slowly seep in, filling a silent, private, seemingly bottomless reservoir of anguish. I knew I should be more honest with Andy about the time I was spending with Rupert, even if we weren't seeing much of each other, even if we weren't talking frequently, and even if we had agreed to see other people. We were still connected, both of us holding on to the possibility that we were meant to be together.

By the time I pulled into the driveway of Jewett House, it was 1:30 a.m.—not late by most young people's standards, but I was happy to be home. Isaac was sitting silhouetted in the window when I opened the door, his head swiveling in the dark like a tiny owl's. I scooped him up and turned on the lamp; then I changed back into the rumpled T-shirt, which I had casually tossed on the bed. I padded quietly into the small kitchen just outside my door and opened the refrigerator—hoping for what, I wasn't sure, but whatever it was, it wasn't there. I settled for a glass of water and some peanut butter on a couple of crackers, which I carried back to my desk. "You hungry, bud?" I asked Isaac. He didn't answer, but I put a little food in his dish anyway. Popping a cracker in my mouth, I took off my earrings and tried to brush the goo out of my hair; then I collapsed on my bed on the floor.

Leaning back against a mishmash of pillows, I exhaled into my space, which was dark with the exception of the circle of light from the desk lamp. Isaac was alert and in full kitten mode now. As I stared out the window watching the night breeze rock the branches of a large tree, I became his living playground. He would spring across my chest, swipe at my hair with his little paws, or knock things over on the windowsill. Sometimes, while I stroked him absentmindedly, he would wrap his whole body around my hand, his back feet furiously kicking in tandem like a crazed bunny's, his razor nails and baby piranha teeth digging into my skin. The next day, this play would be mapped on my hand in embarrassing red scratches, which seemed to be renewed daily. If I happened to meet someone for the first time, I could count on hearing the familiar phrase *So . . . you have a cat?* One of these days, I intended to respond, "No, they're stigmata," but it hadn't happened yet.

Like Isaac, I suddenly felt restless and awake—too awake to just turn off my lamp—so (call me a glutton for punishment), I reopened the book on medieval women and began reading where I had left off. This worked better than a sleeping pill. I suppose it should have made me feel lucky not to be living in the Middle Ages, but instead I felt irritated.

In other words, the ideas about women were formed on the one hand by the clerkly order, usually celibate, and on the other hand by a narrow caste, who could afford to regard its women as an ornamental asset, while strictly subordinating them to the interests of its primary asset, the land. *

Sometimes it seemed the "clerkly order" was still regulating ideas about women, or maybe it was the clerkly voice in my own head that was regulating me. The church, celibacy,

---

* Eileen Power, *Medieval Women*, ed. M. M. Postan (Cambridge: Cambridge University Press, 1975), 9.

women as property or ornament . . . I had to force myself to concentrate. It was hard not to see the world of religion as dry and restrictive, oppressive even, especially with my ears still ringing from Jack's. Whenever my mind drifted to images from earlier in the evening, I would wrangle it back to the page. My eyes eventually grew weary and it became a struggle to retain the meaning from a single sentence. Exhausted at last, I turned off the light and surrendered to sleep, while Isaac still prowled the edges of the room looking for imaginary foes.

A couple of weeks later, I was talking with Michael about my misery regarding relationships. I told him that I was spending time with Rupert, but that I was conflicted because of Andy. "Do you think you could ever be serious about Rupert?" he asked. We were sitting in his car looking at the rocky shoreline of Lynn Harbor. Michael had suggested the drive when he could see that I was struggling and needed to talk. I didn't answer right away. Instead, I watched the tide go in and out, its foamy ghost fingers dragging bits of sand back into the sea with each retreating wave. My knees were drawn up on the seat and my arms were wrapped around them. The waves continued to toss and drag, to give and take, to pound and caress, with mesmerizing, irregular constancy. Watching from the car, I became a particle of sand, a tumbling dot of spirit.

"No," I finally answered him, still staring at the sea. "I don't think it would work in the long run."

"Then ditch," he said softly, turning in his seat to look at me.

"What?"

"Then you have to ditch, kid. Why waste your time or his?"

His voice was caring but firm. I knew he was right, but I still found myself arguing. "But, Michael, he's really sweet. And I like spending time with him. It's fun and different, and sort of an escape . . ."

"I know—and I understand. But you've got to keep your eyes on the prize," he said in his sweet West Virginia accent. It was "old school" kind of talk, talk using words that were familiar to me, harkening back to my childhood. They were not easy words, but they were aimed to center me. "You've been called," he continued softly. "God's plan is unfolding for you now. If you know it's not gonna include this guy, best to end it before it gets any harder."

He drove me back to Saugus, where I got in my own car and headed back to Cambridge. During the drive, I kept thinking of a particular moment with Rupert, an insignificant, random moment—the kind that appears when the light looks a certain way, or you stumble upon the smell of fresh-cut grass, or an old song comes on the radio; the kind that makes you stop to linger in the wonder of it. These are some of the most important moments because they are not obviously significant. When our minds latch on to one of these little snapshots and then spring it on us, like a bouquet of flowers whipped from behind one's back out of the blue, it means there's some treasure buried there. It means we have preserved it, not because it was life changing necessarily, but because it was lovely or re-vealed a sliver of holiness.*

It had been a lemon-yellow kind of day. The sky and trees and houses and people's faces were whitewashed in light. Kath-erine, Rupert, and I were coming from a trip to the factory

_____
* Our minds can latch on to painful images, too, but that's a different story.

store where I had gotten my black leather pants. She had been looking for a leather jacket, so we decided to go there together in the hope of finding something she liked. The store, which was more like a warehouse, was large and very bare bones but it was filled with racks and racks of leather goods in all shapes, colors, and sizes. Once inside, we split up and wandered around, trying things on and pressing our noses to everything we touched to inhale the distinctive smell of new leather. Katherine eventually settled on a sunny yellow jacket, and Rupert surprised me with a pair of purple pants.

Happy with our purchases, we were even happier to walk out of the odd cavernous store into the bright sunshine. Katherine was driving, I sat in the front next to her, and Rupert was lounging across the seat in the back. Until today, they had not spent any significant time together, although each certainly knew of the other. On the surface, the atmosphere was light and breezy, but in the spaces between each sentence, I could hear Katherine steadily tapping out Morse code—to me and to the universe: *Who is this guy . . . is he safe . . . what is she doing with him . . . I don't get it . . . fascinating . . . oh, okay . . . I get it a little . . .* I wanted them to like each other, even though each of them had reason to be concerned. Rupert knew that she was my confidante, my sounding board, and my most trusted counsel. If she didn't like him, it would not bode well. As for Katherine, she fully understood my struggles when it came to relationships, as I understood hers. We had discussed all of this ad nauseam over the past two and a half years, taking turns being the wise or the tortured, the sage or the confused. Perhaps to prove to her (and to myself) that I was not completely out of my mind, I turned around in my seat to face Rupert and asked him to sing for us—not just anything, but something that he used to sing absentmindedly sometimes. For some reason, when he did, I could feel his sweet, private self emerge, and I wanted her to feel this, too.

"Hmmm . . . what would you like me to sing, sweetheart?" he asked with a little arch in his voice.

"Would you sing 'Swinging on a Star' for Katherine?"

He looked slightly uneasy but willing. "Yes, right . . . okay then," he said. Still sprawled across the seat, his arm draped loosely along the back, he paused, letting his gaze drift out the open window. Then he began singing with an easy lilt in his voice, as if he had caught the gentle updraft of the breeze.

Would you like to swing on a star?
Carry moonbeams home in a jar . . .*

When he finished the first verse, he said, "There, now you have it, and Bob's your uncle." But Katherine said, "More! I want more," which is exactly how I always felt. I loved his voice and his gorgeous accent, but mostly I loved seeing this part of him revealed. After some pleading from us, he offered up another verse, followed by others that we made up. When we dropped him off at his apartment and watched him walk away, Katherine nodded. "I get it now. There is something really lovely about him." Perhaps (in part) because of this, it was not such an easy proposition to "ditch," as Michael had so bluntly put it; in fact, it would take me quite a while to cut ties with Rupert.

As we sat on the blue denim couch a few months later in my room at Jewett House, I tried to explain more about Andy,

---

* "Swinging on a Star," by Jimmy Van Heusen and Johnny Burke.

more about my desire to see if there was any hope for that relationship if he moved to Cambridge. Understandably, Rupert did not take this well. Although I had been slowly pulling away, this was the first time we had talked in earnest about not seeing each other. Unbeknownst to me, he was wrestling with other demons, and this change seemed to push him over the edge. He seemed lost for a time in his hurt and his anger and in his own vulnerabilities, and I felt miserable, knowing I had not handled things well. Worried about him, I called Karen, his bandmate and friend, asking for her help. Initially she was guarded and short with me. I understood why—I was not too popular with her at that point—but the situation seemed to be spiraling, and she knew it, too. She agreed to give him support, and I kept moving forward. Unlike Lot's wife, I did not look back.

21

before and afterlife

For every *before* there is an *after*. And every *after* indicates that a myriad of events, energy, and karma have been set into motion, propelling one along in what becomes known as a life. There is no getting around this. The nano-sized dot between before and after—the moment of intersection, of the stone hitting the pond, of conscious decision or unconscious reaction—is the point of entry for all mystery. It is the epicenter of divine fission. We turn left when we could have turned right, we hear a voice, ignore a voice, act with love, lash out in hate. We are curled in the womb, pressed like an ear against God's beating heart; we uncurl and are born. A breath goes in, a breath goes out—and eventually it keeps on going, fanning out into the atmosphere, never to return to the lungs again. Who were we before this moment or that; who will we be after?

Looking backward through the twisting wormhole of the past, we can begin to identify the moments that subtly shaped us, those that nudged us or altered our course in some way. If we squint our spiritual eyes, perhaps we can even begin to intuit the path that was being forged, consciously or unconsciously, as we moved toward our destinies. And if we are able to accept the *all* of it, with gratitude, then we will be able to accept ourselves, and we will more keenly feel the love of God, which has no before or after, but has always been.

This is where I have often failed. I have swung the heavy axe of judgment, aiming directly for my heart, till the blade is dull and the handle's been worn smooth. I have wrung my hands over relationships, over decisions that I have made, over how others may perceive me, over how I perceive myself. I've replayed moments, wishing I could do them over because the *after* was hard to deal with or because I'd like to do them better. But this is a futile exercise: the past cannot be undone—it can only be accepted and ingested as lesson.

We talk of *befores* and *afters* to understand the present, saying things such as, "Before I met my husband . . ." or "After I had children . . ." or "Before I got sick . . ." or "After my mother died . . ." In doing so, we place ourselves in the intersection, teetering on that dot, to survey the mottled landscapes of our lives. From this vantage point, we have several choices. We can drown ourselves in regret, thump our chests in pride, or recognize that our lives have their own unique beauty, continuity, and grace. Whether we find meaning in our lives, whether we can connect the dots that form our paths, is up to us. Meaning is there, waiting to be uncovered. Beauty is there, waiting to be recognized. We are a tune that will never be sung again, a single brushstroke on the canvas of the universe.

As I moved toward the *after* part of my divinity school education, I found myself hopping from dot to dot, trying to understand how I got to where I was. My life was essentially divided into three parts, and they weren't necessarily harmonizing. I still had my roots and my family in Ohio, my education and my career unfolding in Boston, and my relationships, which were scattered like buckshot across a few states. Although I hadn't seen much of Andy during the past year, he was planning on auditioning at Longy. If he got in, we would finally be living in the same city. I was nervous about this but excited, too. Somehow, over the past three years, we had managed to hold on—at least to our sense of potential.

Every relationship has a *before* and an *after*. Before we meet someone, we cannot imagine them—they are always a surprise. It is as if our eyes have not yet developed the ability to see a certain color, as if our ears have not yet learned how to decipher a particular sound. Then we meet this other—and we are immediately, if imperceptibly, changed. Energy fields collide, like waves crashing upon a rocky shore, splashing color down our chests and staining our lips with an undiscovered shade of fuchsia or silver blue. Our eyes acclimate and we begin to notice things we have never seen, because we are seeing things with their eyes, too; our ears pop, and we begin to hear things we have never heard, because we are hearing sounds with their ears, too. We are more than we were before, in the aftermath of a relationship's *after*.

Although I'd spent most of my romantic life pulled in several directions, I found myself deeply grateful for the men whom I had met. Each one had enhanced my life, had taught me about love, and had given me the opportunity to discover something about myself. As I moved toward the next chapter in my life, however, I realized that I was tired of subdividing my heart. With fear and trepidation, I wanted to try something new—like actually committing myself to someone—and

I kept coming back in my mind to Andy. I felt like I was in a recovery program—Relationships Anonymous. It was one day at a time for me when it came to love.

Graduation, Harvard's 350th, came on a rainy Thursday afternoon in June. The first part of the ceremony was in Harvard Yard, with all of the students from the college and various graduate schools present. A number of us from the Divinity School had made halos out of wire wrapped with tinsel to wear on our caps. These provided a nice contrast to the waving of money from the business school and the unfurling of red tape from the school of government. I found it almost surreal to be sitting there in the Yard, in my cap and gown, surrounded by thousands of brilliant minds and proud families. The moment hung there, bouncing in the breeze like a giant balloon whose string I held lightly in my hand. I looked around at the people with whom I had spent the past three years and felt deeply grateful for them—grateful for their brains, their hunger for understanding, their integrity, and their kooky individuality. I made a conscious effort to soak it all in, allowing the morning to permeate my mind and my body. I invited the images and the feelings and the vibration to seep into my cell memory so that they might be preserved. Experiencing such moments is like trying to hold a rainbow beam of spectral light in your hand. You can wonder at it, you can appreciate its beauty, but you cannot close your fingers around it; you cannot stash it away for the future to experience and live again. I was bathing in the light of a moment for which it seemed I had worked my whole life—not that I knew, at five or fifteen or twenty, what that moment would look like, but I recognized it when it came. What took me by surprise was the way it felt—not like an ending, a final point on the journey, but rather the threshold of the next. All of the hard work I had done in my life, all that I had experienced, and everything that had happened to me was for this moment—and, more important, for all that was yet to come.

After the proceedings in the Yard, my parents and I headed into Harvard Square to find the car. We needed to make our way back to the Divinity School for the second part of the graduation ceremony, where I would be awarded my diploma. It was drizzling a little, but the mood was festive. As we walked and chatted among the lively throng of caps and gowns, suits and ties, grandparents and students, I suddenly spotted Tomas. He was slowly pushing his bike along the crowded sidewalk. Wearing a T-shirt and jeans, with his familiar bag draped across his chest like a sash, he looked very much the same as he did on that first day we met. When he saw me, he stopped and squared his shoulders—and I noticed an involuntary narrowing of his eyes and a flash of emotions cross the surface of his face like an electrical current. Standing there, while a steady stream of people continued to flow around and past him, he looked both guarded and proud. Then I watched helplessly as the drawbridge of his heart closed with a subtle lift of his chin, and I could see the conquistador in his eyes. We hadn't spoken or even run into each other for months. And now we were face-to-face, each of us on the threshold of another life.

My parents waited on the bustling sidewalk while I dashed over to him, zigzagging through the living current of people like a salmon swimming upstream. My black graduation gown was unzipped and flapping in the breeze, exposing the white cotton sundress I had on underneath; the cap, with the halo still attached, was in my hands.

"Tomas . . . how are you?" I asked, feeling stupid as soon as the words came out. I knew instantly, of course, that he couldn't possibly answer me—not there, anyway, not then. It was too little too late. Still, I searched his face for some connection.

"I'm fine," he replied coolly, with that look in his eyes.

"It's graduation," I said (duh), trying to sound cheerful. "Those are my parents over there." I pointed in the direction of my mother and father, who were standing close together, as if they were stranded on a rock in the middle of the stream. "What are you doing?"

"I gave my final recital at Longy, so I'm finished with the program. I'm graduating—and I'm moving back to Bogotá."

"What? Really?" I stumbled on his words with the blunt force of stubbing my toe on a rock. "When? I hope we have a chance to say good-bye." I reflexively glanced over my shoulder to check on my mom and dad, who were looking a bit annoyed and anxious to get going.

"Your parents are waiting, Andrea. You'd better go."

I deserved his detached dismissal. I had pushed him away the past couple of years when I could have been spending time with him. Looking back, I'm not even sure why I did that. Mostly, I think, it was because I was afraid—afraid of what I was capable of feeling for him.

My parents didn't ask me much about him as we made our way back to the Divinity School. Fewer questions meant less approval, which meant less encouragement, I guess. The attitude I sensed from them at this point was just "I don't want to know."

Chairs were set up in the backyard of Jewett House—and for once I was not responsible for setting them up or wiping them off. Just as the ceremony began to get going, however, it started to pour, prompting everyone to scramble across the street to the chapel in Andover. My grandmother had come with my parents, although she had skipped the big ceremony in the Yard, and Andrea and Michael's wife, Ella, were there as well. As we all dashed inside, the exuberant energy of the day was compressed and concentrated somehow by being forced into a space with walls and a ceiling. It was like trying to contain the Holy in a shoebox—joy was spilling out of the cracks.

Once seated inside, I looked up at the pulpit from which I had preached during my homiletics class, and where great spirits such as Gustavo Gutiérrez and Desmond Tutu had spoken. I looked up and down the aisles, where Katherine and I had tried and failed to inspire liturgical dance, and I looked around at my fellow students, shoulder to shoulder in the pews. *This ark has sustained us*, I thought. *It has sustained me, through storm and calm, through darkness and light.* As we came forward one by one to receive our diplomas, Professor Guy Martin announced what each person would be doing after graduation. Not only was this interesting, but it also functioned as a reassuring reminder that there was life after Harvard Divinity School. Many obviously needed reassurance, as evidenced by a familiar joke around campus. It went something like this: In New York, the question is "What do you do?" In D.C., it's "Who do you know?" And at Harvard, it's "How long have you been here?" There was some truth in this—it was hard to leave, but it was time.

Out of the one hundred or so graduates, only about ten were going on to become ministers. Most were either entering doctoral programs, planning on teaching, or pursing work with various nonprofit organizations. I did not have a job lined up yet, nor was I sure what I was going to do with the next year. So, when it was my turn to come forward, my tagline was simply that I would be continuing on the path toward ordination in the United Methodist Church. Hearing that said aloud resonated somewhere in the deepest part of me, but it still had an unreal, far-off quality to it—like an army recruit who can't fathom going to war. Ordination was possible in the way that getting married was possible—one had to be very sure before taking the plunge. At the moment, the Methodist church and I were merely engaged.

After graduation, my parents and grandmother returned home, and I moved into an apartment in Somerville with Katherine. The two-bedroom apartment sat atop a steep hill on Summer Street, between Davis and Porter Squares, about a mile from the Div School. We could see the Boston skyline from the front balcony, which could be accessed by climbing through Katherine's bedroom window. There was also a small, shady balcony off my bedroom in the back, accessible in the same way through my window. Somehow we managed to drag the blue denim couch from Jewett House over to the apartment and stuff it out my window. We hung up wind chimes, added some candles and plants, and spent a lot of time curled up there, talking about our lives. It made sense in a way that Katherine's bedroom was in the sun while mine was in the shade. It fit our personalities and the way we balanced and complemented each other.

The only furniture in my room was a mattress on the floor (also a donation from Jewett House) and a couple of plastic milk crates. I lived out of the boxes that I never fully unpacked, using them as drawers and end tables and whatever else I needed—which was not much at the time. Katherine got a kick out of this, often laughing at how I would emerge from my room looking professional and ready for work when, behind the door, it was a whole different story.

Soon after we moved in, Katherine must have scrounged up some furniture, because we did have some odds and ends in our living room (things that seemed to just appear). It was a large, sunny room with a bay window, one that ushered in great gulps of light, flooding the room like an open dam. One of the nicest things about the apartment besides the view was the fact that the beautiful blond hardwood floors had just been redone (except in the kitchen, which was pretty grim). We kept the apartment fairly sparse, adding to it as we went along, never worrying about checking with each other first. It was a shared and evolving canvas, one in which we delighted. Some might have considered our decorating rather haphazard, but I thought it inspired. There was a Hula-hoop hanging on the wall and a woven cotton rug on the floor. When a small window broke, we stuffed a decorative pillow in the hole and considered it art with a sense of humor. It blended in so well that we often forgot about it until someone asked us why it was there. I suppose we could have called the landlord to come fix the window but we grew fond of the way it looked.

There were a few other oddities that made the apartment (in my opinion) magical. For instance, one day I came home to find a full-sized shopping cart in our very small kitchen. Katherine swore she didn't know how it got there, but it became part of the décor. Whenever either of us shopped for food (which was fairly rarely), the cart was used as a sort of open-air cupboard. It was usually filled with assorted cans of green beans and the occasional jar of peanut butter. For all I know, it might still be there.

Even the bathroom had a story. When the lightbulb burned out sometime in the fall, we (naturally) resorted to lighting a candle in there at night. Wouldn't anyone? When this was deemed potentially hazardous—no one wanted her hair to catch fire while in a compromising position—we employed a flashlight instead. We thought nothing of this, but our evening guests would occasionally be startled when we jumped up and handed them the flashlight as they headed to the bathroom. Noticing their expressions, one of us would try to explain, saying, "Sorry! You have to use the flashlight because we're out of matches for the candle." It was Andy who finally brought over a new bulb, answering the age-old question, How many intelligent people does it take to change a lightbulb? Answer: just one, but he's got to be tired of whizzing in the dark.

Our bohemian sensibilities were sometimes viewed with polite curiosity. On one such occasion, my sister Jennie and her husband, Tom, were visiting from Kentucky. Tom is a lawyer and Jennie a nurse, and they already had a lovely home on a tree-lined street just outside of Lexington. They understood that coming to see me did not mean staying in luxury accommodations, but that didn't matter; we were excited to be able to spend some time together. As they were preparing for bed on that first evening, Tom (in his soft Kentucky accent) asked me for a washcloth. Simple enough . . . well, sort of. The conversation that followed went something like this:

ME (SHOUTING TO KATHERINE IN HER BEDROOM): Hey, Katherine, do we have a washcloth?

KATHERINE: Hmm . . . I think it's dirty.

TOM: *It's?* You only have one?

The next day, he and Jennie went out and bought us a couple of lovely washcloths as a housewarming gift.

Good thing they weren't allergic to cats because we had two . . . and then three . . . and, for a short time, four. Katherine, of course, had Lorna, her lovely marmalade tabby, and I had my yin-yang faced Isaac. They adored each other. Then we acquired Big Fat Joey Cat from a sweet but tortured lesbian heroin addict I knew from church. She had tearfully pleaded with me to take her beautiful twenty-two-pound kitty because she was concerned that her fellow drug users were abusing him. Joey came to us shy and traumatized, but blossomed into his gentle-giant self and soon fit right in. Later, in the spring, I stumbled across Arthur, a tiny gray tabby who had been abandoned at a gas station. *He* turned out to be a *she*, somehow getting pregnant a year later, although he/she never left our third-floor apartment. Some feline Romeo must have scaled the trees to be with his Juliet; either that, or it was immaculate conception. Whatever the case, they all became fast friends, grooming each other in the sun and lounging on the white futon folded on the floor. Not only was that our couch, where we played guitar, sang, prayed, meditated, and talked, it was also a reminder of the last time I saw Tomas.

Before he disappeared into the secret treasure chest of my memories, a place from which I would sometimes summon him like a genie from a bottle when I was feeling lonely, I saw Tomas one more time. I'm grateful that the last visual I have of him is not of that defiant stance in the Square, although the replacement image came at a bit of a price. Tomas and I had talked only a couple of times after our chance encounter on graduation day. The first time he called was to tell me that he was moving out of his apartment. Knowing that Katherine and I had just moved in together, he offered to sell me his futon for practically nothing. Although on the surface I felt a little awkward about it, deep down it was comforting to think of having that link to him. The day that his friends delivered it, however, I didn't have any cash on hand (big surprise), so I owed him about forty dollars.

The second time he called was the night before he was to fly back to Bogotà. This time, there was an edge in his voice as he reminded me that I still owed him the money for the futon. Of course, I'd like to believe that he was mostly calling to see me and to say good-bye. Genuinely embarrassed that I had neglected to pay him—something that I'd been putting off in order to deny the fact that he was leaving—I promised to bring it to him that night. He gave me the address of the friend's apartment where he was staying, and where an impromptu going-away party was also in progress.

Meanwhile, Andy had been accepted into Longy School of Music, where Tomas had just graduated, and had moved into his own apartment about three blocks away from Katherine and me. Initially, I felt panicky having him so close. Going from three hours to three blocks apart (after three years) was going to be a trifecta of change, and I wasn't sure I was ready to bet on it. I was still very skittish and jumpy regarding relationships, like a racehorse being led into the starting gate, but I was determined to give it a fair chance. *There must be a reason*, I thought, *to have hung on to him so long, through time and distance*, especially since my usual MO was to cut ties and disappear. Trying to hold fast, I asked Andy to go with me to drop off the money. I knew that saying good-bye might be emotional, and I was afraid of the lingering feelings I still had for Tomas. Unfortunately, it was like a thief bringing a policeman to a jewelry store. I didn't want to be tempted to do anything I would regret—but I should have known better.

Andy drove me to the small apartment building where Tomas was staying. While we were driving, he asked me a couple of times about the nature of our friendship, but I was decidedly vague. *What does it matter now?* I reasoned. He was leaving and I would probably never see him again. Still, my heart was racing when we pulled up and I felt a tinge of regret about having asked Andy to accompany me. Fortunately, he agreed to wait in the car while I delivered the cash. The atmosphere was warm but slightly melancholy when I went inside. People were scattered about the apartment, chatting quietly. There were open takeout containers in the kitchen, as if no one had the heart to cook, and some music was playing on a small boom box. When I handed Tomas the money, he took my face in his hands and kissed me. Really kissed me. It was one of those good-bye kisses you see in the movies—tender and passionate and sad and full of emotion. It also happened to be taking place in front of a large bay window that was visible from the road. It shouldn't have surprised me, then, when a loud banging could be heard coming from the door downstairs a few minutes later. Realizing what must have happened, I ran downstairs with Tomas trailing me, curious and unaware. When I opened the door, Andy was standing there with a furious look on his face.

"I was just saying good-bye . . ." I stuttered.

"That's not the way you say good-bye!" he shouted, his blue eyes burning like twin lasers, cutting through the doorway and hollowing out my eye sockets. Tomas stood behind me looking a little stunned . . . and then guarded. The conquistador was back.

"Good-bye, Andrea," he said quietly, after a few painful seconds.

With that, the harness was slipped on and I was led to the car, feeling miserable and sad and mad at myself. It would take quite a few years before Andy could forgive me for that little display in the window—and it took me some time as well to sort out what had happened and how I felt about it. I'm not sure I completely understand it even now, but I have come to accept and even treasure that moment. Maybe that's wrong of me . . . but it's part of my tapestry. If I took out that stitch, who knows what might unravel?

There were other good-byes as this time in my life came to a close, and other last glimpses of people who had been important to me. My clearest last memory of John, the medical student, was in my room just before graduation. I was introducing him to my parents, simply because I adored him. Sitting on the blue denim couch, he put his arm around me in the sweetest way and said to them, directly and earnestly, "Mr. and Mrs. Ruehrwein, I want you to know that I am crazy about your daughter." I thought this was one of the nicest and most genuine things anyone ever said about me to my parents. And I loved him for that. After graduation, we just drifted apart, like two sailboats set on slightly different courses.

A few months later, I ran into Ernie near the Orpheum Theatre in Boston. He was walking with Frank, a guest from the shelter, one who was more like a friend than a client, and I was on my way to talk with Rupert, who was preparing for a gig. Things had not been going well since our breakup, and I was worried that he was unraveling. Deep in thought, I was startled when Ernie and Frank suddenly appeared in front of me, walking down a wide alleyway between two buildings.

How ironic—back to the alley. It was a sun-drenched, color-saturated day. The sky, an illuminated blue, was propped open overhead like a giant beach umbrella, but the alley was in shade. When I saw them walking toward me in that cool, clear-eyed space, I didn't have to squint—there were no sunspots; everything was in sharp focus.

During my first year at Pine Street, Ernie and I had become close—well, as close as he would let me. I was drawn to his odd and intelligent humor, his kindness toward the men, and probably the lockbox of his inner self. I liked his company but often felt that he would throw me off-balance with an intentionally insensitive remark or some odd behavior. I could never understand this. And perhaps because I couldn't understand it, I kept trying to fix it, which wasn't always the smartest move.

In the five seconds that it took him to approach, a particular memory superimposed itself in the space between us. It had to do with the time he asked me to accompany him, in the middle of winter, to a rather remote spot in order to watch the sun rise. This was typical of Ernie. On the surface, it was a sweet, one could even say romantic, gesture, but underneath it evoked a level of squeamish uncertainty. When I told Katherine about his invite, she begged me not to go with him that morning. She told me that she had a very bad feeling about it. "I just keep seeing gray," she shuddered. "It's just a very bleak and gray feeling." Although I completely trusted her intuition, for some reason I went anyway, promising to be on my guard. I always believed in Ernie's innate goodness—perhaps more than he did—even when he went out of his way to prove he wasn't the person I thought he was. I found this infuriating, which he found funny, which wasn't a great combination.

When the day came, he picked me up and we drove and we hiked in the snowy, silent morning to a hill in the middle of nowhere, to watch the sun rise. Standing knee-deep in shimmering white-blue snow in the predawn hour, he looked at me with a strange smile. "I could kill you right now and no one would ever know," he said. My stomach lurched, but I quickly regained my balance, drew back my bow, and shot back, "I could kill you, too, you know. Just remember that." Then he tossed back his head and laughed.

On that sunny day in the middle of Boston when I saw him for the last time, I'm sorry to report that not much had changed. I searched his face for any crack in the surface, any green shoot, but he opted for the opaque, mocking mask that always drove me crazy. This was too bad, although in some ways it imparted an important lesson; namely, that I couldn't fix or change anybody, nor was that my responsibility. After a few awkward moments, we turned and walked in opposite directions. I snipped any remaining threads that might tether me to him and pledged to stay in the Light. It was time to stick with people I trusted, people who wouldn't try to hurt me, people who could help me grow. I was tired of dancing around the edges, tired of flirting with danger. I was growing up. After divinity school and before ordination, I had some soul searching to do—and walking on either side of me, through the dark alleys and into the sun, were Katherine and Andy. I decided to reach for their hands and keep them close; luckily they reached for mine.

22

the year between

I began scouring the paper for jobs a week after graduation. For the first time in my life, I had rent to pay, a cat to feed, and the very real pressure of paying my bills. Sitting cross-legged on the floor in our new apartment, I opened the Sunday *Globe* without a clue as to what kind of job I could get with my divinity degree. I was still a year away from being eligible for ordination, I wasn't a teacher or a nurse, I knew nothing about computers, and I had no interest in business. The sun was streaming through the large bay window, Lorna was grooming Isaac on the futon as if he were a king, and Katherine was out for a run in the early summer morning. I folded myself in half, elbows on the floor, as I scanned the paper and sipped my coffee. Rather than being nervous or overwhelmed, I was young enough to believe that the possibilities were endless.

Because there didn't seem to be any employment categories entitled "Religious" or "Spiritual" or "Jobs for a Good Person," it made sense to begin by looking under "Social Services." I

still felt the pull of doing socially relevant work but hoped to
do this from a spiritual perspective. I had considered applying
for a job at Pine Street, but the shelter was not hiring full-time
help at the moment. This was fine with me because I was excited about trying something new. Running my finger down
the columns, it was clear that I would have had numerous interesting options if I'd gotten a degree in social work. These
were the jobs that most appealed to me, but they were out of
reach without an MSW. As I continued scanning the paper,
three words set in bold type caught my eye: PROTECTIVE SER-
VICE WORKER. The image of a personal bodyguard immediately flashed through my mind. Somehow "Protective Services"
sounded exciting to my naïve ear, as if the job would require
wearing a black suit and a pair of dark sunglasses. Reading the
rest of the job description dispelled this notion fairly quickly.
It indicated that the position involved working on behalf of
senior citizens who were being neglected or abused in their
homes. I was surprised to find that the small blurb did not
specify whether one needed a social work degree to be eligible
for the job, so I decided to apply.

The morning of my interview, I hopped the T out of
Porter Square in Somerville, my new home base, changed
trains a couple of times, got out at Government Center, and
walked the remaining blocks. I arrived at Senior Home Care in
downtown Boston armed with my résumé, my hope to do
something positive in the world, and a little chutzpah. The
office was in a large building located at 600 Washington Street,
hovering on the edge of what was commonly known as the
Combat Zone. The Combat Zone had once been a thriving
mecca of X-rated movies, strip clubs, peep shows, and prosti-
tution. Not surprisingly, in its heyday, it had also been a favor-

ite spot for sailors and soldiers on leave. Between the crime, the danger, and the presence of men in uniform, it was aptly named. The Combat Zone had been cleaned up quite a bit by the time I was headed in that direction, but there were still remnants of its past—a peep show here or there, a couple of adult movie theaters, seedy erotica stores, and a few remaining strip clubs, such as the Naked I and the Glass Slipper. I arrived for my interview just as a well-dressed businessman ducked into an adult bookstore across the street. Before he disappeared, he glanced around to see if anyone was watching. I pretended I wasn't.

Stepping off the elevator, I was surprised to find that the young woman with whom I would be interviewing appeared to be around my age—and yet she was the social work supervisor for the home care agency. She was petite and straightforward, with eyes that seemed to take in more than what was said on the surface, and she had an aura of integrity. She struck me as someone who was serious and kind and who kept her feelings rather close to the vest. Maybe she had to create some professional distance because she was so young. Her name was Charnan (a combination of her parents' names, Charlie and Nancy), and she had the grace not to flinch when I told her that I had no idea what a home care agency was, what it offered, or how it functioned. Charnan explained that the agency served elderly clients who were living in their own homes (or in their children's homes) by offering nursing, personal care, and social services; then she explained that one of the agency's responsibilities was also protective services. On the home care side of the agency, a well-staffed crew of nurses, home health aides, and social workers tried to field and address the multiple challenges that come with age; on the other side were a small core of protective service workers whose job it was to investigate reports of abuse or neglect. These reports could come from a doctor, a neighbor, a family member, or the person being abused. It could be as rough as a drug-addicted grandson putting his cigarettes out on Grandma for her Social Security check or as sad as an overwhelmed working daughter who thought she had no choice but to leave her sick father home alone.

The job sounded challenging—and I liked the idea of being out in the community rather than stuck in an office all day. Charnan informed me that this position was usually filled by a social worker, but she was open to the possibility of hiring me. I told her about my work at Pine Street, which showed that I was not afraid to jump into a difficult situation, and the fact that I had a Harvard degree certainly carried some weight. But I believe that what actually landed me the job was my saying, "Charnan, you can teach me the necessary paperwork, I can learn the regulations that a social worker might already know, but I am bringing some things that cannot be taught: I am bringing the strength of my intuition, my ability to be present, and my intellect." A few days later, she called to offer me the position. The salary was a rather modest $19,000 per year, but it was enough for me to live on, at least most of the time.

Thus began my year at Senior Home Care. I loved my work, even though it was sometimes rough and a bit scary. I took the T everywhere I went, getting to know Boston from the inside out. On any given day, I might find myself in the moneyed section of Beacon Hill in the morning and the most impoverished section of Dorchester by the afternoon. Abuse knows no race, gender, or economic status; this I learned first-hand. Part of my job was helping to identify whether abuse or neglect was actually happening, and the other part was working to relieve the situation. Sometimes this meant helping a victim obtain a restraining order; other times it involved putting support services in place that a family didn't know were available. It was heartbreaking and disturbing to encounter cases of domestic violence that had been going on for forty or fifty years. As the victim (usually a wife) aged, her bones became more fragile and the abuse more deadly. In one home, I witnessed a man in his eighties, whose left side was paralyzed from a stroke, still manage to pick up an iron burner from the stove with his right hand and swing it at his wife. The defeated look on her face said it all.

In my first months on the job, I found myself thinking and worrying about my clients all weekend long; by the time I got back to work on Monday, I was already exhausted. And so I learned how to let them go on Friday so that I could have the energy to help again come Monday—but not before gently turning them over to bigger hands than mine. Each Friday afternoon, as the T rocked me toward home, I would shut my eyes and pray for them. I would picture each of my elderly clients resting in a beautiful luminescent balloon. One by one, I would let them go, envisioning them floating up to the heavens, and praying, "Please God, hold them in your tender hands. Watch over them, take care of them; let no violence come to them this weekend. Fill me with your love and light and help me to be your servant. Amen." Sometimes I would have to repeat this meditation several times over the weekend, but it allowed my spirit and psyche to return to work on Monday energized and ready to start another week.

One morning as I was heading out to work, Katherine offered to walk down to the T with me. While sipping our coffees and deep in discussion, the train pulled into the station. We were still talking as I boarded and as she stood on the platform, trying to get in every last word. Just as the doors were about to close, Katherine suddenly jumped onto the train, coffee in hand. It was more of a reflex than an intentional decision. It startled us both, as if she had simply been picked up and put there, but we immediately and seamlessly resumed the conversation. That I'll-just-come-with-you moment was the first of many happy mornings that Katherine rode with me to work. When we would arrive at 600 Washington Street, I would go upstairs to my office and she would often sit in the lobby making calls on the pay phone or meet up with another friend. Occasionally, if I was in the office at the end of the day instead of being out in the field, I would come down to the lobby to find her still there.

Katherine did not have a regular job during the year that we lived together, which afforded her the opportunity to accompany me to work. She was painting, writing, and doing a unit of Clinical Pastoral Education (CPE) at Brigham and Women's Hospital. I shared what it was like to do protective services, to find myself in disturbing or sad or dangerous situations, and she ran everything that was going on in her life by me. We were a checks-and-balances system; a validation, recommendation, or caution bureau. Although we lived together, we often did not see that much of each other because our schedules were very different. This made our occasional morning rides or evening meditations a treat. There was a natural ease about living with one another. It helped that we were both independent and had a lot going on in our lives. We trusted in our love for one another, which let so much light into our friendship that there was always room to grow.

One of the few things we actually put on our schedules and committed ourselves to was a small prayer group that consisted of the two of us—and sometimes Michael's wife, Ella. Sitting on the floor in the living room, we would light a candle, and begin by sharing what was going on in our lives, especially the things that were weighing on us. We might discuss a passage of scripture, sing together, play guitar, or sit for long periods of silence, but we would always close with a shared prayer. This was not, of course, the only time that Katherine and I prayed together. We did this frequently and spontaneously, and our conversations—even if they were about men—were always filtered through a spiritual lens. In fact, our lives were seen through a spiritual lens. We were saturated with the Divine and with a desire to be forces of good in the world.

It was during one of these evening gatherings that I requested prayers for the mice living in the walls and ceiling of my office building. Reminiscent of what had happened in the dorm during my first year in div school, the home care building was having a mouse problem. To combat this, they employed the familiar but horrifying sticky traps. During this slow, torturous extermination, I could hear the desperate screams of the mice in the ceiling above me as I was sitting at my desk. It was unbearable. How could anyone possibly think this was okay? "Please pray for the mice!" I said one night to Katherine and Ella. "Pray for the poor mice in the ceiling." We did . . . and our hearts broke open a little more, expanding to embrace the suffering of the smallest of creatures, and deepening our compassion and reverence for life.

During this time in my life, I probably came closest to knowing what it is to "pray without ceasing." Whether walking to the T, buying cat food, working, or relaxing, I had an ongoing dialogue with God. My thoughts were continuously floating upward, while my heart was listening for the answers that were returning to me in a circular flow. In this space, I contemplated my call to ministry and I sought guidance in my personal life. Both paths were becoming clearer. Even though the road to ordination meant enduring a challenging process with the church, I was feeling more and more certain of my call. And even though I was still disentangling myself from a couple of murky situations, one relationship was becoming clearer. Both of these—my calling and my relationship with Andy— were beacons for me. They were lights helping me to navigate my way. As I drew nearer, they grew stronger; as they grew stronger, I grew clearer.

The first few weeks after Andy's move to Somerville had not been pretty. I felt crowded, he felt hurt, and we were both adjusting to living in the same neighborhood. He had a new chapter beginning in his life, but I felt like a chapter was coming to a close. He was starting school, I had finished school; he was moving toward me, I was moving away from the craziness of past relationships, but not yet toward him.

After the fiasco with Tomas, I had one more close call tidying up the past. Rupert and I were still speaking occasionally, although it was becoming increasingly uncomfortable. One evening, I came home to find a message from him on our answering machine saying that he wanted to speak with me and was going to stop by later. I went into a panic. I was pretty sure that Andy had said that he was coming by at around the same time. I couldn't reach either of them by phone, and I just kept picturing both of them walking up and trying to press the same buzzer. Katherine was out somewhere so couldn't help me. Frantic, I called Andrea, who (*whew*) picked up the phone. I explained the situation to her and she started to laugh.

"It's not funny!" I said, laughing in spite of myself.

"Oh, yes it is. Serves you right," she teased.

"Help me! Can you drive over? Like, immediately?"

Andrea was there within twenty minutes. She was that kind of friend. The kind who would drop everything if you were in trouble, even if it was stupid trouble, trouble of your own making. She picked me up in her car and we drove a few blocks before pulling over. Andrea was levelheaded and much stronger than I was in many ways. Where I would want to pull the covers over my head, avoid, or disappear, she would stand her ground, face things head on, just deal with it.

"Look," she said, facing me in her seat. "You know you have to straighten this out. You have got to make it clear to Rupert that you don't want to see him, even if it means hurting his feelings."

"I know," I moaned. "I thought I did. I tried to, anyway."

"Does Andy know about him?"

"Well, sort of. We don't really talk about who we've dated over the past three years. We're finally starting to get close . . . I don't want to blow it."

"So, what do you want to do?" Andrea looked at me with her blue-green kaleidoscope eyes and her pretty mouth, which was trying hard not to smile too broadly.

"Will you just drive around the block a couple of times and see if anyone is at my door, while I lie down in the back?"

At that, she couldn't hold back the laughter that burst like a champagne cork from her body. "You are a mess! Get in the back."

I could always count on Andrea. Even if she didn't agree with me, even if she thought I was making a mistake, she was there for me. And somehow her presence made even this moment of nerves tolerable and even funny. As I flattened myself in the back of her little hatchback, she reported to me what was happening on the steps of my apartment. "So far, nothing," she said. Around the block we crawled again.

"Anything?" I asked anxiously from my prone position.

"Nope. Oh, wait . . ." she said. "I see two guys with flowers in their hands reaching for the buzzer."

"What? What? Who?" I asked, panic-stricken.

"I'm just kidding. No one is there."

"I'm gonna kill you."

"You're the one lying in the back of my car."

And so it went like that for about a half hour, until it was pretty clear that a crisis had been averted. Before she dropped me off, we sat for a while in her car, talking.

"Don't you think it's about time you straighten all this stuff out?" she asked, genuinely concerned. "Just come clean with Andy."

It was solid advice. When I took it, my relationship with Andy began to have a fighting chance. He was stronger than I had given him credit for, more loving, more accepting, and more determined to be my shield and my shelter. After this, it was as if all the static in the air, the noise and the distraction, the subterfuge and the stress, had evaporated between us. I exhaled into the safety and the peace of our relationship, and we began to grow like a plant that's finally been given enough water and sunlight. By Christmas, we were inseparable. I gave him a kitten, which I felt he needed because he lived alone, and he accepted her, even though he'd felt perfectly fine with his piano and plants. Jesse would be the first of many animals that I would inadvertently thrust into his otherwise contented life. It became a rather uncomfortable pattern, but one could argue that he should have seen it coming. At the time, I wasn't really thinking that our cats Jesse and Isaac would spend most of their lives together; I was just thinking that Jesse would be good company for him—which she was.

As each of our paths became clearer—his in music and mine in the ministry—our identities were also growing stronger, and the future was beginning to click into focus. Not that it would be free of challenges, but we were strengthening ourselves for the journey. Andy's musical knowledge and abilities were growing exponentially at Longy. This was as vital a time for him as divinity school had been for me, albeit a little less raucous, a little less of a wild river ride. He was solid and steadfast, while I was learning not to disappear into my shell. Day by day, we were growing closer, we were learning about ourselves, and we were having a lot of fun in the process. We were moving forward, swinging vine to vine—until the next vine I reached for took me away again.

23

---

send me

"Are you sure you're not interested in applying to a doctoral program?" It was my mom's voice on the other end of the phone. "If you don't go for it now, you might never go back." I was stretched out on my bed, gazing at the unpacked boxes that lined the wall of my bedroom. A breeze was blowing through the open window, the chimes were ringing like tiny calls to prayer, and the green leaves were waving good-naturedly at me. I could not have been happier.

"I know, Mom, you're probably right—but I have no desire to be in school right now. Besides, I don't want to be one of those people who has a doctorate but no life experience." She listened, but I could tell she was disappointed. Had I continued on in school, I would have been the first person in our family to earn a PhD. But I was tired of studying, and I was anxious to get out into the world. My parents' support and their faith in my abilities had been a guiding force all my life. They inspired me to be my best, academically, personally, and spiritually; to strive for excellence and to

266

achieve my goals. They believed in me, holding me to standards that were difficult but never out of my reach. Sometimes I would grumble about feeling pressured—but I knew, in reality, it was not my mother or father who was pressuring me, but the voice inside my own head. I was more driven than I would have liked to admit. For some reason, I had trouble reconciling being ambitious with being humble, and so I tried to go about my life and my work quietly, steadily, without calling too much attention.

The idea of having a doctorate, of placing those letters behind my name, was very tempting; the reality of what it would take to get there was not. What's more, I felt absolutely no calling to the field of academia. I did not aspire to be a teacher or a professor—I'd rather be sitting on a smoky bench with Stevie at Pine Street. Perhaps this wasn't clear to me until my mother pushed me on the issue. Sometimes we go through periods of wringing our hands, of feeling lost, of wondering what direction to go in, when suddenly the air clears and our whole bodies resonate with a definite *yes* or *no*. Talking to my mom was one of those moments. Looking out the window, the leaves a thousand friendly hands, chimes sending ripples of energy across the expanse, I felt my life was in harmony with Divine purpose. Not that *I* was always in harmony with the Divine, but the river carrying me was—and I was not going to fight the current. My ego was tempted by the promise of more academic achievement, but my spirit had already surrendered to the call of ministry. Ironically, *I* could wrestle with my calling, like Jacob squaring off with the angel, but when someone else challenged it, the mist cleared and I felt the strength of my conviction, as well as a dogged determination to follow the path that was unfolding for me.

We got off the phone as we always did by saying "I love you." I pictured my mom in our kitchen back home, her petite frame and pretty face a lifelong camouflage for her formidable strength. Only those who did not know her would be fooled by this delicate exterior. Placing the phone back on the cradle, she would continue the conversation in her head behind the locked doors of her private sanctuary. There, she would be holding me in her heart, worrying about me, fretting over me, missing me, a highlight reel of images playing on a loop in the back of her mind. The kitchen walls would reverberate with an echo of laughter, with countless suppers around the table, where there was always room for one more plate, and where a pot of chili simmered every Friday night, as we ran in and out of the house on the way to high school football games and dates. Those years were like Fourth of July sparklers, crackling with energy, light, and excitement—but gone in the blink of an eye. What was left in your hand was the bare remnant, evidence that this moment had actually existed, while the ghost sparks quickly faded, leaving only the memory of light. In the company of these ghosts, she might pour herself another cup of coffee, decaf, and open the Sunday paper, reading it cover to cover with her elbows on the table and her face resting on her open palms, one leg tucked under her, like a little girl.

I shut my eyes and continued to lie there for some time, pondering my future and trying to breathe into the center of myself, into the silvery depths resting in silence, eons and fathoms under the surface. Images came and went, like old slides without sound. I saw myself at four sitting in the grass, my arm around our boxer, a breeze ruffling my unbrushed flaxen hair; and at eight, squealing in disbelief when my father brought a pony around the side of the house to surprise us. There I was at ten in my softball uniform, running as fast as I could around the bases, feeling as fleet and nimble as a deer. At twelve, I was weeping over the death of my cat, looking up toward the empty ceiling of my room, where God should have been listening. The images tumbled into each other, seamlessly telling the story of my life, without judgment or editorial comments. In this wordless place, I felt myself resting in the iridescent, pearly womb of God, home of my spirit before there was an *I* or a *my*. Energy was pulsing through me, igniting my cells and knitting me together. Then, like the reverberation of distant thunder, words (which were not words at all, but only the awareness of meaning) came into my mind: *Trust me*. At some point, I became aware that my body, my physical body, was vibrating. Lingering in that awareness, eyes still closed, a smile spread across my face like the first rays of the dawning sun across the earth. Trust, I would need. Trust in God, trust in my ability to hear God's voice, trust in the future.

This became my mantra as I went about my life. It was harder in reality than it seemed in the vibrant fuchsia pulse of my meditation. Some things were clearer than others. For instance, I trusted that I was in the right place with my work at Senior Home Care. Sitting in the roach-infested apartment of an elderly woman in a wheelchair, her legs lost to diabetes, her body to alcoholism, I felt perfectly centered. As she told me her story of being bullied by her son, I tried not to flinch at the feces that she'd tracked on the floor with the wheels of her chair. "Whom shall I send [to her]?" asked the Almighty. *Send me* was my heartfelt reply. Walking through the crime-ridden streets of Roxbury, I stayed alert but also remained aware of God's presence. *Living or dying, I am in God's hands*, I would remind myself. Trusting God did not mean having a bullet-proof vest; it meant not feeling alone or forgotten as I went about doing the work to which I felt called.

And trust was required as I continued moving through the process mandated by the church to become an ordained United Methodist minister. Every step of the way, there were stumbling blocks and helping hands. It was like running a spiritual obstacle course. My papers and course work were complete, but there were interviews to go through where I would be surrounded by people who looked a lot more legit than me. Surprisingly, I found that my strongest allies and supporters were not necessarily my peers or other women—quite the contrary. They were people of a variety of ages, men and women, who had bravely forged new roads or who had fought for change, challenging the church to become a true force of peace and justice.

Michael Curry, of course, was always in my corner, but another cherished mentor was a pastor in his sixties, the Reverend Dick Harding. I truly don't know if I would have made it through the process and through my first few years of ministry without him. Dick is a large, white-haired man with a friendly face and the kindest eyes. To be enfolded in his bear hug is to know something of that loving father energy of God. Dick marched with Martin Luther King Jr. and others in Alabama and has been fighting for the rights of the marginalized ever since. In him I saw a kindred spirit, a wise guide, and an inspiring example of how one could work within the boundaries of the church to bring about change. Perhaps he saw in me a little of that same fight, as well as a stubbornness to be myself, and the fierce determination to articulate my convictions. All I knew for sure was that whenever Dick was in the room, I felt supported, encouraged, safe—and I never felt alone.

I have walked some scary paths—the alley at Pine Street, the twisted corridors of strange relationships, the steps leading to an abuser's home, and the road toward ordination. They all share a common thread, that of trying to understand myself, to express myself, and to grow into the person I was meant to be. I wanted my life to unfold like a flower, organically, naturally, my face to the sun, arms reaching toward the heavens, and my ears attuned to the whisper of God. *Which way should I go? This way? That?* I wanted to leave the sludge of confusion behind me, arm myself with the lessons that I had learned, and follow the trail out of the woods and into the Light. Of course, in order to do this, I would have to stay alive, physically and spiritually, which was proving no easy task.

Almost as metaphor, the memory of one night when I was walking home from the gym came to my mind. I had joined a small women's gym on the edge of Central Square, not because I was an exercisaholic, but because I needed the physical outlet. I was not a runner like Katherine but I still felt like an athlete, and the only exercise I was getting was walking to the T on my way to and from work. I probably chose the all-women's gym in part because of my experience with Bobby. Needless to say, there was no hot tub. A couple times a week, I would tote my sneakers and spandex to work so that I could take the train straight to Central Square. From there, I would have to walk quite a few long blocks to get to the gym. I could have gone home and driven my car, but parking was always a problem, and if I went home, there was a pretty fair chance I would just stay put.

When I reached the gym around 5:30 p.m., the sun was still illuminating the sky. I changed into my workout clothes, got on the treadmill, and smiled at the woman next to me when our eyes got snagged on the space between us, but I didn't linger. I was distracted by a case I was working on at Senior Home Care, which was going to require initiating an order of protection.

By the time I left the building, it was dark. Not only had I lost track of time, but it had also slipped my mind how much earlier the sun was setting as fall began its steady surrender to winter. Pulling my blazer a little tighter around my chest (I had changed back into my work clothes, with the exception of the sneakers and white ankle socks), I slung my gym bag over my shoulder and headed into the night. My route took me parallel to the Charles River for a couple of blocks, then I turned right at a corner and started the long stretch toward Mass Ave and the lights of Central Square, lights that were still too far away to see. The road was fairly desolate, with closed, darkened buildings, stretches of parking lots, and very few houses lining the street. Although my radar was on high alert, I had no choice but to just keep walking with eyes ahead, hoping that Central Square, with its noise and its bustle, would soon come into view. Then I got a sick feeling.

Coming up behind me was a man whose voice made the blood rush to my head, drowning my ears in their own pulse. I did not turn around, but I could hear him. He was calling to me, teasing me, in a perverse and dangerous way. The next thing I knew, he was beside me, matching me stride for stride and swinging a lead pipe that was about three feet long. He was a young, stocky man, probably younger than I was, with a closely shaved head and menacing eyes, and he was clearly enjoying this. I did not speak to him but kept moving forward, my eyes scanning the darkness ahead for any possibility of help or refuge, but there was none. The man would trot ahead of me a few paces, clicking his tongue and inviting me to move toward him, all the while swatting that pipe into his hand, as if I needed to be reminded that it was there. Then he would disappear behind me and say nothing. The silence and the unknowing was the scariest part of all.

This went on for a couple blocks, during which time several things ran through my head . . . including the very real possibility that this would not end well. My mind became extremely focused and adrenaline pumped through my body as I considered my options. Rapidly shuffling through my mental Rolodex, I remembered reading somewhere (or maybe someone told me) that one way to handle a situation such as this is to try the unexpected—throwing up, for instance, collapsing like Jell-O, acting insane. Before I could think these through, I noticed a car slowly pulling up alongside of us; it was filled with his buddies, and they were starting to laugh. The guy trotted ahead of me again, gripping that pipe and leering at me. *This is it,* I thought. *The crucial moment, the only chance I might have; and I refuse to just stand here and go down without a fight.* With that, I felt the generations of strong, midwestern stock coursing through my veins. My people had plowed fields, fought wars, survived floods, endured hardship. They wouldn't start a fight, but they wouldn't run from one, either; and they would not go quietly. With that (and all the ghosts who live in my lifeblood), I silently shouted my prayer, *Give me strength, O God, Creator of the universe.* Then, with a tremendous roar and eyes of fire, I rushed head-on toward him, my clawed hands outstretched.

He was so taken by surprise that he toppled backward onto the sidewalk, dropping the pipe, with a look of complete terror on his face. Disarmed and suddenly looking up at *my* face, he appeared for a split second like a frightened boy, and a lightning bolt of compassion inadvertently shot from my eyes. It didn't come *from* me—it came *through* me. His friends pulled to a stop, momentarily confused by what had just happened, and even more confused when he jumped into their car shouting, "Go, go, go! She's crazy!" I didn't wait around to hear their response. By then I was flying, running as fast as I ever had in my life, toward the lone light of a bodega ahead. I would be safe at home. Safe. Saved.

I suppose their car must have passed me, but I didn't see it. All I saw was that little light on the corner. Bursting into the bodega, I clearly startled the Latino man working behind the counter because his eyes widened; then they returned to their half-mast resting place. He seemed pleasant enough but did not ask questions about why I was out of breath—perhaps language was a barrier or perhaps he didn't want to know. After a minute of awkward silence, I stuck my head out the door and looked up and down the street. The lights of Mass Ave were visible now, a testament to how far I had run, and I considered resuming my footrace to the T.

As I calculated the distance, the face of my would-be attacker flashed in my mind. I realized that somehow, in my peripheral vision, I had caught a glimpse of him after he jumped in the backseat. He was peering out at me with the hurt eyes of one who had been exposed; oddly enough, he looked like a lost child who needed his mother. I knew this hurt would be stuffed down rather quickly, transforming back into cold bravado and dangerous rage. If they circled back around, I wouldn't stand a chance. With this in mind, I asked the man behind the counter if I could make a call and he quietly directed me to a pay phone on the wall. My hands were shaking a little as I dialed Andy. "Hey, do you think you could come pick me up? I just had the scariest experience." I explained to him where I was, and he promised to be there right away. Feeling a little self-conscious as I stood waiting inside the shop, I bought a bottle of water and pretended to browse. Before I knew it, Andy's blue Toyota Celica had pulled up and I sealed myself inside it.

There will always be dark alleys. There will always be that accidental miscalculation, that random stranger who threatens to undo us, that corner that we cannot see around, but there will always also be light—and when we see it, we should make a run toward it with everything we have. Sometimes we have to call forth all of our strength to face the darkness—within and without. We have to gather it up from our fingertips and toe tips, from our innards to our open pores, so that we can face that which frightens us, that which threatens to undo us, that which hits our most vulnerable spots—bull's-eye. This is easier said than done. Running from a dangerous stranger toward the light of a safe haven is a fairly clear choice, one that is made in the heat of the moment. It is not so much a calculated risk as it is animal instinct. But what of moving from the murky waters of self-doubt and confusion toward confidence and inner peace, or from fear toward faith? Perhaps this is also instinctual, but our reaction time is often set on snooze. The alarm goes off time and again, saying things such as "This person is not right for you" or "That cigarette is killing you" or "You deserve to be happy" or "Don't be afraid to try," but we delay, delay, delay when it comes to running toward authentic existence, toward true happiness, toward life. Why? Because we do not trust ourselves or God. At least, this has been true for me.

When the voice in my mediation said *Trust me*, a light came on in the distance. Trusting meant moving toward that light with the same commitment, the same singleness of purpose that I had when running toward the bodega. It meant following my instincts, even when they seemed crazy or counterintuitive. Rationally there was a sea of reasons for me to question my calling and to do something else with my life. But the Voice had not spoken to my brain—it had spoken to my heart. And so I began to drop the travel trunks of doubt and worry that I had been carrying—one by one, I began to lay them down. They were weighty and burdensome, and I realized that they were not going to change my course; they were only going to slow me down. I suddenly saw myself as the Frenchman from long ago in Harvard Square, straining under a ridiculous mountain of indecision and lugging around more worries than I could reasonably carry. Then I thought of the words from Matthew 11:

*Come to me, all who labor and are heavyladen, and I will give you rest. Take my yoke upon you, and learn from me; for I am gentle and lowly in heart, and you will find rest for your souls. For my yoke is easy, and my burden is light.**

On a deep level, I began to find rest for my soul; unburdened, my spirit exhaled and the questions that had plagued me for so long grew quiet. My path toward ordination was illuminated, and my safe haven was a blue Toyota.

---

* Revised Standard Version.

24

winnowing the spirit

Twenty-two of us sat in a large arc, while members of the Board of Ordained Ministry were seated across from us with expressions that ranged from encouraging to guarded to poker-faced. Other clergy members of various boards sat behind and around us, observing the proceedings that were part of the mandatory retreat for candidates for ministry. This was the last hoop I would need to jump through before being approved for ordination—but approval wasn't a given. Because Methodist ministers are not hired by individual churches but, rather, are appointed by regional conferences, the number of us who could be ordained, regardless of whether we were deemed qualified, would hinge on available placements. This year, the numbers were tight in Southern New England. This might happen in any given year due to fewer retirements or more clergy seeking reassignment to church ministry after working in other settings or even the closing of a church. It was the conference's responsibility to find an appointment for all current clergy members. Because there seemed to be more clergy than available appointments this year, only a small number of the twenty-two of us could be ordained; the others would have to wait until next year. This made the process particularly brutal. During the weekend, various committees had already interviewed me about my personal background, my faith, and my theology. I had been grilled on Methodist doctrine and polity, my understanding of scripture, and my commitment to ministry. It was challenging and a bit nerve-wracking, but it also helped to reinforce just how clear I had become about my desire for ordination.

Now, sitting in the arc, we were on the last leg of the examining process. What's more, this part was supposed to be almost ceremonial, perfunctory, and certainly not difficult. We were wrapping up the weekend by answering simple yes or no questions, questions that are posed to every candidate for ordained ministry. We did not answer in unison, but rather one by one in rapid fire down the line; questions such as

- Do you have a personal faith in Christ?
- Will you nurture and cultivate spiritual disciplines and patterns of holiness?
- Are you persons in whom the community can place trust and confidence?

These and others were easy yeses. Everyone was smiling as we participated in this final ritual, each round of twenty-two yes, yes, yeses building to a soaring crescendo. The feeling among the candidates was that we just might get out of there alive. Then came the rake in the grass—at least for me:

- Will you agree to exercise responsible self-control . . . [through] fidelity in marriage and celi-

bacy in singleness, social responsibility, and growth
in grace and in the knowledge and love of God?

Down the line, the automatic yeses flew—ten voiced and
twelve to go. Like a train, the question was coming closer,
gathering momentum. I was supposed to wave it on from the
platform, but instead I jumped on the tracks, bringing it to a
screeching halt with a single word: *No*. The questioner stumbled a little. "No?" he said, eyes widening. Suddenly, I was
Oliver with an outstretched bowl asking for more. The room
lapsed into squirmy silence. "Are you saying that you do not
believe in fidelity in marriage and celibacy in singleness?"
asked the minister, sounding genuinely curious. The faces of
friends I have known materialized in my mind—Terry, Tim,
Silvia, and others—people who were equally qualified for ministry, but who would find the doors closed to them because of
their sexual orientation. If this wasn't bad enough, were they
also to be sentenced to a lifetime devoid of physical intimacy,
even with a loving partner? Since the doors of marriage were
also locked to them, how could I say that I believed in celibacy
in singleness?

"Of course I believe in fidelity in marriage," I began
thoughtfully, but with conviction. "What I am uncomfortable
with is the way the phrase *celibacy in singleness* further margin-
alizes and condemns our gay and lesbian brothers and sisters."
There was a brief pause, during which I became aware of my
fellow candidates gaping at me (it's hard to look away from a
train wreck) and members of the Board of Ordained Ministry
tumbling my words around like a hot potato. Then the speaker
simply said, "Thank you," and kept going down the line, col-
lecting eleven more yeses.

The Methodist church officially denounces homosexuality as not in keeping with Christian teaching, and it denies ordination to "self-avowed, practicing homosexuals." But the New England Conference, like the New York Conference and others, was more progressive on the issue, challenging the church to change its stance. I suppose there were enough silent supporters in the room who respected my honesty, because somehow, miraculously, I was one of six candidates approved for ordination as a deacon that year. Three others were accepted for elders' orders.

Until 1996, the United Methodist Church had a two-tiered system of ordination. Candidates for ministry had to be ordained a deacon first, which carried the right to perform all rituals and sacraments; then, after serving for two years in a church, one was eligible for ordination as an elder, which meant full connection in the conference (similar, in a way, to tenure). When I received word of my approval, I was startled at how happy I felt. I called my parents to share the news and to tell them the date of the ordination ceremony, which would happen at the Annual Conference in Springfield, Massachusetts. They were thrilled, and I could feel how proud they were of me.

My approval for ordination, however, also carried the reality of difficult changes. Because I was going to be appointed to a church somewhere, the location of which was out of my control, I would have to leave the sanctuary of the lovely apartment that I shared with Katherine. I don't think either of us really wanted to acknowledge this until it was actually happening. Our year together would remain one of the most magical, fun, and spiritually expanding times of my life. From the look of the boxes that had never been unpacked in my room, perhaps I had intuited that I would not be there long. As my time in Somerville drew to a close, I tried to drink in the colors of the apartment, the creative freedom of life there, and the peaceful community of cats that had come to live with us. Isaac and Joey would come with me; Lorna and Arthur would stay with Katherine. The only thing I left behind was the blue denim couch.

Leaving Somerville also meant being separated once again from Andy. In the past, I would have welcomed the distance, welcomed the chance to have more space, but this time, I was honestly sad. I noticed it within myself, marveling at how much I had changed and how far we had come. The last nine months had been a time of growing closeness for us. We were both evolving as people, and we were happily sharing the journey. My ordination would affect his life, too, and he would have to honestly consider what it would mean for him. Although we hadn't spoken of it, we both felt there was a possibility of a future together—and, let's face it, few people in their right minds would choose to marry a minister. All we could do was cross our fingers and hope that I wouldn't be sent to a church too far away.

Everything seemed to be moving at an accelerated pace now. I had to give my notice at Senior Home Care, which was even more difficult than I had anticipated. When I told Charnan, she winced a little, as if I had landed a soft punch to her solar plexus. She looked at me with those intelligent eyes, searching my face in stunned disbelief, hardly bothering to conceal her disappointment. After all, she had taken a chance on hiring me, and now I was leaving after only a year.

I would like to believe that she was also sorry to see me go because I was good at the job and added something to the team. I felt bad about it, and I tried to explain to her that I had wrestled with the idea of ordination for three years; now that it was here, the timing was out of my control. In the end, I doubt she ever realized how much she had taught me, how grateful I was for that opportunity, or how much of what I learned there would contribute to my work in the future. Ironically, the class that I had taken at the med school (on the problems of the aged) had helped to prepare me for my work at Senior Home Care. And both of these, the class and my work with seniors, foreshadowed what would become a large part of my life's calling as a hospice chaplain. As in the class, I would be working alongside doctors and nurses to alleviate the suffering of mostly elderly people; and as in my protective service job, I would be going from home to home, working with families as well as patients, many of whom were stressed and despairing. But this was all ten years in the future—and *hospice* was a word that I hadn't even heard yet.

A few weeks after being approved for ordination, I got a call from the district superintendent. He told me that the bishop and cabinet wanted to send me to a church in West-field, Massachusetts. Although I wasn't exactly sure where this was, my heart sank a little. I had been hoping, albeit unrealistically, to be assigned a church in the Boston area. I took out a map, tracing my finger along the smooth surface that hid the hills and valleys, the cities and people; I scanned the paper horizon of unfamiliar names and discovered that Westfield was about ninety miles west of Cambridge. *It could be worse*, I thought. At least it was a straight shot on the Mass Pike, where the traffic moved at breakneck speed. *Looks like I could do it in an hour and a half.*

I knew I didn't have much of a choice. In the appointment system, you are guaranteed a job, but you pretty much have to go where you are told—especially in the beginning of your ministry. It wasn't totally a blind date with destiny, however. Out of courtesy to the congregation and to the prospective pastor, an interview would take place on site. If the pastor felt strongly that this was not the right appointment for some reason—and it had to be a valid reason—or if the congregation felt similarly, then the cabinet might reconsider. This system has its benefits and its challenges. On the one hand, churches that might never have hired a woman or a person of color as their pastor are strong-armed into accepting whomever the bishop and cabinet send. This often challenges congregations in a positive way, resulting in spiritual growth, personally and communally. On the other hand, at least for me, it was difficult knowing that I had little control over where I was going to live.

"I think you'll like Westfield," said the superintendent. "It's a pretty little town nestled at the foot of the Berkshires. The population is primarily working class, with a junior college and a decent school system." Then he told me that I would be appointed as an Associate Pastor, which meant that I would be working alongside someone who had been there for several years. This would be a new position for the church, which had long relied on the efforts of a director of Christian education, who had decided to retire. The thinking was that the church would benefit from another ordained pastor, one who could officiate the sacraments, preach, and, it was hoped, get a youth fellowship going. I liked the idea of starting out as an associate. It seemed less daunting somehow. I had had such a positive experience working with Michael, but I felt as if I still knew virtually nothing about how to run a church. "At least I'm an expert at weddings, funerals, and liturgical dance," I joked with Katherine.

A time was arranged for my interview in Westfield. Well, it was called an interview but was more like a meet and greet. Everyone knew that the district superintendent would essentially be introducing the church to its new pastor and vice versa—unless, of course, there were huge red flags. In this case, I would also be meeting the pastor with whom I would be working. Little did I know that he was not particularly thrilled about having a new colleague. No one thought to inform me that he had had a rough spring, mentally and emotionally, or that he was considering the summer to be his "recovery time." I believe that at heart, he was a decent man, but in the end, he made my life difficult.

Driving west, I tried to measure the distance that was unfolding between myself and Boston—not in miles, particularly, but in spirit. I couldn't quite believe that I would be leaving Boston, leaving a place that I had loved and that had been so important to me; leaving my friends, my relationship, my job, and my apartment. I prayed as I drove; prayed for courage, prayed for a clear mind and an open heart, prayed that I was on the right track.

The First United Methodist Church of Westfield sat on a circle near the center of town. As soon as I saw it, I knew that I would be serving there. It wasn't a particularly pretty building from the outside, but it looked friendly and inviting. The district superintendent was already there when I arrived. He met me in the parking lot, extending his hand with a warm smile. "You ready?" he asked, with the same cheerful tone a skydiving instructor might use before pushing you out of a plane. "Ready as I'll ever be" was my reply.

We walked into the empty church, where the air seemed noticeably cooler, and where our footsteps echoed on the smooth tile floor. We passed the sanctuary, whose angled pews and large windows gave it an airy openness that I hoped was indicative of the congregation. The pastor-parish relations committee, composed of about nine church members and the pastor, was already assembled in one of the church school rooms. Everyone stood up when we walked in, shaking hands all around. The only person with an odd expression on his face was the pastor. He seemed drawn up into himself, clearly un-convinced that (a) he needed an associate pastor, and (b) he needed me. When one is not feeling secure or good about one-self, it is almost impossible to be open toward another person. I was twenty-five, naïve, idealistic, hopeful, and green, while he was in his midfifties and apparently feeling a little beat up. I was single, with few responsibilities other than paying off my student loans and feeding my cats; he was happily remarried but obviously had much more on his plate. Maybe at another time or another church, we could have made a good team, but our trouble began before I even walked into the room.

The committee members were warm, welcoming, and openly enthusiastic about me. Their questions seemed to spring from genuine interest and were the antithesis of a grill-ing. They did not ask me my views on any controversial issues, and they seemed unfazed by the fact that I would be coming to them with virtually no experience other than my time with Michael as a student. When they were satisfied with the question-and-answer part of the interview, we moved on to the next—which was not only a bit awkward, but inadvertently threw a few nails onto the already tenuous road between the pastor and me. I had been asked to bring an audiotape of a sermon I'd given. I'm not sure if this was standard protocol or if this particular church felt that preaching was a priority. I'd chosen a sermon that had been recorded at my home church in Cincinnati, in part because of the quality of the recording and in part because it was representative of my thinking and theology.

The room grew quiet as the committee chairman popped the cassette into a small black tape player in the center of the table. I felt nervous and embarrassed and had an overwhelming urge to crawl under the table, allowing my disembodied voice to fill in for the rest of me, but I stayed in my seat, eyes fixed to the box from which that one moment in time was summoned.

As everyone leaned in to listen, I could picture myself in the pulpit of Groesbeck United Methodist Church. It was here that I had been baptized; here that I had played in the nursery while my mother attended Women's Society; here that I had been confirmed, participated in youth fellowship, Bible study, and church plays. My closest friends in high school were a part of this church. We would all sit together in the front pews, aware of the smiles that followed us as we walked down the side aisles en masse. The only exception to this was when there was a soccer game. On these Sundays, I would come to church with my sister Jennie and my best friend, Wendy, dressed for the game—shin guards, cleats, and all. We would sit in the last pew, nervously jiggling our legs until the final hymn began. It was only then that we were allowed to hightail it out of there and get to the game. My parents were firm about the priority of church over sports, even if it meant that our team would be missing its best forward, wing, and goalie. As soon as the coach saw our car pull up, he would frantically wave us onto the field; then he would look to the heavens with a sigh. "Are you sure you girls can't go to the Catholic church on Saturday?" he'd ask, only half joking.

In the echo of the recording, I could see the light through the rectangular stained-glass windows, which were not particularly pretty but which I had come to love. Like radar, the sound waves of my voice bumped against the images of people I knew and loved, people who sat in the same pews each week, many of whom had watched me grow up and had been my teachers, my mentors, and my cheerleaders. For me, this church had been second in importance only to my family— and there was no separating my family from this church. *Can they hear this?* I wondered, as I snuck a look around the table at the committee. *Can they hear the cradle of my spirit rocking? Can they see the wisdom of my elders and the shimmering depths of their love and support? Can they fathom the road that has brought me here? Can I?*

The sermon ended, followed by a click of the cassette player. There was a momentary pause; then someone at the table said, "Well, looks like we've got ourselves a preacher." Those words, while affirming and slightly embarrassing to me, were like a dagger in the heart of the senior pastor. On some level, I was aware of this, but things were moving too quickly for me to fully process it. The district superintendent then asked me to step out of the room so that the committee could discuss the interview. During this time, I sat in the empty sanctuary, tried to breathe, and just surrendered to the process. Before too long, I was called back into the room. Everyone was smiling. I would like to say that the pastor was, too, albeit in a rather pained way, but I could be seeing that through the lens of everything I know to have transpired after this moment. "Welcome to Westfield," said the chairman, a tall, sweet-faced man in his late thirties. And, just like that, my road turned west.

25

in the company of angels

By the time Annual Conference arrived in late June 1987, I had moved most of my things out of the apartment in Somerville and into a small two-bedroom town house in Westfield. Because all church appointments began on July 1, I still had some time to linger in my old life, which was both sweet and rather melancholy. In those waning days of June, I felt neither here nor there. I didn't regret the choice I had made to follow the call to Westfield, but I wasn't exactly itching for it to begin. The wheels of change were in motion, wheels that I had helped to propel through a fair amount of hard work and determination; the only thing I could do was to hope and pray they were spinning in the right direction.

My new apartment complex was down a winding country road about two miles from the church. Since there had never been an associate pastor before (and hence no parsonage), I had the rare opportunity to choose my own place to live. The church gave me a budget for the rent, which was modest but reasonable, and I scanned the local paper for housing options.

I had chosen the town house because it afforded me some privacy, both because of its location in relationship to the church, as well as the fact that it had a communal parking lot. The other cars provided the camouflage that a single driveway could not have. I didn't necessarily want everyone in the congregation watching me come and go.

My unit had a small powder room and a galley kitchen on the first floor, opening onto a long dining and living room area. It had the unfortunate but requisite shag carpeting in a lovely shade of rusty orange, but it was freshly painted and in good condition. The living room faced the river, which was pretty during the day but felt rather wild and menacing at night. This feeling was amplified by the whispers I'd heard about a woman who'd been raped recently in the complex. Rumor had it that the perpetrator had come right through the sliding doors in the living room, past the woman's husband, who'd fallen asleep on the couch, and upstairs to her bedroom. Obviously I found this very disconcerting. To make matters worse, it was incredibly quiet compared to Somerville, and I would be living by myself for the first time. The fact that I had neighbors on either side of me, who might be able to hear me scream through the thin walls, offered at least some measure of comfort. There was a small balcony off my bedroom upstairs, which looked out onto the river—and I would sometimes stand there like a ghost, watching people float by on rafts or canoes, laughing, living, and having fun.

On the morning of my ordination, I awoke feeling clear minded, at peace, and positively buzzing with nervous, happy energy. There was not a moment of inner hand-wringing or second-guessing. I got on my knees and prayed, prayed myself into silence, prayed until I became aware that I was communing (at least momentarily) with the Divine. *Make me an instrument of your peace.* These were the words that resonated from within.

I got dressed, threw my white alb over my arm, and grabbed the stack of pink triangles that another ordinand and I had painstakingly cut out. Being accepted for ordination while others continued to be denied, based on their sexuality alone, presented a moral dilemma for me. It was difficult not to feel like a sellout, like one happily accepting membership in a club that slams the door in the faces of others. As a witness to our hope for change, a fellow ordinand and I planned on handing out hundreds of the pink triangles, a popular symbol of the gay rights movement, to those attending the ordination service. Not surprisingly, she and I would be the only ordinands who would pin one to our white albs.

My parents had arrived the day before and were staying at a hotel nearby. We agreed on a time and place to meet before the proceedings, not only to give each other a squeeze, but also because my mom would be participating in the service with me. Each person being ordained was allowed one special person to stand with them as the bishop and members of the clergy offered the official blessing. At first I hesitated about whether to ask my mom or my dad. Both had been equally instrumental in my spiritual development, in supporting me throughout my life, and in offering me an endless wellspring of love and wisdom. As I thought about this, I suddenly envisioned my father walking me down the aisle at my wedding—whenever and with whomever that would be. My dad and I would most certainly share that publicly private moment, that long walk, the *before* and *after* that changes your life. That's why I decided to ask my mom to stand with me now. Ordination offered a chance for me to share a similarly life-changing moment with her. When I asked her, she was deeply touched—and I was happy knowing that she would be there once again, holding my hand as she always had throughout my life.

As people began streaming into the large gymnasium that had been transformed for the purposes of the service, I stood at the door, passing out pink triangles with my friend. Some people just took one without thinking, the way one might accept a flyer handed out on the street; others politely declined; while still others asked what it meant, and made their decision accordingly. I was so giddy with excitement and nervous energy that even the sour faces did not faze me. When my parents found me at the door, I gave them a huge hug and handed them each a triangle. "What's this for?" asked my dad, his sweet warmth and openness oozing out of his pores. I suggested that he just put it on, promising to explain it to him later, but my mom was savvier. "You're not wearing that, Richard," she said, with a little roll of her eyes. She handed her triangle back to me, but I noticed that my dad put his in his pocket. This made me want to laugh. Everything made me want to laugh. Even the sight of Andy nervously coming around the corner made me want to laugh. Instead, I ran up to him and we wrapped our long arms around each other in a quick embrace.

This was only the third time he and my parents had seen each other in the past four years—and so far, it had been no laughing matter. The first time they met had been at the infamous Parents' Weekend; the second time was a month later at our Denison graduation, memorable for its iciness and its thinly veiled hostility; and the third time was now, at my ordination. I admired Andy for making the drive from Boston. I knew he was nervous but was coming anyway to support me. This was a defining moment not only for me, but also for us— could we endure it? Could our relationship sustain another separation, much less make the transition from me being essentially a free agent to being a United Methodist minister? It was daunting, and because it was daunting, I needed him (*and* my parents) to know that he was important to me. I might be moving to Westfield, but I wasn't running from him. This alone was a miracle.

When it came my turn to come forward and kneel, my mom and I walked hand in hand. Even in her heels, she was much smaller than I, but when she gave my hand a little shake, I could feel the transmission of her strength. I glanced over my shoulder, where my dad and Andy were sitting. My father nodded at me with a smile, his warm cocoa-colored eyes emanating love and support. Andy gave a little wave and leaned over to whisper something in my dad's ear. When my name was called, members of the First United Methodist Church of Westfield stood in the bleachers. It was a startling and touching display of solidarity, one that said to me, "We are here. You are ours, and we are yours, and we will stand with you."

I looked toward the center of the room, where members of the clergy were waiting, including Michael Curry. He was grinning at me from within the wilds of his curly hair and thick beard. He looked like an excited kid about to wave me onto a roller coaster. His eyes were alive and knowing; he'd been on this ride for a few years now and still found it fun. I knelt, and immediately many hands came to rest on my head, my shoulders, my back. I had thought that this would be awkward, but instead found it strangely comforting. It was like being caressed by a dozen doting angels. Perhaps I was. Perhaps that is what happens during the laying on of hands—they mysteriously become the hands of angels. I could feel my mother's small, familiar hands resting on my right shoulder. I knew her eyes would be closed and her head bowed. Between each word that the bishop spoke, she would have a hundred others flying up toward the heavens on my behalf. Swaddled in prayer, surrounded by hope, lifted by spiritual forces unseen, I surrendered to the mystery and the power of the moment. And when I opened my eyes, I did so to a new dawn—and I was ready.

26

broken pieces

A Postlude Twenty-five Years Later

"Do you believe in miracles?" The question left the man's lips like an arrow shot from a bow. They quivered slightly, his eyes widening, as if surprised by the sheer force of it. I must have flinched, or at least he sensed that I did, because he squared his shoulders and raised his chin with some defiance. "Well, *do* you?"

Although I tried not to show it, the arrow had hit its mark (around the center of my chest), and I floundered for a moment to find an answer I could live with. Just down the hall, his twenty-nine-year-old daughter was fighting for her life. Melanoma. The disease had already engulfed most of the muscle and tissue of her right thigh; now it was greedily gobbling up her lungs and even sneaking into her brain. She was in the hospital for what seemed to be the millionth time this year, and she was getting tired. Scary tired.

I knew what he was asking; he was asking me whether I thought God could and/or would heal his daughter—and if God couldn't, or wouldn't, then what was the use of faith, of the church, and even of my presence there? I was careful not to answer with some watered-down platitude about the miracle of God's grace or the mystery of God's Way. He wasn't interested in a metaphorical type of healing, as in the healing of her spirit; he wanted his daughter to be rid of the cancer—immediately—despite the odds.

As he waited for my answer, the man sent ripples of pain through the air like a silent scream—and part of me wondered what I was doing there. What *did* I believe? I was raised as much on miracles as I was on heartbreak; on prayers that seemed to be answered (favorably) and on the myriad that were not. Despite the years that I have spent thinking about God, talking to God, listening for God, I knew I didn't have the answers for this man, and I certainly didn't have the power to change his daughter's circumstances. Maybe God didn't, either.

For a moment, I felt embarrassed for God. Once again He/She would appear impotent and callous in the face of suffering, and I would be left to come up with a reasonable explanation for God's silence. Sometimes my role as a chaplain felt more like divine damage control. The man's eyes bore into my skull like a blowtorch, searing my defenses and burning away any flimsy paper answers I might have been tempted to pull from my spiritual Rolodex. I felt my cheeks flush. His teeth were clenched in animal desperation, and it crossed my mind that he might spring off the couch in the hospital lounge and take me by the throat. Well, not me, exactly, but God. Since he couldn't get his hands around God's throat, mine just might have to do.

I never intended to be God's throat; never intended to be a human stand-in, press secretary, interpreter, lawyer, or flesh and blood sponge to absorb the pain and anguish of the spiritually disenfranchised—but here I was. Here I am, more than twenty-five years later. And it's sometimes a very strange place to be. When the father of a dying girl asks me a question about miracles, he doesn't really give a damn about whether *I* believe in them or not—he just wants one of his own. That's why he goes to Mass every morning and pounds his fist as he prays. He is too afraid to stop asking and too mad to listen for the answer. And so he squares off against the closest thing he has at hand to God—me. By now, I have been a chaplain long enough to understand it. I do not take it personally. I know this father is not interested in my personal theology; he's probably not even interested in my answer—he just needs to ask the question. He needs someone to see that he is broken.

For some reason, I have always been drawn to the broken places. Maybe there is something in me that needs fixing, maybe there is someone I have always wanted to fix, or maybe I have intuited what Leonard Cohen meant when he wrote

> There is a crack, a crack in everything
> That's how the light gets in.*

I have spent my life following the beams of light that seep from our cracked perfection. I don't know how else to live. This is how it has always been with me. When I was small, for example, the remnants of a robin's egg always held more unbridled mystery than one that was unbroken. Delicate and beautiful, the broken shell pointed toward life—a baby bird had been born. Holding the pieces in my hand, I would gently

---

* "Anthem" by Leonard Cohen.

run my finger over the smooth surface and the jagged edges. I knew that when the first ray of light appeared through the cracks it meant life for the bird. The blue of the egg was the color of the sky, a clue from God about where this bird was heading—one world opening to another, one home making way for the other. I would look up at the trees and smile, knowing I was a part of nature and nature was a part of me; we had an ongoing, unspoken dialogue. Sometimes we mourned. Finding a whole, unbroken egg on the ground meant that things hadn't gone right. A seamless shell meant that something had died—or would die—imprisoned in its own arrested beauty, its own blue heaven.

Broken shells did not necessarily prepare me for broken fathers or mothers, for dying children, or for the pain of broken humanity, but they are part of my mosaic. I cannot remember a time when I was not aware of God. And God was always most real, most accessible to me, in the natural world. When I was young, every small thing felt like a miracle. Finding a robin's egg was a miracle. Seeing the sun break through the clouds was a miracle. Each discovery was like a secret message sent from God for me to decode. Sometimes the message was simply that I was loved. Sometimes it was that God was near. Once in a while, the message was, "Remember Who's in charge." That could be scary or reassuring, depending on the circumstances. But I always felt in communion with the Divine.

Feeling connected to God and the natural world did not mean that I wanted to be a minister—far from it! My earliest aspirations were to be an artist or a poet, although (I confess) I did tell my second grade teacher that I wanted to be a missionary. This was primarily because two of my mother's sisters were missionaries in Costa Rica at the time. I'm not sure exactly what was so captivating about this, but it made a deep impression on me.

The stories that my aunts told were interesting, but it was my aunt Virginia—Ginny—in particular, whom I found utterly mesmerizing. She was petite, like my mother, with dark curly hair, intelligent green eyes, and a beautiful smile. She was the oldest of the five children in my mother's family, my mom being the youngest. Ten years and many lifetimes seemed to separate them. At that time, my mom was raising six children, lived within an hour of where she was born, and was constrained by finances and responsibilities. My aunt, on the other hand, was unmarried, she had a couple master's degrees, and she was free to travel and seek adventure. During her visits with us, she would often become so animated in her storytelling that she would slip into rapidly spoken Spanish. When we would point this out to her, she'd say, "But I can talk so much faster in Spanish!" This would make everyone laugh. I would laugh, too, but mostly I would see the light dancing in her eyes, and want to follow it—or her.

When Ginny moved to California after returning from Costa Rica, she continued her life of spiritual exploration. We used to look forward to her visits because she was usually on some new "kick." That's how my grandmother explained it, anyway; that's how she could accept it. I, however, took her and her newest ideas very seriously, even as a child, because what she said usually resonated with me. Whether she was extolling the importance of a healthful diet or teaching me about acupuncture and kinesiology, the chakras, and reincarnation, Ginny's visits were always fun. She was ahead of the curve in terms of embracing organic food and holistic health. She brought the New Age movement of California right to our Ohio door, special delivery. Sometimes she would bring duffel bags full of clothing, usually of one particular color, that she no longer wanted. "I don't wear red anymore," she might explain, "bad for my aura." Or "I'm only wearing white and lavender right now." We never knew what we would find in her bag.

One summer she showed up with unmistakably orange skin from drinking too much carrot juice. Everyone, including my grandmother, thought this was hilarious. On another visit, she tried to convince us of the benefits of drinking small amounts of our own urine (very sterile, she assured us). I decided to stick to the carrot juice. This was also the summer she introduced me to spirulina, a strong, blue-green algae, which I dutifully stirred into my juice every day, simply because she said it was good for me. I was about twelve years old at the time. My siblings thought I was crazy, but my mom would smile and say, "You're just like your aunt!" She was diagnosed with stage 4 colon cancer at about the same age that I was when I was diagnosed with breast cancer. She rather miraculously survived, hand-over-fisting her way into remission, and married for the first time at fifty. Fourteen years later, the cancer reared its ugly head again, and she died. I hope to have more life ahead of me than she did.

Ginny was anything but orthodox. Although she was raised on the same Kentucky farm with the same no-nonsense Methodist principles, and by the same strict mother as my mom, she always moved to the beat of her own drum. I didn't become a minister because of her, but I know that she is there somewhere. Not only was she spiritually open, she was bold about this; she didn't try to hide or apologize for it, which was something one often did in my house. Unlike Ginny, we carefully guarded our spiritual "weirdness" from most people, especially from my grandmother. We didn't tell her, for instance, about our family séances, which (one could argue) was understandable. Not everyone, especially not every Christian, is comfortable with that kind of spiritual exploration. But my grandmother was so conservative that we didn't even tell her that my sister and I took ballet, because that was considered dancing! The fact that Aunt Ginny was clearly comfortable with who she was, even if it meant disagreeing with my grandmother, made her endlessly intriguing, heroic even. She was light and lilting, breezing in and out of town with her new ideas and her duffel bag full of magic, like a traveling mystic. She never seemed bothered by what others thought of her and would just sort of giggle when confronted on her ideas—a response that was sweetly disarming, even to my grandmother. How do you argue with stardust?

Although I didn't see her very often, I was very aware of her presence in my life, and I found comfort in her odd wisdom. For example, when she heard that I had decided to drop my bio major in college, abandoning my plans to become a doctor, she told my mother not to worry. "My guides said to tell you that Andie has been a doctor in many lifetimes," she said confidently. "That's why she feels this impulse now. She *could* do it, but something else is planned for her. She will discover her path." Three years later, I found myself at Harvard Divinity School.

Ginny died six months after I graduated from HDS. I was devastated. To make matters worse, the last time I saw her, we'd had the only strained conversation I can ever remember having with her—naturally, it was about spiritual matters.

She'd gotten involved in a religious cult on the West Coast, which frightened me and consumed her. As with all of her newest "kicks," she was completely committed and absolutely undeterred by the raised eyebrows and the genuine concern of those who loved her. I admired her conviction but her once-dancing eyes now had a flatness I didn't recognize. She was still sweet, still lovely, but something was missing. A part of *her* was missing. Call it coincidence, but it was a couple years after joining this cult that her cancer came back with a ven-geance . . . and killed her. The cult killed her. That's how I always thought of it, anyway.

Is this what happens when you take a detour off the straight and narrow? I wondered. Do you get lost? Do you find yourself without a map in a field of land mines? My parents were also spiritually open, but they had always remained grounded in the Christian tradition. Somehow this made their spiritual exploration safe; they never traveled so far that they couldn't find their way home. Home was in the church, it was in the spirit and the figure of Christ; it was not in some modern-day prophet who wanted her followers to store up food and weapons for the end of the world as we know it. I couldn't help but think that my aunt Ginny had gotten lost along the way. It feels judgmental to say that now—and it makes me wish I could speak with her again. I don't think I'd debate any theological points this time. I think I'd ask her to tell me a story about Costa Rica, tell it until she gets going so fast that she laughs her way into Spanish. That's at least a lan-guage I can understand, even if I don't speak a word of it.

I'm often asked why I decided to become a minister. Do I say it's because of my aunt Ginny, who was a missionary in Costa Rica, who went to California, found karma but lost her compass, who survived cancer but died from a fractured identity? Do I say it's because my parents lived their faith, fed us on spiritual food, made life an adventure, and encouraged me to spread my wings? Maybe I should try to explain what it was like to find a piece of shell, hold it in my hand, and feel the ripples of living energy emanating from it. I guess the easiest thing to say is that I was terrible at chemistry, so I had to drop the bio major and figure something else out. Luckily, I landed at Harvard.

"God has a sense of humor" is how I usually respond, and perhaps that's the closest thing to the truth. By most accounts, I still don't look like a minister—or at least most people's conception of one. My hair has been too long, my skirts too short, and my theology too broad. I have struggled with the projections and the expectations that come with the role, which include being a sanitized version of myself. This was more the case when I started in ministry at the age of twenty-five. Now, that many years later, it's disappointing—alarming, even—when people do not act surprised when I tell them what I do. If they flinch, it's usually because I tell them I work with the dying; the fact that I'm ordained elicits a mere shrug. Benefits of age, I guess.

Why did I decide to become a minister? Maybe it was decided for me in every little twist and turn of my life, as all of our ways are decided in every moment, at every bend in the road. My journey went one way, my sisters' went another, my brothers' still another. What looked like an unmarked path when I was young now appears as a smooth and carefully carved road. I didn't become a doctor, as I had planned when I was young, but I work as part of a medical team. My area of expertise is not caring for the body but, rather, caring for the soul. Because my family was open to such things as séances and communication with the dead, I had probably thought more about death and the progression of the soul than most and consequently felt right at home with the dying. And although I didn't become a missionary like my aunt, the idea of doing spiritual work with those in need is deeply rooted in me. Stepping back, I can see that the pieces of my puzzle fit together without effort—I just have to remind myself of this when I am struggling in my life.

The truth is I never really wanted to become a minister; I just wanted to become myself. That's why I went to divinity school—to figure out what it is I'm supposed to do with this life. Ordination was never in my plans when I applied to school; in fact, I made a point of reassuring my friends that this was not a possibility. Being ordained, however, has allowed me to intersect with others in meaningful ways. It has opened doors and has challenged me to think about life, about God, and about our connection to one another.

I am still learning to stand, like Martin Luther, before the powers that be without apologizing for who I am. "Sin boldly," he said, meaning "Take risks." If you're going to go out on a limb for what you believe in, go *all* out. Believe so passionately, so fearlessly, that you are willing to be condemned as a heretic or a madwoman. Martin Luther faced death for his beliefs; most of us face only shame and judgment when it comes to being honest about who we are. At the heart of things, I am still just a person who is trying to follow the nudges of the Spirit, who feels Living Energy in every nook and cranny of our existence and seeks to share this reality with others, especially those who are suffering. This is what I was destined to do.

I didn't get ordained to wear the robe and the collar, or to prove to the world that I am a good person. It has taken me a while to understand this. At first, I questioned whether this was the case: had I been guilted into it because of things that had happened in my life? Or maybe I was afraid that I was tottering too close to the edges of my faith and was in danger of getting lost, like my aunt. Perhaps I allowed myself to be collared, literally, because I was afraid that my secret would be exposed; namely, that I was a free spirit. Maybe I corralled myself, like a wild pony, so that I wouldn't open myself to judgment. The church was the fence that defined my life and promised safety—but the open plain and the hills beyond are where my spirit lives. This is part of my story, anyway, part of my truth.

When I question my calling, when I feel like a charlatan in the clergy collar, I think of the places I have been led and the people who have opened their doors and their hearts to me. In those interactions, I know that I am home—home in my own skin, home in the world—and every moment of my life has brought me to this perfect place. Then I understand that I became a minister so that I could sit with a father whose daughter is dying, because it is a hard and holy thing to do. When he asks me if I believe in miracles, I can look into his blue eyes and see the remnants of a robin's egg. I can see life, even there, amidst the jagged edges of his spirit, and answer, "Yes." The authentic intersection of our spirits has created a mirror of light. It is *his* truth that I will reflect back, it is *his* answer, not mine. Perhaps he will see, as I do, that love has cracked him open. He is not dead inside, he is only broken, and this is a miracle. "I will lift you up on eagle's wings," writes the Psalmist. I am praying these words as I turn and walk down the hall, holding the pieces in my hand.

acknowledgments

I would like to express my heartfelt gratitude to Cynthia Manson, literary agent extraordinaire, to whom I am eternally indebted. Without her, these words would not be in print. Thanks, Cynthia, for your expertise, your friendship, and your unwavering faith in me.

A warm thanks, also, to my wonderful editor, Beth Adams, whose keen eye and attention to detail, not to mention her patience, helped shape this story into a better book; and to Jessica Wong for lending a special hand.

Thank you to Jonathan Merkh and Becky Nesbitt from Howard Books for taking a chance on me. Your creativity, your faith, and your daring spirits were evident from the first time we met. Thank you for being leaders in the field, and for giving me the opportunity to tell my story.

An ongoing wave of gratitude is extended to Judith Curr and Peter Borland of Atria Books. You changed my life when you opened the door to *The Voice That Calls You Home*, and I am forever in your debt.

Thank you to Louise Burke for her generosity of spirit and her professional guidance. Your silent contribution is immeasurable.

Finally, my deepest gratitude to my wonderful family and to my dear friends, who support and encourage me, who laugh and suffer with me, and who continue to make life a spiritual adventure.